Coykendall's
Complete Guide to
Sporting Collectibles

Coykendall's Complete Guide to Sporting Collectibles

Ralf Coykendall, Jr.

WALLACE-HOMESTEAD BOOK COMPANY
Radnor, Pennsylvania

Published in Radnor, Pennsylvania 19089, by Wallace-Homestead, a division of Chilton Book Company

Designed by Stan Green/Green Graphics

Manufactured in the United States of America

Library of Congress Cataloging-in-Publication Data
Coykendall, Ralf W. (Ralf Wales), 1929–
    Coykendall's complete guide to sporting collectibles / Ralf
Coykendall, Jr.
        p.   cm.
    Includes index.
    ISBN 0-87069-736-6
    1. Hunting—Collectibles—United States. I. Title.
NK6077.5.C68   1996   95–53850
799'.075—dc20   CIP

On the cover, clockwise from top left: Carved fish, old binoculars, cobalt blue target ball, 1940s Wildfowler blue-wing teal decoy, old fish net, stag-handle hunting knife and sheath, 1800s shotgun and rifle cartridges, cast-iron shooting gallery target birds, sporting magazine with cover by William H. Foster (inventor of skeet), tin yellow-legs decoy by Stratier & Sohier, bait casting rod and reel together with an early brass reel and automatic fly wheel, miniature wood duck decoy by the author, one of five Heddon Punkinseed lures, fly-tying feathers with turn-of-the-century gut-eye salmon flies, and split-willow creel with Charles F. Orvis fly box and leaders. The tweed hat is the author's favorite and the red-and-black hunting shirt was lost on the campaign trail.

The Wildfowler decoy is from the extensive collection of Jim McGovern of the Hermitage in Wilmington, Vermont; the stag-handle hunting knife was provided by A. G. Russell of Springdale, Arkansas; the brass reel is from Charles "Buzz" Eichel of Dorset, Vermont; The Heddon Punkinseeds are from dealer/collector Greg Hamilton of Vergennes, Vermont; and the salmon flies are from bookseller Ken Callahan of Peterborough, New Hampshire. All other items are from the author's collection.

1 2 3 4 5 6 7 8 9 0   5 4 3 2 1 0 9 8 7 6

A dedication is a simple matter, but now as I keep earlier promises and dedicate this volume to my numerous grandchildren, I will leave each of them my yesterdays as well. Life was simpler when I was young. People cared about one another and sporting collectibles were actually used. I cannot turn back the clock, but I can hope that my grandchildren will look back every now and then and find the warmth of the golden age of American sport that warmed me in my youth.

Contents

Acknowledgments

No one can write a book alone, and so it is with this volume. Harry Rinker, the noted antiques columnist, believed in the idea from the very beginning, and the people at Chilton Book Company have worked with me harmoniously to bring this volume to fruition. To Harry, Jeff Day, Troy Vozzella, and Susan Clarey go my thanks and appreciation. Special thanks to Harriet Goldner who corrected my errors and made the book make sense.

I may pass myself off as an expert, but without the help of the real ones, this book would not exist. And so, in no special order, my sincere thanks go to Henry A. Fleckenstein Jr., Bob Lang, Lou Razek, Martin J. Keane, Henry Broggi of South Bay Auctions, Michael Jaffe, and Teri Bell of the Fish and Wildlife Service and her boss who is still my favorite bartender.

Others include Gary Guyette and Frank Schmidt, A. G. and Goldie Russell, Gary Randall, Thomas A. Daly, John Shoffner, Greg Hamilton, Richard Oliver, Skip Woodruff, Bob Hanafee, Jack Ordeman, Sally Bockus, Buzz Eichel, Ken Burkhardt, Judith and Jim Bowman, Colonel Henry Siegel, Ken Callahan, the friendly folks at The Orvis Company, and Jim McGovern of the Hermitage in Wilmington, Vermont, whose decoy collection is exceeded only by his wine cellar.

And last, but far from the bottom of this list or any other list, a special thank you to each of my five children who have stood by me and encouraged my writing.

Photo Credits

The following have provided photos or items for use in this book or on the cover. Many thanks to them for all their help: Greg Hamilton; Ken Callahan, Callahan & Company Booksellers; James McGovern, Hermitage Inn; Charles R. Eichel; Robert Hanafee; Pat Theodorus, The Orvis Company; Ken Burkhardt; Thomas A. Daly; Caroline Birnbaum, Swann Galleries, Inc.; Henry Broggi, South Bay Auctions; Gary Guyette, Gary Guyette & Frank M. Schmidt, Inc.; A. G. and Goldie Russell, A. G. Russell Knives, Inc.; Sally H. Bockus, Hickok-Bockus; Gary Randall; Teresa M. Bell, Federal Duck Stamp Office, U.S. Fish and Wildlife Service; John E. Shoffner, American Fish Decoy Association; Richard Oliver, Oliver's; Martin J. Keane; Richard E. Oinonen, Oinonen Book Auctions; and Bob Lang, Lang's Sporting Collectibles, Inc.

—Ralf Coykendall

Introduction

All books have a beginning and an end, but this may be unique in that I am writing this introduction after all else is complete and at the publisher's. I have written about firearms, duck stamps, prints and etchings, and all the other stuff sportsmen and women collect, yet I find that I have neglected the most important things of all: the warmth of bygone campfires, a small boy's eyes on Christmas morning, and the friendships sealed by a fireside on cold winter evenings. In a way, decoy collector Joel Barber was at his very best when he wrote his thoughtful description of an old decoy. With your kind indulgence, it serves:

Americana
"Americana," the catalog runs
And down below:
"Canvasback decoy from Maryland."
Watching the dust rise and settle again
On faded curios.

Americana! And I had rather lie
At anchor off Havre de Grace,
Or drift to leeward, derelict,
And spend my days
Stored away on the Eastern Shore
In a shanty.

Americana? Why, spent shot
Is better off than I
On the bottom of the Chesapeake.
And that's where I would rather be,
Water-logged and bound in tendrils
Of wild celery.

Americana? No! But lying there,
Shadows would pass above,
Wild geese and canvasback,
Phantom boats and me
And, now and then, the white breasts
Of rafting swan.

It was my good fortune to know Joel Barber and enjoy his wonderful collection of waterfowl decoys. But when all is said and done and I think back to the times my wife and I shared manhattans with this famous man, it is his prose that I remember. I hope in your quest for material things you, too, will discover the real values that are so important. People, and not things, are the real collectibles.

I

PART I
PAPER

CHAPTER 1

Prints

ſporting prints come in all shapes and sizes, in color and in black and white, and in limited and unlimited signed and unsigned editions. No one can hope to learn all there is to know about sporting prints, but I hope that the information presented here will help beginning collectors and would-be collectors and will provide the do's and don'ts that often find the buyer—rather than the print—being hung.

The earliest sporting prints were woodcuts and steel engravings that were sometimes hand colored. Virtually all of the hand-colored trout and salmon fly prints we come across today were originally illustrations for books. Collectors prize the works of Henry Alken and John James Audubon; and the multitude of sporting prints produced by Currier and Ives beginning before the Civil War are both collectible and costly. Artists A. B. Frost and Winslow Homer began their careers as illustrators for the *Harper's*

A. B. Frost's "Good Luck" (right) and "Bad Luck" are from the 1903 set of prints entitled "A Day's Shooting" published by Scribner's. These particular prints were from Eugene Connett's collection and sold (framed in oak) as a pair for $1,400.00 plus a 10% buyer's fee. *Photograph courtesy of Richard Oinonen Book Auctions, Sunderland, Massachusetts.*

Weekly publication, and, interestingly, their prints are among the very few unsigned prints that have real value. Another illustrator whose unsigned prints have value is the late Lynn Bogue Hunt who was and is perhaps America's best-known sporting artist. I remember meeting Hunt at his New York City studio in the 1940s, and now, as I write about the value of sporting prints, my mind turns back to other artists' homes and studios, and I realize how fortunate I was to meet and know Roland Clark, William

This Derrydale Press hand-colored print was the only print done for Eugene Connett's famous press by William J. Schaldach, and in a limited/signed edition of only 200 it sells for $2,000.00 to $2,500.00. *Illustration courtesy of John T. Ordeman.*

Schaldach, Carl Rungius, Ogden Pleissner, and the other artists who gave warmth to the golden age of American sport. But enough of sentiment—it's time to return to today and the dollars and cents of sporting art.

No discussion of sporting prints could be compiled without a listing of many of the prints produced from 1928 to 1941 by Eugene Connett's Derrydale Press, nor is it possible to overlook the many rare etchings that are, perhaps, the finest and most valuable of all sporting prints. Certainly, etchings and dry points by Frank Benson, Roland Clark, Carl Rungius, and others fit this description handsomely. Works by all of these fine artists are listed in the value guide that follows, but before jumping into the listings, I respectfully suggest that you consider not only what you hope to collect but also how to protect yourself before you buy and how to care for your property afterwards.

Frank W. Benson's most popular etching, "The Gunner," was published in an edition of 50 signed prints and is valued between $6,500.00 and $7,500.00. *Illustration courtesy of John T. Ordeman.*

DERRYDALE PRINTS

A number of Derrydale Press prints are listed in this section. A complete listing has been compiled by John T. Ordeman and is available through sporting-books dealers. The complex process of making aquatints is explained in this worthwhile publication.

Modern limited edition prints in editions of more than a few hundred tend to have little, if any, resale value. If you are considering buying for investment purposes, I suggest you look elsewhere to feather your nest or to provide a nest egg for your offspring. This is not to say that if you find a sporting print that you truly like you should not buy it and hang it proudly, but bear in mind that you will probably pay more to have a so-called "limited edition" sporting print framed than it will ever be worth on the resale market. Sporting print dealers come in many shapes and sizes—it is up to you as the buyer to know what you are buying and who you are buying it from.

Roland Clark's "The Last Round" is a scarce large (15″ × 12″) drypoint executed in 1928. It sells for about $2,000.00. *Illustration courtesy of John T. Ordeman.*

DUCK STAMP PRINTS

Many of the artists listed in this chapter also designed one or more state or federal duck stamps and are, therefore, also mentioned in Chapter 2.

Fine sporting prints require proper care and handling. All too many fine prints are ruined by improper shipping, storing, and/or framing methods. Prints should always be shipped and stored flat and should be protected by acid-free coverings. Acid-free matting and backing boards should also be used in the framing of sporting prints and etchings, and they should be sealed to protect their backings from moisture. Sunlight and bright lights are the enemies of fine prints—display prints so as to avoid any unwarranted fading.

The following sporting artists are names to be reckoned with. Most are represented in print form, and although we will not cover this complex subject here, their original art is valuable. This listing includes information to give you an idea of who is who in this field. When available, representative prices are given for examples sold through auctions and/or catalogs. The

SIGNED PRINTS

A signed print is one that has been signed by the artist *after* it has been printed. Many, many prints are made from artwork that carries the artist's signature as part of the original. To be considered a signed example, the print must be signed and (usually) numbered after completion.

10% to 15% buyer's fee added to nearly all auction sales is *not* included. Unless otherwise stipulated, the prints are artist signed, unframed, and in very good or better condition. Figures in parenthesis indicate the number of prints produced.

Robert Abbett—A contemporary artist whose color prints of birds and bird dogs are popular with sportsmen and women.

Black Lab Family (850) 135.00
Close Honor (1,000) 825.00
Hillside Woodcock (850) 125.00
Setter and Woodcock (500) 400.00
Theodore Gordon Flyfishers (300) 140.00
Trout Unlimited print and stamp for 1981, framed. 150.00

Harry C. Adamson—Contemporary artist who portrays game birds and animals in their natural settings.

After the Storm—Pintails (850)
  Framed, sold at a decoy auction, excellent condition 60.00
  Unframed 150.00
The Loafing Bar—Mallards (580) 165.00
Wild Bounty—Black Ducks (450) 125.00

Henry Alken, Sr.—Best known for his equestrian scenes, this English artist also captured the spirit of early 1800s sports.

John Atherton—A dedicated fisherman and fly tier, this talented artist's work is scarce and desirable.

John James Audubon (1785–1851)—An artist who dedicated his life's work to depicting America's birds and animals. His early prints are priceless.

Robert Bateman—A very popular contemporary sporting artist whose use of light and shadow is highly regarded.

High Kingdom—Snow Leopard (580) 725.00
Midnight—Black Wolf (580) 675.00
Other signed prints . . . . 100.00 to 1,500.00

JOHN JAMES AUDUBON

The "Birds of America" prints by Audubon and produced by Havell from 1827 through 1838 consist of 435 hand-colored rarities. There are Audubon prints and there are Audubon prints. Anyone interested in the real thing should buy only from a trusted dealer.

Frank W. Benson—John T. Ordeman's book titled *Master of the Sporting Print* says it all about this great artist. Another of his books, *Frank W. Benson's Etchings, Drypoints, and Lithographs,* lists and depicts all of Benson's prints and is a must for serious sporting art collectors. See the appendix for this and other information about prints.

Etchings and drypoints
Cloudy Dawn (150) 950.00
Marsh Gunner (150)
    Framed and faded 1,550.00
    Unframed. 2,450.00
Old Tom (150) 5,000.00
Wildfowler (150 . . . . 4,200.00
Yellowlegs Alighting (100) 1,700.00
Yellowlegs #2 (150) 1,650.00

Richard E. Bishop—An important wildlife artist who, unfortunately, failed to limit and/or sign his prints (making them of limited value only).

Color prints
Signed, rare and should be authenticated . . . . to 500.00
Unsigned . . . . to 100.00
Etching and drypoints
Blacks and Greenheads 170.00
Bog Sprites. 275.00
Timber Mallards. 300.00

Herb Booth—A contemporary artist who is at home in the uplands and wetlands of America.

The Home Place (450)
    Framed. 250.00
    Unframed 125.00
Mill Pond Mallards (450) 85.00
Split Covey (600). 110.00

"Going North" etching by Frank W. Benson was published in an edition of 150 signed prints in 1919. The current estimated value of this depiction of Canada Geese is approximately $750.00.

Frank W. Benson's 1923 etching "Setting Out Decoys" was printed in an edition of 150 signed prints and is valued at upwards of $1,000.00 in today's marketplace. *Illustration courtesy of Hickok-Bockus, Summit, New Jersey.*

"Woodcock," published in an edition of 150 signed prints, has proven to be one of Frank W. Benson's more popular etchings and is valued at $5,000.00. *Illustration courtesy of Hickok-Bockus, Summit, New Jersey.*

Ralph Boyer—An artist whose talents are obvious in his prints and etchings for the Derrydale Press.

Etchings and drypoints. . . . . 300.00 to 500.00
Prints
    After a Big One (200) 450.00
    An Anxious Moment (250) 450.00
Fathers of American Sport (250 sets of six) . . . . to 1,000.00

Paul Brown—An equestrian artist who also illustrated hunting and fishing articles, including one by my father.

Limited edition Derrydale Press prints. . . . . 250.00 to 500.00

Ken Carlson—A contemporary wildlife artist with a feel for the woods, fields and waters.

Rainbow Trout (300)
    Matted and framed 210.00
    Unframed 85.00
Woodcock (600) 145.00

Roland Clark (1874–1957)—An artist/writer/sportsman whose work is eagerly sought by knowledgeable collectors. (See also listing in Chapter 3, Books.)

Derrydale prints, "single duck" series (250)
    The Alarm 1,225.00
    Sanctuary 975.00
    The Scout 900.00
Others . . . . 450.00 to 1,000.00
Etchings and drypoints
    Before the Squall 425.00
    Captain Billy's Rig 1,750.00
    The Feeding Ground. 550.00
    The Ice Hole. 375.00
Others . . . . to 2,000.00

Guy Coheleach—A contemporary artist who has become very well known for his African game animal paintings and prints.

African big-game prints . . . . 250.00 to 750.00

Arthur Cook—A contemporary artist who has become well known for his portraits of birds in natural stormy settings.

After the Storm (350) 90.00
Arctic Tern (450). 110.00
Others . . . . 50.00 to 225.00

John Cowan—Another contemporary wildlife artist who is equally at home with fish or fowl.

Currier and Ives—Early and important contributors to the sporting scene, their work is very valuable when in good condition.

This etching by Roland Clark entitled "Inbound" was the signed frontispiece for his book *Gunner's Dawn* **published in an edition of 950 copies by the Derrydale Press in 1937.** *Illustration courtesy of Ken Callahan, Peterborough, New Hampshire.*

Roland Clark's drypoint "Sanctuary No. 2" is a fine example of this artist's work and sells for up to $1,200.00. *Illustration courtesy of John T. Ordeman.*

Thomas Aquinas Daly—An outstanding contemporary artist whose work is collected and coveted by many.

Aquatints and etchings
Georgia Pines (60) 350.00
Limestone (60) 425.00
Others. .... to 750.00

CURRIER AND IVES

A complete listing of the many sporting prints produced by Currier and Ives from the works of a variety of artists, such as Arthur Tait and Fanny Palmer, can be found in a number of books including the scarce *Currier and Ives Sporting Prints* by Peters. Many original prints have been reproduced time and time again, and collectors should deal only with reliable and trustworthy specialists. Caveat emptor. The three sizes are estimated in value as follows:

Small folio	to 750.00
Medium folio	to 2,500.00
Large folio	to 10,000.00

Trimmed, stained, and otherwise damaged prints are worth far less.

Churchill Ettinger—A dedicated sportsman who fished, hunted and skied, his prints and etchings are increasing in price and popularity, as is usually the case after any talented artist's demise.

Prints
Rainy Day—Restigouche River 400.00
Worn Rock Pool 275.00
Etchings. . . . . 150.00 to 400.00

A. B. Frost—Aptly called "America's artist," his scenes capture sports and sportsmen in a very special manner.

John Frost—The son of A. B., he is a fine artist in his own right and is said to have colored his father's Derrydale prints.

Derrydale prints (Note: Frost's and Currier and Ives's prints are the only examples of sporting prints that are worth these high prices *without* the artist's signature.)
A Chance Shot While Setting out Decoys (200) . . . . to 2,500.00
Coming Ashore (200). . . . . to 2,500.00
Grouse Shooting in the Rhododendrons (200) . . . . to 2,500.00
October Woodcock Shooting (200) . . . . to 5,000.00
Scribner's 1895
Individual prints. . . . . 300.00 to 500.00
12-print portfolio. . . . . to 10,000.00
Scribner's 1903 (Note: "Good Luck" and "Bad Luck" from this series are increasingly popular.)
Individual prints. . . . . 250.00 to 500.00
6-print portfolio. . . . . to 5,000.00
Winchester Press reproductions . . . . to 25.00

"October Woodcock Shooting" by A. B. Frost, published by the Derrydale Press in an edition of 200 hand-colored copies, has become the most expensive of the 90-odd Derrydale Press prints. This copy from Eugene Connett's collection sold for $1,800.00 plus a 10% buyer's premium. *Illustration courtesy of Oinonen Book Auctions, Sunderland, Massachusetts.*

Nancy Glazier—A fondness for big game in its Western American settings has brought fame to this talented lady.

King's Crossing—Elk (600)............................150.00
Morning Glory—Mule Deer (600)......................285.00

Francis Golden—A onetime Connecticut neighbor this talented artist/illustrator is at home with both field and stream.

Angus Pool (100) 300.00
Canadas and Young (850) 125.00

Phillip R. Goodwin—Increasingly popular as north-woods scenes and settings from the 1920s and 1930s have grown in stature.

Owen Gromme—This fine artist's bird and game-bird prints have captured America's fancy and become costly.

Bird and sporting-bird prints .... 200.00 to 1,000.00

John Groth—A favorite of fly fishermen, Groth's prints and etchings have a feel of their own.

David Hagerbaumer—A watercolorist and etcher of note, his waterfowl and upland game-bird representations are important.

Prints
    Foggy Morning—Mallards (400) 225.00
    Gathering Storm—Pintails (450) 175.00
    The Old Duck Camp (450) 210.00
Etchings . . . . to 200.00

Winslow Homer—This artist needs no introduction other than to tell you that he did not sign his prints (had he done so, these low prices would be in the thousands).

Canoe in the Rapids 85.00
Leaping Trout by the Angler's Club 350.00
Other Adirondack prints . . . . 75.00 to 125.00

Lynn Bogue Hunt—Best known for his prolific illustrations for books and magazines, his prints are nonetheless important. He is probably America's best-known sporting artist, and his work is very popular. His signed prints and etchings are rare. See also Chapter 2, Duck Stamps and Prints.

Etchings and signed prints . . . . to 400.00
Prints
    DuPont 18-print portfolio, 1918 . . . . 500.00

"Sharpshooter" is a steel engraving made from a painting by Winslow Homer for *Harper's Weekly* during America's Civil War. This example was clipped from a copy of the magazine and is valued at $85.00.

Field and Stream portfolios
Game birds. . . . . to 250.00
Game fishing . . . . to 350.00

Francis Lee Jaques—A self-taught talent, his art reflects the knowledge gained through 20 years at the American Museum of Natural History.

James Killen—A prolific contemporary sporting artist whose style has proved popular with collectors. He was the artist for the first four Vermont state duck-stamp prints and stamps.

In the Feed—Canada Geese (500). 125.00
That's My Dog, various breeds, unsigned. 35.00

Edward King—One of the Derrydale Press artists who became famous through Eugene Connett's efforts in the 1930s.

Derrydale Press prints . . . . 200.00 to 800.00

Marguerite Kirmse—Justifiably famous for her sporting and non-sporting dog prints, her work is gaining in popularity and price.

Derrydale Press prints
The Fox (250). . . . . to 750.00
The Hounds (250). . . . . to 750.00
Etchings. . . . . 100.00 to 450.00

J. D. Knapp—One of the early Federal Duck Stamp program participants, his prints are of the waterfowl he knew and loved.

All Clear 350.00
Reflections. 275.00
Others . . . . 150.00 to 350.00

Robert Kuhn—A contemporary and popular sporting artist who knows the outdoors as few others, and his work reflects this knowledge.

Jaguar and Egret (100) 150.00
Sunshine and Shadow (500) 185.00
Others. . . . . to 350.00

Lee LeBlanc—Upland birds and waterfowl are this contemporary artist's bag, and his prints are collectible.

Arkansas Mallards (400) 235.00
Busted Covey (800). 85.00
Cache River Memory (800) 110.00
Others. . . . . to 300.00

David Lockhart—Another contemporary sporting artist with a talent for painting waterfowl and upland game birds.

David Maass—A well-known and prolific sporting artist whose "Misty Morning" prints are very desirable and costly. Maass was the artist chosen for three Federal and many state duck-stamp prints and stamps.

Early Winter Morning—Bobwhite (850) 325.00
Early Winter Morning—Turkey (950) 210.00
Misty Morning—Green Wing Teal (580) 600.00
Misty Morning—Woodcock (450) 1,000.00

Edwin Megargee—A well-known sporting artist who is best known for his fine portraits of sporting dogs.

Derrydale Press prints
November Morn (250) 550.00
Staunch (250) 475.00
Steady (250) 475.00
Others . . . . to 1,000.00

Rosemary Millette—A talented lady with a soft treatment of both winged and hooved wildlife.

Abandoned Homestead—Pheasants (580) 175.00
Autumn Encounter—Pheasants (1,200) 80.00
Others . . . . to 500.00

Gustav Muss-Arnolt—An artist whose paintings of gun dogs have appeared in many forms. His prints are scarce.

Edmund Osthaus—Another artist whose works depicting gun dogs led him to capture field trial dogs on canvas.

Roger Tory Peterson—Best known for his famous field guides, this artist's work is collected by many enthusiasts.

Richard Plasschaert—Game birds are this contemporary artist's game, and he plays it very well indeed.

Moonam Marsh—Green-Wing Teal (580) 225.00
Moonam Marsh—Mallards (580) 185.00
Moonam Marsh—Wood Ducks (580) 225.00
Others . . . . to 275.00

Ogden M. Pleissner—It was my good fortune to conduct the last interview with this world-famous artist before his death in 1983.

Etchings
Salmon Guide 1,100.00
Others . . . . to 1,750.00
Prints
The Battenkill at Benedict's Crossing (270) 1,000.00
Beaverkill Bridge (221) 1,800.00
Blue Boat on the Saint Anne (270) 3,250.00

Dawn on the Duck Marsh (270) 650.00
Hillside Orchard—Grouse Shooting (275) 1,400.00
Woodcock Cover (270). 1,500.00

Alexander Pope—This artist's detailed 1800s chromolithographs of game
are collectible and becoming expensive.

Waterfowl and game bird chromolithographs. . . . . . . 200.00 to 350.00

Maynard Reece—A well-known contemporary portrayer of game and fish
in natural settings. Reece is a four-time Federal duck stamp competition winner.

Against the Wind—Canvasbacks (55) 400.00
Dark Sky—Bobwhites (950) 225.00
Dark Sky—Ruffed Grouse (950) 225.00
Dark Sky—Snow Geese (950) 150.00
The Sand Bar—Canada Geese (950) 110.00

Frederick Remington—This well-known Western-scene artist also produced worthy Adirondack woods and waters.

Chet Reneson—A talented watercolorist whose contemporary paintings
have wide appeal with sportsmen.

Alder Brook (200) 200.00
Early Season (400) 175.00
Neighbor's Field (400) 150.00
Summertime (200) 200.00
Winter Grouse (400) 200.00
Others. . . . . to 500.00

A. Lassell Ripley—"Gunning in America" was a *Field and Stream* portfolio, but it aptly describes all of this artist's fine contributions.

Etchings. . . . . to 1,000.00
Prints
   Field and Stream "Gunning in America"
     Individual prints, framed. 75.00
     Portfolio 250.00
   Frost and Reed
     Covey by the Cabin 675.00
     Grouse Cover 750.00
     A Turkey Drive. 625.00
     Others . . . . to 750.00

Carl Rungius—Considered by many to be our finest big-game artist, his
work continues to escalate in value.

Etchings . . . . 1,000.00 to 3,500.00

William J. Schaldach—This late artist's work depicts game birds and fish with the skill of the sportsman he was. See Chapter 3, Books, for more about this artist/writer/sportsman.

Prints
    Derrydale Press, American Game Birds—Woodcock
    (250) . . . . to 1,500.00

William J. Schaldach's "Leaping Quananiche" portrays the excitement of the landlocked salmon when hooked. One of an edition of 50 prints, this rare etching sold for $550.00. *Courtesy John T. Ordeman.*

Theodore Gordon Flyfishers
    Brook Trout 85.00
    Eastern Brook Trout (300) 400.00
Etchings and drypoints . . . . to 500.00

David Shepherd—A serious and accurate portrayer of African big game in its natural settings.

African game prints
    Signed. . . . . to 750.00
    Unsigned . . . . to 100.00

Peter Scott—A talented English artist whose work is sought by collectors throughout the world.

Michael Sieve—A contemporary artist who is best known for his paintings of American game animals.

Alaskan Classic—Dall Sheep (850) 110.00
Alpine Meadow—Elk (850) 150.00
Fast Break—Whitetail Deer (850) 125.00
Others. . . . . to 350.00

Gary Sorels—Another contemporary painter who specializes in American big game.

Early Winter—Whitetail Deer (600) 145.00
In the Clearing—Elk (850) 85.00
Others. . . . . to 350.00

Arthur F. Tait—This talented artist's contributions are clearly represented in his work for Currier and Ives.

Milton C. Weiler—Classic decoys and shorebirds are only a portion of this late artist's sporting output.

Classic Decoys portfolio 750.00
Classic Shorebirds
    Individual prints. . . . . 25.00 to 50.00
    Portfolio 500.00
Matapedia Mist (250) 700.00
Upper Twin Pool—Henryville (125) 1,000.00
Upstream and Down plate, signed by artist and author 450.00
Others . . . . to 1,000.00

Confucian wisdom tells us that a picture is worth a thousand words, but I beg to differ and suggest you read anything and everything about sporting prints you can lay your hands on—preferably before you buy anything. You should not be satisfied with the limited information I have provided in these all-too-few pages, not when the shelves of libraries and bookstores are filled with so much more information. Pick an artist and chances are good to excellent that someone has written about him. Ordeman's books on Benson, Clark, and Schaldach are of great merit, as is Schaldach's book about Carl Rungius. A. B. Frost is the subject of several volumes and Peter Bergh's book about the late, great Ogden Pleissner cannot be overlooked in spite of its poor color reproductions. Abbett, Bateman, Coheleach, and others are covered in the series *Masters of the Wild,* and a trip to your local library or bookseller may uncover just the information you are looking for. If all else fails, contact the art and/or book dealers listed in the appendix at the end of this book. A few thousand words may prove to be worth a few thousand dollars in savings.

REMARQUED PRINTS

A remarqued print is one in which the artist has added to the border a small original sketch in black and white or color. Remarques often add to a print's value but are not always worth the additional cost if one is thinking in terms of investment.

CHAPTER 2

Duck Stamps and Duck-Stamp Prints

et's get right to the point of this four-part chapter and admit that all too many collectors have been taken in by the hyperbole that is a part of today's duck-stamp print marketing of "limited edition" artwork, which is worth next to nothing on the secondary market where real values are set. But wait! Many duck stamps and duck-stamp prints are of value, as the figures on the following pages indicate, so before you line your parrot's cage, read on. I sometimes wonder if anyone reads prefaces and introductions, but if you do, what follows may surprise you.

Federal Duck Stamps

During the late 1920s and early 1930s the waterfowl population of North America shrunk to new all-time lows as more and more acres of potholes and wetlands turned to dust. Something had to be done! Sportsmen and sporting magazines helped with the solution, but it was through the efforts of one man—Jay Norwood "Ding" Darling—that the dusty corner was turned. Working with Franklin Roosevelt and his Secretary of Agriculture (who was of little, if any, help), Darling pushed for and finally got FDR's approval to charge the princely sum of $1 for the "duck stamp" that would permit waterfowl gunners the right to hunt migratory ducks, geese, and certain species of shorebirds. Jay Norwood Darling, working against time, drew and designed the first Federal Migratory Waterfowl Stamp himself so as to have it ready for the 1934–1935 season.

For most of us the "permit" will always be the "duck stamp" and its innovator just plain "Ding." A truly fine example of that very first duck stamp can cost $500 on today's market, but more important in the overall scheme of things are the countless waterfowl the original cost of $1 saved so many years ago. Were it not for those efforts, I can almost guarantee the haunting honking from autumn- and spring-time skies and the happy quacking of nestlings in the twilight would diminish our lives by their absence.

The duck stamp worked. By the end of the 1930s the crisis with ducks and drought was over and the stamp itself had become an established and desirable collectible. During these early years—and hoping to attract non-hunters to the stamp—famous sporting artists were asked to contribute their energies to the program, and this too worked. Designs by such notables as Frank W. Benson, Roland Clark, Richard Bishop, and Lynn Bogue Hunt all added to the worth of an already worthwhile program and ensured its success. Things changed rapidly in the 1940s when so many artists wanted to "do" the duck stamp that by 1950 confusion necessitated a contest to determine the "winner." In that first year of the contest, 88 designs were submitted by 65 different artists. Although it was a far cry from the original one-artist, one-design concept, it has become an event that continues to this day with thousands of entries. Many winning duck-stamp designs from the 1970s and 1980s sold in "limited editions" of as many as 30,000 prints and the artists who caught the judges' eyes became millionaires as a result. One wonders what Ding Darling would have to say about that hyperbole.

Federal Duck-Stamp Prints

Most people think of the federal duck stamp and its corresponding duck-stamp print as being akin to peas in a pod, but nothing could be further from the truth.

Duck-stamp prints were not offered for sale until 1940, when Ed Thomas and Ralph Terrill of Abercrombie & Fitch's art department convinced Richard Bishop to make an etching of his 1936–1937 duck stamp. In 1942 Thomas was able to get Frank Benson to follow suit, and by the time

Federal Duck Stamp print by Bruce Miller depicts a pair of canvasbacks. Issued in 1993–1994, it was the sixtieth stamp in the Federal series of stamps and, later, prints.

Jay N. Darling turned out an estimated 300 prints of his duck-stamp design in 1944, duck-stamp artists were routinely making limited-edition prints of their designs. Darling turned out the aforementioned 300 prints and Frank Benson only 100; but Dick Bishop, who did not believe in limiting his prints, turned out not one but two unlimited editions of his stamp art—today's values reflect that long-ago decision. J. D. Knapp produced 260 prints, Lynn Bogue Hunt came up with two editions of 100 each, and Francis Lee Jaques turned out three editions with a total of 260 prints.

This pattern of truly limited editions continued through the 1960s, with print editions climbing slowly to an average of 600 or so each. This changed with the 1970–1972 duck-stamp print when artist Ed Bierly turned out 1,000 of his winning watercolor stamp design at $60 each. The print sold out quickly, and the handwriting was on the wall: Color had come to the duck stamp, and collectors craved color.

In 1971–1972 and 1972–1973, duck-stamp prints in color editions of 950 each sold out almost immediately, as did Lee LeBlanc's winning design of Steller's eiders in 1973–1974 in an edition of 1,000 prints. Grabbing the bull by the horns, David Maass then offered his winning wood-duck stamp design to all who ordered it before a given deadline. Twenty-seven hundred prints were sold, and the meaning of "limited-edition print" was changed forever.

From then on, duck-stamp prints were turned out in ever-increasing numbers, and in 1980–1981 Richard Plasschaert's design sold 12,950 print copies. Two years later, David Maass's winning design sold a record-setting 22,250 copies, to be bested in 1983–1984 when 31,900 copies of the year's duck-stamp print were sold in all editions. Duck-stamp print sales might well have spiraled to unheard-of numbers had not some well-meaning official closed the barn door and limited the number of prints produced to 20,000, beginning with the 1987–1988 print. But it was too late. The horse was gone and the truly limited-edition duck-stamp print was lost forever.

State Duck Stamps and Duck-Stamp Prints

Forty-nine of the fifty states have state duck and/or conservation stamps that accompany them, with only Hawaii happily out of step as I write these words. Why happily? Simply because these so-called sporting collectibles are, for the most part, worthless. Few do anything for waterfowl or our wetlands, let alone improve gunning conditions for waterfowlers. And, more to the point, fewer still reap any benefits for sporting print collectors. Examine the following lists of state duck stamp and duck-stamp print prices, but bear in mind that they are top-of-the-line retail prices. Anyone wishing to sell should expect not more than half of the retail value, with many of the more plentiful prints and canceled (signed) stamps worth next to nothing on the already crowded market. Perhaps if you consider that every year 50 duck stamps and duck-stamp prints are added to the plethora out there already, you will understand why.

FEDERAL DUCK STAMPS

Year	Used*	Unused**	Fine***
1934–35	$ 95.00	$125.00	$425.00
1935–36	100.00	180.00	400.00
1936–37	50.00	85.00	225.00
1937–38	30.00	60.00	195.00
1938–39	30.00	60.00	195.00
1939–40	20.00	40.00	125.00
1940–41	20.00	40.00	125.00
1941–42	20.00	40.00	125.00
1942–43	20.00	40.00	125.00
1943–44	20.00	30.00	50.00
1944–45	18.00	25.00	45.00
1945–46	13.00	18.00	30.00
1946–47	10.00	18.00	30.00
1947–48	10.00	20.00	30.00
1948–49	10.00	20.00	40.00
1949–50	8.00	22.00	40.00
1950–51	8.00	22.00	45.00
1951–52	7.00	22.00	45.00
1952–53	7.00	22.00	45.00
1953–54	7.00	22.00	45.00
1954–55	6.00	24.00	55.00
1955–56	6.00	24.00	50.00
1956–57	6.00	22.00	55.00
1957–58	5.00	25.00	55.00
1958–59	5.00	25.00	50.00
1959–60	5.00	35.00	65.00
1960–61	7.00	35.00	65.00
1961–62	7.00	35.00	65.00
1962–63	7.00	45.00	75.00
1963–64	7.00	55.00	70.00
1964–65	7.00	50.00	70.00
1965–66	7.00	55.00	70.00
1966–67	7.00	55.00	70.00
1967–68	6.00	50.00	70.00
1968–69	5.50	35.00	50.00
1969–70	5.00	30.00	45.00
1970–71	4.50	30.00	45.00
1971–72	4.50	18.00	25.00
1972–73	4.50	12.00	18.00
1973–74	4.50	12.00	14.00
1974–75 through 1994–1995			to 25.00

*Signed by hunter.

**Not signed but good to very good condition only.

***Fine stamps that have been hinged. Never-hinged stamps in excellent condition are more expensive.

To end this dissertation on a happy note, I suggest you look into the value and availability of Native-American Indian reservation duck stamps, which are an interesting and often valuable collection. Write to Michael Jaffe, Box 61484, Vancouver, Washington 98666. Michael has a wonderful catalog and has been a friend, indeed, to this writer.

FEDERAL DUCK-STAMP PRINTS
(Prices are for unframed prints without stamps.)

Year and Artist		Quantity	Value
1934–35: Darling		300	4,400.00
1935–36: Benson		100	8,000.00
1936–37: Bishop		unlimited	850.00
1937–38: Knapp		260	3,000.00
1938–39: Clark		300	3,800.00
1939–40: Hunt	(1st ed.)	100	7,500.00
	(2nd ed.)	100	7,000.00
1940–41: Jaques	(1st ed.)	30	10,000.00
	(2nd ed.)	30	7,500.00
	(3rd ed.)	200	3,500.00
1941–42: Kalmbach	(flopped)	100	4,500.00
	(2nd ed.)	unknown	1,300.00
1942–43: Ripley		unlimited	1,200.00
1943–44: Bohl	(1st ed.)	290	1,500.00
	(2nd ed.)	unknown	500.00
1944–45: Weber	(flopped)	100	4,700.00
	(2nd ed.)	200	2,700.00
	(3rd ed.)	90	700.00
1945–46: Gromme		250	6,500.00
1946–47: Hines	(1st ed.)	300	1,600.00
	(2nd ed.)	380	200.00
1947–48: Murray		300	2,700.00
1948–49: Reece	(1st ed.)	200	1,500.00
	(2nd ed.)	150	1,000.00
	(3rd ed.)	400	600.00
	(4th ed.)	300	500.00
1949–50: Preuss	(1st ed.)	250	3,000.00
	(2nd ed.)	395	200.00
1950–51: Weber	(1st ed.)	250	1,500.00
	(2nd ed.)	300	250.00
1951–52: Reece	(1st ed.)	250	1,200.00
	(2nd ed.)	400	600.00
1952–53: Dick	(1st ed.)	250	2,100.00
	(2nd ed.)	300	150.00
1953–54: Seagers	(1st ed.)	250	2,000.00
	(2nd ed.)	1,500	150.00

Year and Artist		Quantity	Value
1954–55: Sandstrom	(1st ed.)	275	1,600.00
	(2nd ed.)	400	150.00
1955–56: Stearns	(1st ed. 1st prt.)	250	1,200.00
	(1st ed. 2nd prt.)	53	1,100.00
	(2nd ed.)	100	600.00
1956–57: Bierly	(1st ed. 1st prt.)	325	1,000.00
	(1st ed. 2nd prt.)	125	800.00
1957–58: Abbott	(1st ed.)	253	1,000.00
	(2nd ed.)	500	300.00
	(3rd ed.)	1,500	150.00
1958–59: Kouba	(1st ed.)	250	1,300.00
	(2nd ed.)	250	1,000.00
	(3rd ed.)	300	300.00
1959–60: Reece	(1st ed.)	400	4,000.00
	(2nd ed.)	300	2,000.00
	(3rd ed.)	400	1,500.00
1960–61: Ruthven	(1st ed.)	400	1,000.00
	(2nd ed.)	300	600.00
	(3rd ed.)	400	500.00
1961–62: Morris		275	1,500.00
1963–63: Morris		275	1,500.00
1963–64: Bierly	(1st ed. 1st prt.)	550	1,000.00
	(1st ed. 2nd prt.)	125	800.00
1964–65: Stearns	(1st ed.)	665	1,100.00
	(2nd ed.)	100	650.00
1965–66: Jenkins	(1st ed.)	700	850.00
	(2nd ed.)	100	600.00
	(3rd ed.)	250	250.00
1966–67: Stearns	(1st ed.)	300	1,100.00
	(2nd ed.)	300	400.00
1967–68: Kouba		275	900.00
1968–69: Pritchard		750	1,200.00
1969–70: Reece		750	1,000.00
1970–71: Bierly	(1st ed.)	1,000	2,500.00
	(2nd ed.)	2,150	200.00
1971–72: Reece		950	5,200.00
1972–73: Cook	(1st ed.)	950	2,700.00
	(2nd ed.)	900	150.00
1973–74: LeBlanc	(1st ed.)	1,000	2,000.00
	(2nd ed.)	900	150.00
1974–75: Maass		2,700	1,100.00
1975–76: Fisher		3,150	1,000.00
1976–77: Magee	(reg. ed.)	3,600	800.00
	(medallion ed.)	1,000	1,300.00

Year and Artist		Quantity	Value
1977–78: Murk		5,800	450.00
1978–79: Gilbert		7,150	450.00
1979–80: Michaelson	(reg. ed.)	7,000	350.00
	(medallion ed.)	1,500	500.00
1980–81: Plasschaert		12,950	600.00
1981–82: Wilson		16,000	350.00
1982–83: Maass		22,250	350.00
1983–84: Scholer	(reg. ed.)	17,400	500.00
	(medallion ed.)	6,700	1,000.00
1984–85: Morris	(reg. ed.)	20,400	175.00
	(medallion ed.)	11,500	350.00
1985–86: Mobley	(reg. ed.)	18,200	135.00
	(medallion ed.)	6,650	250.00
1986–87: Moore	(reg. ed.)	16,310	135.00
	(medallion ed.)	4,670	250.00
1987–88: Anderson, A.	(reg. ed.)	20,000	135.00
	(medallion ed.)	5,000	250.00
1988–89: Smith	(reg. ed.)	22,000	200.00
	(medallion ed.)	6,500	350.00
1989–90: Anderson, N.	(reg. ed.)	20,000	145.00
	(medallion ed.)	7,000	325.00
1990–91: Hautman	(reg. ed.)	14,500	145.00
	(medallion ed.)	5,500	325.00

State Duck Stamps

ALABAMA

1979	10.00
1980–1982	9.00
1983–1987	15.00
1988	12.00
1989–1991	9.00
1992–1995	8.00

ALASKA

1985	15.00
1986	12.00
1987–1988	10.00
1989–1995	7.00

ARIZONA

1987 . . . . 12.00
1988 . . . . 10.00
1989–1991 . . . . 9.00
1992–1995 . . . . 7.50

ARKANSAS

1981–1983 . . . . 60.00
1984 . . . . 22.00
1985–1986 . . . . 12.00
1987–1991 . . . . 11.00
1992–1995 . . . . 9.00

CALIFORNIA

1971 . . . . 750.00
1972 . . . . 3,400.00
1973 . . . . 15.00
1974 . . . . 4.50
1975 . . . . 115.00
1976 . . . . 15.00
1977: $1.00 stamp 55.00
1977: $5.00 stamp 9.00
1978 . . . . 150.00
1979–1983 . . . . 7.50
1984–1992 . . . . 10.00
1993–1995 . . . . 12.50

COLORADO

1990 . . . . 15.00
1991 . . . . 9.00
1992–1995 . . . . 7.50

CONNECTICUT

1993–1995 . . . . 7.50

DELAWARE

1980 . . . . 100.00
1981 . . . . 90.00
1982 . . . . 95.00
1983 . . . . 60.00
1984 . . . . 30.00
1985 . . . . 14.00
1986–1987 . . . . 10.00

The 1993 Connecticut "First of State" duck stamp print by Tome Hirata shows a pair of black ducks over the Saybrook breakwater.

1988.. 9.00
1989–1995.. 7.50

FLORIDA

1979.. 195.00
1980–1981.. 30.00
1982... 50.00
1983... 60.00
1984–1985.. 25.00
1986... 11.00
1987–1988... 7.50
1989–1991... 6.00
1992–1995... 5.50

GEORGIA

1985... 15.00
1986... 11.00
1987–1995... 7.50

HAWAII HAS NO STAMP AT THIS WRITING.

IDAHO

1987	15.00
1988	11.00
1989–1991	10.00
1992–1995	8.00

ILLINOIS

1975	695.00
1976	250.00
1977	195.00
1978–1981	115.00
1979 (error)	750.00
1982	65.00
1983	60.00
1984	55.00
1985	25.00
1986	12.00
1987–1989	10.00
1990–1991	15.00
1992–1995	13.00

INDIANA

1976	10.00
1977–1987	8.00
1988–1991	10.00
1992–1995	9.00

IOWA

1972	175.00
1973	45.00
1974	75.00
1975	110.00
1976–1977	15.00
1978	60.00
1979	425.00
1980	60.00
1981	37.50
1982	17.00
1983	15.00
1984	40.00
1985	20.00
1986	19.00
1987	12.00
1988–1989	10.00
1990	9.00
1991–1995	7.50

KANSAS

1987. . . . . 10.00
1988. . . . . 6.50
1989–1991. . . . . 6.00
1992–1995. . . . . 5.25

KENTUCKY

1985. . . . . 10.00
1986–1991. . . . . 8.00
1992–1993. . . . . 10.00
1994–1995. . . . . 9.50

LOUISIANA

1989
  Resident 11.00
  Non-resident 13.00
1990
  Resident 9.00
  Non-resident 12.00
1991
  Resident 8.50

The 1989 Louisiana "First of State" duck stamp print by David Noll shows a pair of blue-wing teal in flight.

Non-resident 10.00
1992–1995
  Resident 7.50
  Non-resident 9.50

MAINE

1984 . . . . 30.00
1985 . . . . 50.00
1986 . . . . 13.00
1987 . . . . 10.00
1988 . . . . 8.00
1989–1995 . . . . 5.00

MARYLAND

1974 . . . . 20.00
1975 . . . . 8.00
1976–1981 . . . . 6.00
1982 . . . . 9.00
1983 . . . . 12.50
1984–1991 . . . . 9.00
1992–1995 . . . . 8.00

MASSACHUSETTS

1974 . . . . 15.00
1975–1979 . . . . 10.00
1980–1987 . . . . 7.50
1988–1990 . . . . 5.00
1991 . . . . 7.50
1992–1995 . . . . 7.00

MICHIGAN

1976 . . . . 7.50
1977 . . . . 325.00
1978 . . . . 30.00
1979 . . . . 40.00
1980 . . . . 18.00
1981–1986 . . . . 25.00
1987–1988 . . . . 12.00
1989 . . . . 7.50
1990 . . . . 6.50
1991–1994 . . . . 6.00
1995 . . . . 7.00

MINNESOTA

1977 . . . . 15.00
1978–1989 . . . . 10.00
1990 . . . . 20.00
1991 . . . . 7.50
1992–1995 . . . . 7.00

MISSISSIPPI

1976 . . . . 15.00
1977–1990 . . . . 10.00
1991 . . . . 4.50
1992 . . . . 4.00
1993–1995 . . . . 7.00

MISSOURI

1979 . . . . 725.00
1980 . . . . 150.00
1981 . . . . 75.00
1982–1984 . . . . 50.00
1985 . . . . 30.00
1986 . . . . 25.00
1987 . . . . 18.00
1988 . . . . 11.00
1989 . . . . 10.00
1990 . . . . 9.00
1991 . . . . 8.00
1992–1995 . . . . 7.00

MONTANA

1986 . . . . 17.50
1987 . . . . 15.00
1988 . . . . 13.50
1989 . . . . 12.00
1990 . . . . 10.00
1991 . . . . 9.00
1992–1995 . . . . 7.00

NEBRASKA

1991 . . . . 10.00
1992–1995 . . . . 8.00

NEVADA

1979. . . . . 65.00
1980–1986 . . . . 12.00
1987–1988 . . . . 10.00
1989. . . . . 6.00
1990. . . . . 10.00
1991. . . . . 8.00
1992–1995 . . . . 7.50

NEW HAMPSHIRE

1983. . . . . 195.00
1984–1985 . . . . 85.00
1986. . . . . 30.00
1987. . . . . 22.00
1988. . . . . 12.00
1989. . . . . 11.00
1990. . . . . 9.00
1991. . . . . 7.00
1992–1995 . . . . 6.00

NEW JERSEY

1984
   Resident 55.00
   Non-resident 65.00
1985
   Resident 19.00
   Non-resident 25.00
1986
   Resident 12.00
   Non-resident 15.00
1987
   Resident 10.00
   Non-resident 14.00
1988
   Resident 8.00
   Non-resident 12.00
1989
   Resident 6.00
   Non-resident 10.00
1990
   Resident 5.50
   Non-resident 9.50

1991
  Resident 4.50
  Non-resident 8.50
1992–1995
  Resident 5.00
  Non-resident 7.00

NEW MEXICO

1991 . . . . 11.50
1992–1995 . . . . 9.50

NEW YORK

1985 . . . . 15.00
1986–1988 . . . . 12.00
1989 . . . . 9.50
1990 . . . . 8.50
1991–1995 . . . . 7.50

The 1991 New Mexico "First of State" duck stamp print depicts a pair of pin-tails landing in a desert slough.

NORTH CAROLINA

1983. . . . . 120.00
1984. . . . . 55.00
1985. . . . . 45.00
1986. . . . . 19.00
1987. . . . . 14.00
1988. . . . . 12.00
1989. . . . . 11.00
1990. . . . . 10.00
1991. . . . . 8.00
1992–1995. . . . . 7.00

NORTH DAKOTA

1982. . . . . 125.00
1983. . . . . 75.00
1984. . . . . 40.00
1985. . . . . 30.00
1986. . . . . 25.00
1987. . . . . 18.00
1988. . . . . 15.00
1989. . . . . 12.00
1990. . . . . 11.00
1991. . . . . 10.00
1992–1995. . . . . 8.00

OHIO

1982. . . . . 90.00
1983–1984 . . . . 85.00
1985. . . . . 62.50
1986. . . . . 30.00
1987. . . . . 18.00
1988–1989 . . . . 12.00
1990. . . . . 15.00
1991. . . . . 13.00
1992–1993 . . . . 11.00
1994–1995 . . . . 14.00

OKLAHOMA

1980. . . . . 45.00
1981. . . . . 35.00
1982. . . . . 12.00
1983. . . . . 10.00
1984. . . . . 9.00
1985–1991 . . . . 7.00
1992–1995 . . . . 6.00

OREGON

1984	45.00
1985	50.00
1986	20.00
1987	12.00
1988	11.00
1989	10.00
1990	9.50
1991	9.00
1992–1995	8.00

PENNSYLVANIA

1983	35.00
1984	25.00
1985	14.00
1986–1989	10.00
1990	8.50
1991	8.00
1992–1995	7.50

RHODE ISLAND

1989	15.00
1990	12.00
1991	10.50
1992–1995	9.50

SOUTH CAROLINA

1981–1982	95.00
1983	110.00
1984	75.00
1985	70.00
(# on reverse)	90.00
1986	35.00
(# on reverse)	22.00
1987	22.00
(# on reverse)	25.00
1988	30.00
(# on reverse)	30.00
1989	15.00
(# on reverse)	15.00
1990	10.00
(# on reverse)	10.00
1991–1992	8.50
1993–1995	7.50

SOUTH DAKOTA

1976	30.00
1977	20.00
1978	12.00
1979–1985	(none issued)
1986	15.00
1987	8.00
1988	7.00
1989	6.00
1990	5.00
1991–1995	4.00

TENNESSEE

1979	
Resident	225.00
Non-resident	1,295.00
1980	
Resident	75.00
Non-resident	600.00
1981	45.00
1982–1983	85.00
1984	95.00
1985	32.50
1986	20.00
1987	15.00
1988	12.00
1989	11.00
1990	19.00
1991	17.00
1992–1993	16.50
1994–1995	18.00

TEXAS

1981	45.00
1982	40.00
1983	225.00
1984	30.00
1985	18.00
1986	12.00
1987	10.00
1988	9.00
1989	8.50
1990	8.00
1991–1995	10.00

UTAH

1986 . . . . 11.00
1987 . . . . 8.00
1988–1989 . . . . 7.00
1990 . . . . 5.50
1991–1995 . . . . 5.00

VERMONT

1986 . . . . 11.00
1987 . . . . 10.00
1988 . . . . 9.00
1989 . . . . 8.00
1990 . . . . 7.50
1991–1995 . . . . 7.00

VIRGINIA

1988 . . . . 15.00
1989 . . . . 10.00
1990 . . . . 9.00
1991 . . . . 8.00
1992–1995 . . . . 7.00

WASHINGTON

1986 . . . . 11.00
1987 . . . . 10.00
1988–1989 . . . . 9.50
1990 . . . . 10.00
1991 . . . . 9.00
1992–1995 . . . . 8.00

WEST VIRGINIA

(Note: Resident and non-resident stamps were issued each year and are of equal value.)

1987 . . . . 15.00
1988–1990 . . . . 10.00
1991–1993 . . . . 8.50
1994–1995 . . . . 7.50

WISCONSIN

1978	140.00
1979	45.00
1980–1981	15.00
1982–1984	8.00
1985–1986	10.00
1987–1990	6.00
1991	8.50
1992–1995	7.50

WYOMING

(Non-waterfowl issued from 1986 and initially in 1984.)

1985	9.50

State Duck-Stamp Prints

ALABAMA

1979	750.00
1980–1981	110.00
1982	210.00
1983	110.00
1984	190.00
1985–1986	110.00
1987–1990	135.00

ALASKA

1985	700.00
1986	500.00
1987	210.00
1988–1989	200.00
1990	135.00

ARIZONA

1987	200.00
1988–1989	135.00
1990	145.00

ARKANSAS

1981	900.00
1982	250.00
1983	350.00
1984	300.00

1985–1987 . . . . 250.00
1988 . . . . 135.00
1989 . . . . 200.00
1990 . . . . 135.00

CALIFORNIA

1971 . . . . 1,750.00
1972 . . . . 2,500.00
1973–1977 . . . . 300.00
1978 . . . . 900.00
1979 . . . . 850.00
1980 . . . . 700.00
1981 . . . . 200.00
1982 . . . . 175.00
1983–1985 . . . . 150.00
1986 . . . . 190.00
1987 . . . . 200.00
1988 . . . . 135.00
1989–1990 . . . . 145.00

COLORADO

1990 . . . . 145.00

CONNECTICUT

1993–1995 . . . . 145.00

DELAWARE

1980 . . . . 800.00
1981–1989 . . . . 125.00
1990 . . . . 135.00

FLORIDA

1979 . . . . 800.00
1980–1985 . . . . 135.00
1986 . . . . 200.00
1987–1988 . . . . 135.00
1989–1990 . . . . 145.00

GEORGIA

1985 . . . . 300.00
1986–1990 . . . . 200.00

IDAHO

1987	4,000.00
1988	135.00
1989	180.00
1990	145.00

ILLINOIS

1976	4,000.00
1977–1978	500.00
1979–1980	400.00
1981	1,200.00
1982–1989	250.00
1990	135.00

INDIANA

1976	2,800.00

IOWA

1972	10,000.00
1973	700.00
1974	1,300.00
1975	200.00
1976	150.00
1977	600.00
1978	150.00
1979	900.00
1980–1982	150.00
1983–1986	200.00
1987–1990	135.00

KANSAS

1987–1989	135.00
1990	300.00

KENTUCKY

1985	350.00
1986–1988	200.00
1989–1990	135.00

LOUISIANA

1989	250.00
1990	135.00

MAINE

1984	400.00
1985	300.00
1986	275.00
1987–1988	200.00
1989	135.00
1990	145.00

MARYLAND

1974	6,000.00
1975	1,750.00
1976	900.00
1977	700.00
1978	300.00
1979	250.00
1980	450.00
1981	400.00
1982	300.00
1983–1985	250.00
1986–1988	200.00
1989–1990	135.00

MASSACHUSETTS

1974	1,400.00
1975	1,500.00
1976	400.00
1977	4,000.00
1978–1979	600.00
1980	350.00
1981–1982	250.00
1983	200.00
1984	400.00
1985–1987	200.00
1989–1990	140.00

MICHIGAN

1976	4,000.00
1977	1,750.00
1978	350.00
1979	500.00
1980	1,200.00
1981–1982	150.00
1983	800.00
1984	150.00

```
1985 . . . . . . . . . . . . . . . . . . . . . . . . . . . . . . . . . . . . . . . . . . . . . . . 275.00
1986 . . . . . . . . . . . . . . . . . . . . . . . . . . . . . . . . . . . . . . . . . . . . . . . 200.00
1987 . . . . . . . . . . . . . . . . . . . . . . . . . . . . . . . . . . . . . . . . . . . . . . . 350.00
1988 . . . . . . . . . . . . . . . . . . . . . . . . . . . . . . . . . . . . . . . . . . . . . . . 155.00
1989–1990 . . . . . . . . . . . . . . . . . . . . . . . . . . . . . . . . . . . . . . . . . 140.00
```

MINNESOTA

```
1977 . . . . . . . . . . . . . . . . . . . . . . . . . . . . . . . . . . . . . . . . . . . . . 1,800.00
1978 . . . . . . . . . . . . . . . . . . . . . . . . . . . . . . . . . . . . . . . . . . . . . . . 700.00
1979 . . . . . . . . . . . . . . . . . . . . . . . . . . . . . . . . . . . . . . . . . . . . . . . 500.00
1980 . . . . . . . . . . . . . . . . . . . . . . . . . . . . . . . . . . . . . . . . . . . . . . . 600.00
1981 . . . . . . . . . . . . . . . . . . . . . . . . . . . . . . . . . . . . . . . . . . . . . . . 150.00
1982–1985 . . . . . . . . . . . . . . . . . . . . . . . . . . . . . . . . . . . . . . . . . 200.00
1986 . . . . . . . . . . . . . . . . . . . . . . . . . . . . . . . . . . . . . . . . . . . . . . . 135.00
1987 . . . . . . . . . . . . . . . . . . . . . . . . . . . . . . . . . . . . . . . . . . . . . . . 275.00
1988 . . . . . . . . . . . . . . . . . . . . . . . . . . . . . . . . . . . . . . . . . . . . . . . 140.00
1989–1990 . . . . . . . . . . . . . . . . . . . . . . . . . . . . . . . . . . . . . . . . . 145.00
```

MISSISSIPPI

```
1976 . . . . . . . . . . . . . . . . . . . . . . . . . . . . . . . . . . . . . . . . . . . . . 3,000.00
1977 . . . . . . . . . . . . . . . . . . . . . . . . . . . . . . . . . . . . . . . . . . . . . 1,000.00
1978–1979 . . . . . . . . . . . . . . . . . . . . . . . . . . . . . . . . . . . . . . . . . 500.00
1980–1982 . . . . . . . . . . . . . . . . . . . . . . . . . . . . . . . . . . . . . . . . . 300.00
1983–1985 . . . . . . . . . . . . . . . . . . . . . . . . . . . . . . . . . . . . . . . . . 200.00
1986 . . . . . . . . . . . . . . . . . . . . . . . . . . . . . . . . . . . . . . . . . . . . . . . 400.00
1987–1988 . . . . . . . . . . . . . . . . . . . . . . . . . . . . . . . . . . . . . . . . . 150.00
1989–1990 . . . . . . . . . . . . . . . . . . . . . . . . . . . . . . . . . . . . . . . . . 135.00
```

MISSOURI

```
1979 . . . . . . . . . . . . . . . . . . . . . . . . . . . . . . . . . . . . . . . . . . . . . 1,750.00
1980 . . . . . . . . . . . . . . . . . . . . . . . . . . . . . . . . . . . . . . . . . . . . . . . 250.00
1981–1982 . . . . . . . . . . . . . . . . . . . . . . . . . . . . . . . . . . . . . . . . . 125.00
1983–1986 . . . . . . . . . . . . . . . . . . . . . . . . . . . . . . . . . . . . . . . . . 130.00
1987–1990 . . . . . . . . . . . . . . . . . . . . . . . . . . . . . . . . . . . . . . . . . 135.00
```

MONTANA

```
1978 . . . . . . . . . . . . . . . . . . . . . . . . . . . . . . . . . . . . . . . . . . . . . . . 400.00
1979–1980 . . . . . . . . . . . . . . . . . . . . . . . . . . . . . . . . . . . . . . . . . 135.00
1981–1985 . . . . . . . . . . . . . . . . . . . . . . . . . . . . . . . . . . none issued
1986 . . . . . . . . . . . . . . . . . . . . . . . . . . . . . . . . . . . . . . . . . . . . . . . 275.00
1987–1990 . . . . . . . . . . . . . . . . . . . . . . . . . . . . . . . . . . . . . . . . . 135.00
```

NEBRASKA

1991 . . . . 185.00
1992–1995 . . . . 145.00

NEVADA

1979 . . . . 1,800.00
1980–1981 . . . . 300.00
1982–1983 . . . . 135.00
1984 . . . . 200.00
1985 . . . . 150.00
1986 . . . . 135.00
1987 . . . . 200.00
1988–1989 . . . . 135.00
1990 . . . . 145.00

NEW HAMPSHIRE

1983 . . . . 600.00
1984–1985 . . . . 400.00
1986 . . . . 500.00
1987–1988 . . . . 200.00
1989 . . . . 175.00
1990 . . . . 150.00

NEW JERSEY

1984 . . . . 700.00
1985 . . . . 500.00
1986 . . . . 250.00
1987 . . . . 225.00
1988 . . . . 200.00
1989–1990 . . . . 135.00

NEW MEXICO

1992 . . . . 185.00
1993–1995 . . . . 145.00

NEW YORK

1985–1986 . . . . 275.00
1987–1988 . . . . 200.00
1989 . . . . 275.00
1990 . . . . 135.00

NORTH CAROLINA

1983	850.00
1984	300.00
1985–1988	135.00
1989	250.00
1990	135.00

NORTH DAKOTA

1982	450.00
1983–1990	135.00

OHIO

1982	350.00
1983	300.00
1984–1988	153.00
1989–1990	175.00

OKLAHOMA

1980	750.00
1981–1988	125.00
1989	150.00
1990	135.00

OREGON

1984	350.00
1985	250.00
1986–1987	200.00
1988–1990	250.00

PENNSYLVANIA

1983	1,000.00
1984	450.00
1985	200.00
1986	400.00
1987	250.00
1988–1989	200.00
1990	135.00

RHODE ISLAND

1989	200.00
1990	145.00

SOUTH CAROLINA

1981	1,600.00
1982–1983	250.00
1984–1987	200.00
1988	400.00
1989–1990	135.00

SOUTH DAKOTA

1976	2,100.00
1977	900.00
1978	400.00
1979–1985	none issued
1986	150.00
1987–1990	135.00

TENNESSEE

1979	850.00
1980	300.00
1981–1982	125.00
1983	200.00
1984	400.00
1985–1990	135.00

TEXAS

1981	900.00
1982	500.00
1983	700.00
1984	600.00
1985	125.00
1986–1987	250.00
1988	350.00
1989–1990	200.00

UTAH

1986–1987	200.00
1988–1989	135.00
1990	145.00

VERMONT

1986	250.00
1987	200.00
1988	175.00
1989–1990	135.00

VIRGINIA

1988 . . . . 200.00
1989–1990 . . . . 135.00

WASHINGTON

1986 . . . . 275.00
1987 . . . . 200.00
1988 . . . . 275.00
1989 . . . . 200.00
1990 . . . . 135.00

WEST VIRGINIA

1987 . . . . 200.00
1988–1990 . . . . 135.00

WISCONSIN

1978 . . . . 850.00
1979 . . . . 450.00
1980 . . . . 1,000.00
1981 . . . . 150.00
1982 . . . . 175.00
1983 . . . . 200.00
1984–1990 . . . . 175.00

WYOMING

1985 . . . . 250.00
1986–1987 . . . . 150.00
1988 . . . . 135.00
1989–1990 . . . . 200.00

CHAPTER 3

Books

S porting books have been an important part of my life for more than half a century. Ray Bergman's *Trout* taught me to fish and John Alden Knight's *Ruffed Grouse* and *Woodcock* guided me through the colorful covers of autumn. My winters were warmed by the words of Nash Buckingham, Zane Grey, and Colonel H. P. Sheldon, and in the summer of my sixteenth year, I carried my copy of William J. Schaldach's *Carl Rungius—Big Game Painter* to the Canadian Rockies where this great artist added his words to those of my dad and the author on the front endpaper. I have read a great many volumes since those times and written a few of my own; but, most importantly, I have bought, sold, and traded hundreds of sporting books and learned a little bit along the way. I do not pretend to be an expert on the subject of fishing and hunting books. I refer your questions to one or another of the trusted sporting-book dealers listed in this guide's appendix, but I am sure the information provided here will be useful.

Sporting books come in all shapes and sizes and in all kinds of bindings. There are first editions, trade editions, and limited editions; but all have one thing in common: condition. A rare book in poor condition is of no interest to a collector, whereas a common book in excellent condition and with its original dust jacket commands a premium price. If you only learn one thing about sporting books from my recollective ramblings, I would like to be sure that you gain at least a working knowledge of the terms used to evaluate books and are able to recognize and rate condition. If you doubt the wisdom of these words, consider the New England mail-order book dealer who told me his three concerns when buying his stock-in-trade were condition, condition, and condition. He and I have learned the hard way about condition, and I cannot stress its importance too strongly.

First editions and limited editions are two fields of fine sporting book collecting that are worthy of your consideration, but, again, that old bugaboo "condition" plays a role. Serious collectors will insist that first and limited edition sporting books be as close to "as issued" as possible and will not usually settle for less.

First editions are frequently the only edition of many sporting titles with limited appeal. Many of these obscure writings are valuable, as are first printings of popular titles that have gone to second, third, and more printings. The difference between a "first" in fine condition with a dust jacket and a later printing in the same condition can be like night and day. For example, a first edition of my father's *Duck Decoys and How to Rig Them* in

Art added to a given volume adds to the value. This watercolor sketch by A. Lassell Ripley affixed to the pastedown of a book on driven pheasant shooting increased the selling price eightfold.

very good condition with a tattered dust jacket catalogs at $65 to $75, while a near mint copy of the ninth (and last Holt printing) brings from $15 to $20. The first edition collector will pay top dollar for what he or she wants, but only if the condition warrants the expenditure.

Limited edition hunting and angling volumes can be good long-term investments if they are truly limited, but too many publishers have issued "limited editions" of books that are only reprints of scarce early titles. A few of these titles will increase in value, but most will be used books with little, if any, appeal. Those of you who are interested in learning more about the subject of "limited edition" sporting books will do well to consult with one or more of the book dealers listed in the back of this volume. They can, and will, advise you, help you build a collection if that is your desire, and generally add to your knowledge. You, as a buyer or potential buyer of sporting books, are the lifeblood of a select market. Don't be afraid to question these dealers, but don't be a bother, either. Send for their catalogs ($5 to $20) and read them. Chances are it won't be long before you find that you know more

The increasing popularity of "catch and release" fly fishing has reinvented the art of fish carving. This superb trophy brook trout was carved and painted by angler/artist Ken Burkhardt of Collinsville, Connecticut, and sold for $2,400.00.

Federal duck stamp, 1935, by Frank W. Benson depicts three canvasbacks in flight and was printed in a single color. Produced in a limited edition of 100 copies. *Courtesy of the U.S. Fish and Wildlife Service.*

Federal duck stamp, 1971–1972, by Maynard Reece depicts three cinnamon teals about to land. Produced in a limited edition of 950 copies. *Courtesy of the U.S. Fish and Wildlife Service.*

Federal duck stamp, 1991–1992, by Nancy Howe depicts king eiders on the tundra. Production was limited to the number of presale orders, prompting Freddy King to call it "the clear leader in worthwhile modern duck stamp art." *Courtesy of the U.S. Fish and Wildlife Service.*

"Prairie Girl" poster from Hopkins and Allen, 1910, is valued at around $1,000.00. *Courtesy of Robert Hanafee.*

Rare Winchester poster valued at $1,000.00 in good condition. *Courtesy of Robert Hanafee.*

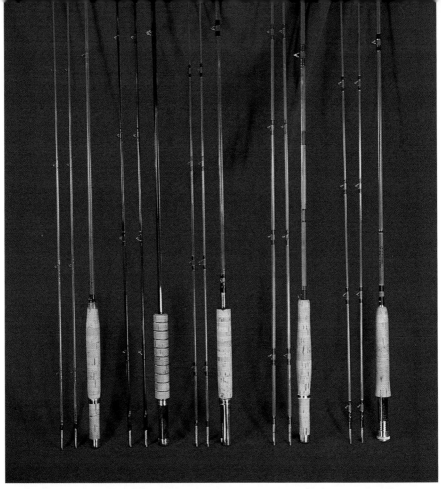

Classic split-cane rods. Left to right: 7' 9" Garrison rod, $4,200.00; 8' R. W. Summers custom-built rod, $850.00; rare Jim Payne rod, 8' 6", detachable handle, $1,550.00; Frank Wire five-strip parabolic, 8' 6", $695.00; superb G. H. Howells rod, 8', "as new" condition, $900.00. *Courtesy of Martin J. Keane.*

A rare and wonderful collection of Edward Vom Hoff fishing reels. The early 1990s prices on these classics ranged from $1,200.00 to $2,600.00 and they continue to increase. As with all truly fine sporting collectibles, these reels are a good investment. *Courtesy of Martin J. Keane.*

The many examples of Steven's work seen here are topped by her internationally renowned Grey Ghost. Values range from $200.00 to $400.00 each. *Courtesy of Martin J. Keane.*

The late Carrie G. Stevens (1882–1970) of Upper Dam, Maine, was and is still considered to be America's preeminent fly tier. Her streamer flies have no equal and her fame is worldwide. The four flies depicted here are (from top to bottom) Lady Miller, Supervisor, Fire Fly, and Will Ketch. *Courtesy of Martin J. Keane.*

Three grades of Cattaraugus's famous Folding Hunter knife, each with bone stag handle. These fine blades range in cost from $50.00 to $200.00. *Courtesy of A. G. Russell.*

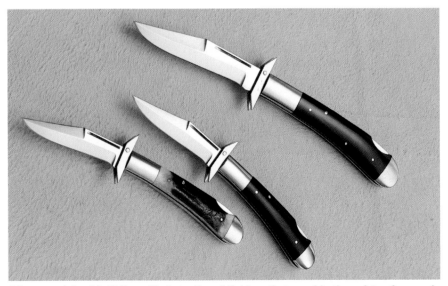

Three models of A. G. Russell's Auto Guard Folders that provide the safety of a guard with the convenience of a pocket knife. These range in cost from $50.00 to $150.00. *Courtesy of A. G. Russell.*

A classic early Delaware River decoy by the famous John Blair of Philadelphia. Sold for $132,000.00 in very fine condition at Guyette-Schmidt's Fall 1994 auction. *Courtesy of Guyette-Schmidt.*

An exceptional pair of bufflehead decoys by Rowley Horner of West Creek, New Jersey, was knocked down for $71,500.00 at Guyette-Schmidt's Fall 1994 auction. *Courtesy of Guyette-Schmidt.*

Increasingly popular and rising in cost are fine examples of Mason factory decoys. These, sold by Guyette-Schmidt in November of 1994, are a premier grade pintail drake (top) that went to a happy buyer for $8,500.00 and a pair of challenge grade blue-wing teal (bottom) that sold for $6,250.00.

CONDITION

Terminology may vary slightly from one sporting book dealer to another, but generally the following terms apply:

Mint
: Used to describe books that are "as issued" and must have dust jackets (if issued) in like condition. "Like new" is an equal term.

Very fine
: Lacks crisp quality of a new book but is without flaws of any kind. Dust jacket can show minimal wear.

Fine
: Not quite up to the above but still a volume to cherish. Any flaws must be noted both in the book and dust jacket if one is present.

Very good
: No serious flaws or damage present. Others must be noted.

Good
: An average used book with all leaves and pages present. All defects must be noted.

Fair
: Must have all its text pages. All defects must be noted.

Poor
: A possible reading copy with rarely any other value. Not to be confused with a binding copy, which has fine leaves but a poor or nonexistent cover.

Bookplates add value to many volumes. These two, one by noted artist William J. Schaldach and another from the famous establishment of Ernest R. Gee, are indicative of many, many other fine examples.

than you once did and have made friends in the sporting book business as well.

The alternative to buying sporting books from one or more of the appendixed dealers is to haunt auctions, house sales, garage sales, flea markets, and any and all places where these sporting collectibles may be found. I have found Corey Ford in a box at a yard sale, Teddy Roosevelt at an auction, and both Jack O'Conner and Roland Ward at flea markets. Sporting books turn up just about anywhere. Read your local newspapers for auctions and sales; let your friends and neighbors know you are interested in acquiring sporting titles at the right price. If you have ever moved any number of books, you know how eager people are to "get rid of the weight" before moving. It's up to you to be there when these collectibles turn up.

I have told this story before; but, in short, it involves the sale of a well-known sporting library within minutes of my home. Each and every book—Derrydales, rare angling volumes, et al.—was priced at $5. I learned about the sale one week after it had been held. As I said, it's up to you to be there.

The following list of fishing and hunting books is alphabetical by author. The prices given are for volumes in very good to fine condition (unless otherwise noted); and, when present, dust jackets (dj's) are noted. These prices are retail and/or replacement values. Those wishing to sell these and other sporting books should not expect more than 30% to 50% of these values. Rare volumes may bring a higher percentage, but, on the other hand, common titles may bring next to nothing. The list is far from complete, but it can, and will, tell you much about today's book market.

Henry David Thoreau wrote, "Books are the treasured wealth of the world, the fit inheritance of generations. . . ." And I can only agree.

Edward Abbey

Desert Solitude, New York, 1968, first edition, fine condition 50.00

ABBREVIATIONS

Abbreviations are often used in descriptions of sporting books in catalogs and advertisement, and, not surprisingly, they are used here as well. You should know that "dj" means dust jacket; "pp" privately printed; and "s/n" stands for signed and numbered. Other common abbreviations are "teg" for top edge gilt; "nd" for no date of publication; and "np" for no place of publication.

Many booksellers use abbreviated condition identification such as "vg/g" to signify a very good book in a good dust jacket and "f/f/f" for a fine copy with a fine dust jacket in a fine slipcase. This last is rare, but you should know and understand all these designations.

Henry Abbott

The Birchbark Books of Henry Abbott
PP, 1914 through 1932, 18 of the 19 birch-bark-covered Christmas greetings published by Abbott in editions of 100 each, lacking the first (1913) title, the set is crisp with minor spine chipping 2,000.00
1980 reprint, Abbott's books in a single volume 35.00
Muskrat City, pp, 1922, one of *The Birchbark Books,* spine chipped 150.00

Carl E. Akeley

In Brightest Africa, New York, 1932, very good condition
First edition 35.00
Later printing 20.00

Mary L. J. Akeley

Carl Akeley's Africa, New York, 1938, photographs, fine endpaper maps, very good condition 25.00
The Wilderness Lives Again, New York, 1940, hard-to-find title about Akeley's life, fine condition 45.00

American Gun, edited by Larry Koller, short-lived publication boasts but three issues, each 15.00

DUST JACKETS

Dust jackets, also referred to as "wrappers," are not to be dismissed lightly. Designed to protect books, as their name implies, these paper covers are considered a part of a given volume by many collectors and are often worth as much or more than the book itself.

American Sportsman

Quarterly publication, this author contributed to the first of 12 issues, fine set of 12 (1968–1970) 150.00
American Sportsman's Treasury, New York, 1971, very fine condition
With dj 45.00
Without dj 20.00

Kenneth Anderson

The Black Panther of Sivanipalli, Chicago, 1960
Fair to good condition 20.00
Fine condition, no dj 40.00

Tales from the Indian Jungle, London, 1970, near mint condition, dj   50.00
The Tiger Roars, New York, 1967, first edition, very good condition, dj 22.00

Bradford Angier

Living off the Country, Harrisburg, 1971, fine condition 12.00
Other titles by Bradford . . . . 10.00 to 20.00

The Angler's Club of New York (see also Atherton, John)

The Angler's Club Story, pp, limited edition of 750, fine condition . . 175.00
The Best of the Angler's Club Bulletin, pp, limited edition of 1,000, fine condition 125.00
Well Dressed Lines, pp, 1962, limited edition of 500 copies, fine condition 225.00

Russel Annabel (Both of Annabel's books have been reprinted.)

Hunting & Fishing in Alaska, Borzoi/Knopf, 1948
   Fine condition, fine dj. 225.00
   Good to very good condition, no dj. 95.00

DERRYDALE

From *American Trout Streams* in 1926 to the second edition of *The Happy End* in 1942, Eugene Connett's Derrydale Press produced 221 of the finest books to be found anywhere. The majority of this output can be considered "sporting," and all of it appeals to the Derrydale collector. A copy of the first book to carry the Derrydale Press imprint, Eugene Connett's *Magic Hours* (89 total copies) sold recently for $10,000. Many Derrydale titles cost far less and are listed by author's name on these pages.

Tales of a Big Game Guide, Derrydale Press, 1938, limited edition of 950 copies
   Fine condition. 550.00
   Torn spine. 235.00

John Atherton

The Fly and the Fish, fine condition
   PP for the Angler's Club, limited edition of 222, rare 600.00
   Reprint, 1971. . . . . 55.00

Lionel Atwill

Sporting Clays—An Orvis Guide, 1990, first edition
  Soiled and shaken 8.00
  Very fine condition. 25.00

Havilah Babcock (*These titles have been reprinted.)

The Best of Babcock, New York, 1974, edited by Hugh Grey, near mint
  condition 45.00
I Don't Want to Shoot an Elephant*, New York, 1958, first edition, fine
  condition 100.00
Jaybirds Go to Hell on Friday*, New York, 1965, second printing, near
  mint condition 85.00
My Health Is Better in November*, Columbia, 1947, first edition, good
  condition, dj. 100.00
Tales of Quails 'n Such*, fine condition
  Limited edition of 299 signed copies, scarce, in slipcase 600.00
  Trade edition, 1951. . . . . 125.00

Charles H. Baker, Jr.

The Gentleman's Companion, Derrydale Press, two volumes, food/wine
  set, fine condition
  1939, limited edition of 1,250 . . . . 110.00
  1946, reprint 60.00

Joel Barber

Long Shore
  Derrydale Press, 1939, limited edition of 750, s/n
    Very fine condition. 400.00
    Tattered cover 60.00
  Mississippi Derrydale edition . . . . 20.00 to 35.00
Wild Fowl Decoys
  Derrydale Press, 1934, limited edition of 55 copies, rare, fine
    condition. 6,500.00
  Dover, paperback . . . . 10.00 to 20.00

Garden City, 1937, dj 100.00
Mississippi Derrydale edition 35.00
Windward House, 1934, fine condition 200.00

Joseph D. Bates, Jr. (Joe Bates was a prolific writer; and as early as the 1960s, he recognized the market for limited, deluxe editions. These printings of 10, 24, and 36 copies cost from $1,000 to $2,500 and are not listed here; but the less-expensive trade editions of these classics are included as are a good many of Bates's myriad books.)

The Art of the Atlantic Salmon Fly, Boston, 1987, first trade edition, mint condition 100.00
Atlantic Salmon Flies and Fishing, Harrisburg, 1970, first edition, fine condition, dj. 150.00
Spinning for Salt Water Game Fish, Boston, 1957, first edition, fine condition, dj 25.00
Streamer Fly Tying & Fishing, Harrisburg, 1966, first edition, fine condition
    With dj 165.00
    Without dj. 100.00
Streamer Fly Fishing in Fresh & Salt Water, scarce, very good condition 50.00
Trout Waters and How to Fish Them, Boston, 1949, scarce, fine condition 50.00

Ray Bergman

Fresh Water Bass, very good condition
    Borzoi/Knopf, first edition. 65.00
    Philadelphia, 1937, first edition, dj. 90.00
Just Fishing, Philadelphia, 1932, first edition, fine condition. 125.00
Trout, fine condition
    Borzoi/Knopf, first edition. 100.00
    First trade edition. 75.00
    Philadelphia, 1938, deluxe limited edition of 149, s/n 1,450.00
With Fly, Plug and Bait, New York, fine condition
    1947, limited edition of 249 copies. 285.00
    First trade edition. 60.00

Richard Bishop

Bishop's Birds, Philadelphia, 1936, limited edition of 1,050, introduction by H. P. Sheldon 300.00
Bishop's Wildfowl, St. Paul, 1948, full mission leather, introduction by Buckingham 275.00

SIGNED COPIES

Author-signed and author-inscribed-and-signed copies of fine sporting books can be of considerable value. Do not confuse these signed copies with limited editions for which all copies are signed and presumed valuable. There is a world of difference between an author-signed *Green Hills of Africa* and one of 1,000 signed copies of *Hunting the African Lion*. With all due to respect to Jimmy Rikhoff, I'll put my money on Hemingway every time.

William J. Blades

Fishing Flies and Fly Tying, Harrisburg, 1951
    One of 100 signed copies 750.00
    Trade edition 100.00

Adam H. Bogardus

Field, Cover, and Trap Shooting, New York, very good condition
    1874 . . . . 85.00
    Later printing 65.00

Boone and Crocket Club

American Big Game Hunting, New York, 1893
    Rare, very fine condition 200.00
    Worn condition 100.00
American Big Game in Its Haunts, New York, 1904, spine faded and corners worn 110.00
Hunting in Many Lands, New York, 1895, scarce, fine copy 350.00
Records of North American Big Game, New York, fine condition
    1952, scarce 350.00
    1958 . . . . 225.00
    1964 . . . . 200.00
    1971 . . . . 85.00

Charles E. Brooks

Larger Trout for the Western Fly Fisherman, New York, 1972, second printing, fine condition, dj. 55.00
The Living River, New York, 1979, first edition, fine condition, dj . . . 40.00
Nymph Fishing for Larger Trout, New York, 1976, first printing, fine condition 50.00
The Trout and the Stream, New York, 1974, first edition, fine condition 65.00

Joe Brooks

The Complete Book of Fly Fishing, New York, 1958, first edition, fine condition, dj 35.00
Salt Water Game Fishing, New York, 1968, first printing, fine condition, dj 25.00
Trout Fishing, New York, 1972, first edition, scarce, very fine condition, fine dj 45.00

Charles Browne

The Gun Club Cook Book, New York, 1934, newer edition of old favorite 15.00

Nash Buckingham (There are enough reprints of Nash Buckingham's books and books about Buckingham to bridge his mighty river. Those listed here are your best bets for investment.)

Blood Lines, fine condition
    Derrydale Press, 1938, limited edition of 1,250 . . . . 400.00
    Putnam, 1947 . . . . 75.00
De Shootingest Gentleman
    Derrydale Press, 1934, limited edition of 950, fine condition. . . . 650.00
    Nelson, 1961, limited edition of 200, signed, very fine condition. 200.00
    Putnam, 1943, very fine condition 75.00
Game Bag, Putnam, fine condition
    1945, limited edition of 1,250 . . . . 150.00
    Trade edition 50.00
Hallowed Years, Stackpole, 1953, Buckingham's 7th book, fine condition 125.00
Mark Right
    Derrydale Press, 1936, limited edition of 1,250, fine condition . . 450.00
    Putnam, 1944 . . . . 75.00
Ole Miss', fine condition
    Derrydale Press, 1937, limited edition of 1,250 . . . . 450.00
    Putnam, 1946 . . . . 75.00
Tattered Coat, Putnam, fine condition
    1944, limited edition of 995, numbered 200.00
    Trade edition 50.00

Raymond Camp

Ducks, Boats, Blinds and Decoys, Knopf/Borzoi, 1952, rare, fine condition 175.00
Game Cookery, New York, great advice and recipes, fine condition
    1958, first edition 45.00
    Later printing, illustrations by Thomas A. Daly 45.00

Roland Clark

Gunner's Dawn, Derrydale Press, 1937, limited edition of 950, fine condition 750.00
Pot Luck, Countryman Press, 1945, fine condition
    Deluxe limited edition of 150, signed, slipcase 850.00
    Limited edition of 460, s/n 250.00
    Trade edition, worn slipcase 45.00
Roland Clark's Etchings, Derrydale Press, 1938, limited edition of 800, worn box, fine condition 900.00
Stray Shots, Derrydale Press, 1931, limited edition of 500, very fine condition 1,750.00

Kit Clarke

The Practical Angler, New York, 1895, worn condition but very good internally 35.00
Where the Trout Hide, New York, 1889, rare
    Missing front cover 45.00
    Tattered and worn condition 30.00
    Very good condition 125.00

Eugene V. Connett, III (author and/or editor)

American Big Game Fishing, Derrydale Press, 1935, limited edition of 850, very fine condition 750.00
American Sporting Dogs, New York, 1948, scarce, fine condition . . 125.00
Any Luck, New York, 1933, first edition, fine condition, dj 125.00
Duck Decoys, New York, how-to book, very fine condition
    1953, first edition 75.00
    Later printings . . . . 20.00 to 25.00
Duck Shooting Along the Atlantic Flyway, New York, 1947
    Deluxe limited edition of 149, signed 1,000.00
    Fine copy, dj 175.00

BOOK SIZES

A number of sporting booksellers still employ the archaic 64mo, 24mo, etc., system of sizing, and, because of this, readers should know the system. Sizes are approximate.

64mo	2 " × 3"	12mo	5" × 7½"
32mo	3" × 5"	8vo	6–7" × 8–10"
24mo	3½" × 6"	4to	9" × 10–12"
18mo	4" × 6"	Folio	12" × 15"
16mo	4" × 7"	Elephant folio	Any book larger than folio

This portrait of Derrydale Press founder Eugene V. Connett, III was a part of his personal scrapbook that brought $8,200.00 at an Oinonen Book Auction in 1994.

Feathered Game from a Sporting Journal, Derrydale Press, 1929, limited edition of 550, fine condition. 400.00

Fishing a Trout Stream, Derrydale Press, 1934, limited edition of 950, fine condition 375.00

Magic Hours, Derrydale Press, 1927, printed for Angler's Club, limited edition of 89 . . . . 10,000.00

My Friend the Trout, New Jersey, very good condition
    1961, first edition, dj. 150.00
    1991, reprint 35.00

Random Casts, Derrydale Press, 1939, limited edition of 950, very fine condition 325.00

Upland Game Bird Shooting in America, Derrydale Press, 1930, limited edition of 850
    Spine and corners worn. 275.00
    Very fine condition 650.00

Wildfowling in the Mississippi Flyway, New York, 1949, very fine condition
    With dj 285.00
    Without dj. 200.00

Wing Shooting & Angling, New York, 1922, Connett's first book, very good condition 100.00

Jim Corbett

Jungle Lore, London, 1953, very fine condition, fair dj 40.00

Man-Eaters of Kumaon, New York, 1946, first American edition, fine condition, dj 20.00

The Man-Eating Leopard of Rudraprange, London, 1949, second edition,
very good condition 50.00
The Temple Tiger & More Man-Eaters of Kumaon, London, 1954, scarce
With dj 50.00
Without dj 40.00
Worn and slightly soiled 25.00
Tree Tops, New York/London, 1955
Soiled book covers, no dj 25.00
Very fine condition, fine dj 50.00

Ralf Coykendall

Duck Decoys and How to Rig Them, New York, 1955
Collector's slipcased edition 90.00
First edition, tattered dj 65.00
Later printing 25.00

Ralf W. Coykendall, Jr.

You and Your Retriever, New York, 1963, corrected first edition
Fine condition 25.00
Worn and soiled 20.00
Wildfowling at a Glance, Harrisburg, 1968, scarce, fine condition . . . 35.00

Rube Cross

The Complete Fly Tyer, New York, 1950 (combination of *Fur, Feather and Steel* and *Tying American Trout Lures*), fine condition 65.00
Fur, Feather and Steel, New York, fine condition
1940, first edition, signed 100.00
1944 . . . . 35.00
Tying American Trout Lures, New York, 1936, very good condition,
dj 35.00

Paul A. Curtis

Guns & Gunning, very good condition
Outdoor Life edition 15.00
Philadelphia, 1934, first edition 25.00
Sportsmen All, Derrydale Press, 1938, limited edition of 950, fine condition 150.00

Byron W. Dalrymple

Complete Guide to Hunting across North America, New York, 1970, very
fine condition 15.00
Deer Hunting with Dalrymple, New York, 1978, very fine condition,
dj 12.50
Doves & Dove Shooting, New York, 1949, very fine condition, dj 35.00

North American Big Game Hunting, New York, 1974, very fine condition,
dj 15.00
Other titles by Dalrymple . . . . 10.00 to 25.00

Harry Darbee

Catskill Flytier, Philadelphia, 1977, scarce
Fine condition, dj 150.00
Limited slipcased edition with fly 750.00

A. W. Dimock

The Book of the Tarpon, New York, very good condition
1911, scarce 150.00
1926. . . . . 85.00

J. W. Dunne

Sunshine and the Dry Fly, London, good condition
1924, first edition 65.00
1950. . . . . 35.00

Ben East

Danger, New York, 1970, first edition, fine condition 10.00
Survival, New York, 1967, fine condition. 10.00

Frank C. Edminster

Hunting Whitetails, New York, 1954
Fine condition, good dj. 20.00
Worn condition, no dj. 10.00
The Ruffed Grouse, New York, 1947, very fine condition, Webb book-
plate 100.00

Robert Elman

The Atlantic Flyway, New York, 1972, first edition, very fine condition
With dj 45.00
Without dj. 30.00
The Great American Sporting Prints, New York, 1972
Deluxe limited edition of 450. . . . . 200.00
Trade edition 50.00

Dr. R. P. Elmer

Archery, Philadelphia, 1926, first edition, scarce, fine condition. 75.00
Target Archery, Borzoi/Knopf, 1945, first edition, fine condition
With dj 75.00
Without dj. 40.00

George Bird Evans

An Affair with Grouse, Clinton, 1982, limited edition of 1,000, slipcased,
fine condition. 200.00

The bookplate of Samuel B. Webb is a plus in a fine sporting book and adds greatly to the value of all books. Webb's sporting library was auctioned by William Doyle Galleries, N.Y.

The Best of Nash Buckingham, New York, 1973, very good condition, dj. 45.00
The Bird Dog Book, Clinton, 1979, limited edition of 1,000, fine condition 200.00
Grouse Along the Tramroad, pp, limited edition of 1,500 . . . . 85.00
Recollections of a Shooting Guest, Clinton, 1978, very fine condition 225.00
The Ruffed Grouse Book, Clinton, 1977, limited edition of 1,000, s/n, slipcased 425.00
The Upland Shooting Life, New York, 1971, signed, fine condition, dj 65.00
The Woodcock Book, Clinton, 1977, limited edition of 1,000, s/n, slipcased 425.00
Other titles by Evans. . . . . 50.00 to 125.00

Fred Everett

Fun with Game Birds, Harrisburg, 1954, fine condition
   Deluxe limited edition 150.00
   Trade edition 35.00

Fun with Trout, Harrisburg, 1952, fine condition
   Limited edition 175.00
   Trade edition 45.00

S. Kip Farrington

Atlantic Game Fishing, New York, 1937, first edition, fine con-
   dition 250.00
Bill—The Broadbilled Swordfish, New York, 1942, juvenile, illustrated by
   Lynn Bogue Hunt 175.00
The Ducks Came Back, New York, the Ducks Unlimited story, fine condi-
   tion. 45.00
Fishing the Atlantic, New York, 1949, first edition, fine condition, dj   75.00
Fishing the Pacific, New York, 1953, scarce, very fine condition, dj   125.00
Pacific Game Fishing, New York, 1942, hard-to-find first edition . . . 150.00
Tony—The Tuna, Southampton, 1975, juvenile, illustrated by A. D.
   "Sandy" Read. 175.00

Art Flick

Art Flick's Master Fly Tying Guide, New York
   1972, fine condition, torn dj 45.00
   Later printing 20.00
Art Flick's New Streamside Guide, New York, 1969, very fine condition,
   dj 25.00
Streamside Guide, New York
   1947, first edition, rare 150.00
   Later printings . . . . 20.00 to 40.00

Corey Ford

The Best of Corey Ford, 1975, very fine condition 35.00
The Corey Ford Sporting Treasury, 1987, fine condition 35.00
Minutes of the Lower Forty, New York, 1962, first edition, scarce, dj   85.00
Uncle Perk's Jug, New York, 1964, more from the "lower forty," mint condi-
   tion, dj 85.00
You Can Always Tell a Fisherman, New York, 1958, first edition, fine con-
   dition, dj. 85.00

William Harnden Foster

New England Grouse Shooting, New York
   1942, first edition, the classic grouse book 250.00
   1947. . . . . 100.00
   Later reprint 45.00

A. B. Frost

A Book of Drawings, New York, 1904, black-and-white drawings from this
   master, cover worn 95.00

A book that would qualify as a perfect blend of author/artist's talents is *New England Grouse Shooting* by William Harnden Foster. His words or his fine drawings would no doubt stand alone, but, fortunately, they meld into what is one of our finest sporting volumes.

E. Garrison and H. Carmichael

A Master's Guide to Building a Bamboo Rod, Harrisburg
    1977, first edition, scarce 200.00
    1985, second printing 100.00

Jim Gasque

Bass Fishing, Borzoi/Knopf, 1945, first edition, dj 50.00
Hunting & Fishing in the Great Smokies, Borzoi/Knopf, 1948, fine condi-
    tion, chipped dj 50.00

Arnold Gingrich

The Fishing in Print, New York, 1974, fine condition, good dj 25.00
The Joys of Trout, New York, 1974, fine condition, fine dj 45.00
The Well-Tempered Angler, New York, 1965, first edition
    Good condition 50.00
    Worn condition 30.00

R. C. Grey (Zane Grey's brother)

Adventures of a Deep Sea Angler, New York, 1930, rare, fine con-
    dition 350.00

Zane Grey (All of Zane Grey's great sporting books are valuable in good
condition. Harper editions are sometimes priced as high as $200 to
$400, and Grosset reprints can run nearly as much, especially those
with dust jackets.)

Roping Lions in the Grand Canyon
  Harper, 1924 (code B-Y), scarce, fine dj 95.00
  Reprints... 40.00
Tales of Fishes
  Harper, 1919 (code F-T), first edition, scarce, dj.............. 150.00
  Reprints... 75.00
The Young Lion Hunter, Harper
  1911, first edition, juvenile, scarce......................... 75.00
  Later reprints 25.00

George Bird Grinnell

American Duck Shooting, New York, 1901, first edition, fine condition 275.00
American Game Bird Shooting, New York, 1910, first edition, fine condition.. 75.00

Roderick L. Haig-Brown

Fisherman's Spring, Fisherman's Summer, Fisherman's Fall, and
  Fisherman's Winter, New York, 1975, reprints, each 35.00
A Primer of Fly Fishing, New York, 1964, first edition, fine condition,
  dj 75.00
A River Never Sleeps, New York, 1946, first edition, scarce, fine condition 85.00
The Western Angler, Derrydale Press
  1939, limited edition of 950 sets
    Fine condition 450.00
    Without maps....................................... 300.00
  1947, trade edition 45.00

Van Campen Heilner

A Book on Duck Shooting
  Borzoi/Knopf, 1943 .... 150.00
  Philadelphia, 1939
    Limited edition of 99, s/n 1,200.00
    Trade edition 175.00
Salt Water Fishing, fine condition
  Borzoi/Knopf
    1943 .... 75.00
    1952, introduction by Hemingway 75.00

HARPER FIRST EDITIONS

Until 1912 Harper and Brothers used matching dates on both sides of the title page on first editions. Beginning in 1912 a two-letter code was employed. The first letter indicates the month of publication and the second letter signifies the year. The first-letter code omitted the letter J and used other letters as follows:

A January	E May	I September
B February	F June	K October
C March	G July	L November
D April	H August	M December

The second letter can be decoded as follows:

M 1912	Q 1916	U 1920
N 1913	R 1917	V 1921
O 1914	S 1918	W 1922
P 1915	T 1919	

Using this method, you will find that MM means December 1912, EO is May 1914, and, more importantly, you will have cracked the mysterious code. If the two-letter code matches the numerical month-year date on the copyright page exactly, you are holding a first edition.

Philadelphia, 1937
    Limited edition of 199 . . . . 250.00
    Trade edition 100.00

James A. Henshall

Book of the Black Bass, Cincinnati, very good condition
    1881, first issue, first edition 225.00
    Facsimile edition 15.00
    Later 1880s 75.00
Camping & Cruising in Florida, Cincinnati, 1888, scarce, fine condition 225.00
More about the Black Bass, Cincinnati, 1889, first edition, fine condition 150.00

Gene Hill

Hill Country, New York, 1978, like new condition. 35.00
A Hunter's Fireside Book, New York, 1972, touching book, fine condition 25.00
Mostly Tailfeathers, New York, 1975, more of Hill's outdoor musings, fine condition 20.00

H. A. Hochbaum

The Canvasback on a Prairie Marsh, Washington, 1944, important book,
fine condition..50.00
The Travels and Traditions of Waterfowl, Minnesota, fine condition
1956, second printing.....................................60.00
Third printing..50.00

Dan Holland

Trout Fishing, New York, 1949, decoration by William Schaldach, photographs by Holland 35.00

Ray Holland

Now Listen Warden, West Hartford, Vermont, 1946
Limited edition of 475....................................125.00
Trade edition 35.00
Shotgunning in the Uplands, West Hartford, Vermont, 1944
Limited edition of 250, s/n, very good condition 175.00
Trade edition, good condition, dj.........................75.00
Shotgunning the Lowlands, West Hartford, Vermont, 1945
Limited edition of 275, s/n, very good condition 150.00
Trade edition, good condition, dj.........................75.00

William T. Hornaday (Hornaday's prolific output was topped by the fol-
lowing, and his other works are valued at $20 to $40 in good condition.)

Campfires in the Canadian Rockies, New York, good condition
1906, first edition 75.00
1907..60.00
Campfires on the Desert and Lava, New York, 1908, scarce, good condition 75.00

Lynn Bogue Hunt

Artist's Game Bag, Derrydale Press, 1936, limited edition of 1,250, num-
bered, very good condition...............................400.00
DuPont Portfolio of Game Birds...................150.00 to 250.00
Field & Stream Portfolio of Game Birds 125.00

J. A. Hunter

Hunter, New York, 1952, very good condition
Good dj...25.00
Without dj...15.00
Hunter's Tracks, New York, 1957
Fine condition, fine dj....................................45.00
Soiled 20.00

Edward C. Janes

Fishing with Lee Wulff, New York, 1972, signed, fine condition 50.00
Fishing with Ray Bergman, New York, 1972, very good condition, good
    dj 20.00
Hunting Ducks and Geese, Harrisburg, 1954, scarce, fine condition   25.00

Preston Jennings

A Book of Trout Flies, Derrydale Press, 1935, fine condition
    Green binding. 600.00
    Limited Crown edition with fly 450.00
    Limited edition of 850, blue binding 700.00
    Trade edition 35.00

Martin Johnson

Lion, New York, 1929, very good condition
    First edition 20.00
    Later printing 10.00
Safari, New York, 1928, fine condition, faded spine 20.00

Osa Johnson (Mrs. Martin)

Four Years in Paradise, Garden City, 1941, very good condition 15.00
I Married Adventure, Philadelphia, 1940, good condition, good dj. . . 20.00

Martin J. Keane

Classic Rods and Rodmakers, Massachusetts, 1992, third edition, as
    new. 50.00

Elmer Keith

Big Game Hunting, New York, 1948, first edition, good condition. . . 65.00
Big Game Rifles and Cartridges, Samworth, 1936, very good condition,
    dj 225.00
Elmer Keith's Big Game Hunting, Boston, very good condition
    1948, first edition, scarce 150.00
    Later printing 75.00
Hell, I Was There, Los Angeles, 1979, first edition, very fine condition,
    dj 45.00
Sixgun Cartridges and Loads, Samworth, fine condition
    1936, first edition, dj. 150.00
    Later edition 25.00

Marguerite Kirmse

Dogs in the Field, Derrydale Press, 1935, limited edition of 685, num-
    bered, boxed 575.00
Marguerite Kirmse's Dogs, Derrydale Press, 1930, limited edition of 750,
    very good condition 550.00

John Alden Knight

Black Bass, New York, 1949
    Limited edition of 150, fine condition 200.00
    Trade edition 35.00
Ol' Bill and Other Stories, New York, 1942, very good condition, dj 35.00
Ruffed Grouse, Borzoi/Knopf, 1947
    Limited edition of 210, slipcased, fine condition 750.00
    Trade edition 100.00
Woodcock, Borzoi/Knopf, 1944
    Limited edition of 275, slipcased, fine condition 500.00
    Trade edition 75.00

Larry Koller

Shots at Whitetails, Boston, fine condition
    1948, first edition 35.00
    Later printing 20.00
Taking Larger Trout, Boston, 1950, Koller's finest book
    Fine condition 150.00
    Soiled 45.00
The Treasury of Angling, New York, 1963, very fine condition, dj . . . 35.00

F. H. Kortright

The Ducks, Geese & Swans of North America, Washington, fine condition
    1942, first trade edition 35.00
    Later printing 20.00

George M. L. LaBranche

The Dry Fly and Fast Water, New York, 1924, first edition, good condition 25.00
The Salmon and the Dry Fly, Boston, 1924, limited edition of 775 . . 275.00
Two titles above combined into single volume, 1951, very good condition 75.00

C. S. Landis

.22 Rifle Shooting, South Carolina, 1922, scarce, fine condition 100.00

Larry Lariar

Fish and Be Damned, New York, 1953, very fine condition 15.00
Hunt and Be Damned, New Jersey, 1956, very fine condition 12.50

William B. Leffingwell

The Art of Wing Shooting, Chicago, 1895, second printing, fair condition 45.00

Wild Fowl Shooting, Chicago, 1890, second printing
    Good condition 75.00
    Fair condition 40.00

James E. Leisenring

The Art of Tying the Wet Fly, New York
    1941, first edition, fine condition, dj. 275.00
    1971
        Fine condition 35.00
        Soiled 20.00

Aldo Leopold

A Sand County Almanac (this writer believes this to be the finest of all
    essays on the great outdoors), very fine condition
    1962, sixth printing. 75.00
    1977, illustrated 75.00

Robert Page Lincoln

Black Bass Fishing, Harrisburg, 1952, first edition, very good con-
    dition 35.00
The Pike Family, Harrisburg, 1953, scarce, fine condition 25.00

Henry Lyman

Bluefishing, Boston, fine condition
    1950, first edition, leather bound. 50.00
    Later printings 20.00

Nick Lyons

Fisherman's Bounty, New York, 1970, anthology of fishing lore
    With dj 65.00
    Without dj. 45.00
Fishing Widows, New York, 1974
    Fine condition, fine dj. 35.00
    Without dj. 25.00
Spring Creek, New York, 1992, like new, fine dj 25.00

Arthur R. MacDougal

Doc Blakessley Angler, Portland, 1949
    Limited edition of 500, s/n, glassine wrapper. 175.00
    First trade edition. 45.00
Dud Dean and His Country, New York, 1946
    Limited edition of 450, s/n. 125.00
    Trade edition 50.00

The Sun Stood Still, Maine, 1939, s/n 125.00
Under a Willow Tree, New York, 1946, illustrated by Milt Weiler, fine condition 45.00
Where Flows the Kennebec, New York, 1947, very good condition
    Good dj 50.00
    Without dj 30.00

Mary Orvis Marbury

Favorite Flies and Their Histories
    Second printing
        Fine condition 350.00
        Very good condition. 200.00
    1988 reprint, very good condition 25.00

Vincent C. Marinaro

In the Ring of the Rise, New York, 1976, first edition, near mint condition
    Fine dj 65.00
    Without dj 40.00
A Modern Dry Fly Code, New York
    1950, first edition, fine condition 125.00
    Later printing 35.00

A. J. McClane

The American Angler, New York, 1954, very fine condition, torn dj. . 20.00
McClane's Standard Fishing Encyclopedia, New York, fine condition
    1965, first edition 50.00
    Later printing 35.00
The Practical Fly Fisherman, New York, 1953, first edition
    Fine dj 150.00
    Very good condition 75.00
Wise Fisherman's Encyclopedia, New York, 1951, first edition, fine condition 35.00

Samuel Merrill

The Moose Book, New York, 1916, first edition
    Truly fine condition 125.00
    Soiled and shaken 65.00

William B. Mershon

The Passenger Pigeon, New York, 1907
    Fine condition, dj 150.00
    Without dj 100.00

Merwin, John

Stillwater Trout, New York, 1980, informative volume, fine condition 25.00

NOM DE PLUME

Many fine sporting books have been written by authors who, for reasons of their own, used pen names instead of their own. Readers wishing to learn more about these pseudonyms should read *A Dictionary of Sporting Pen Names* by Ken Callahan. Write to him at Peterborough, NH 03458-0505.

Jack O'Conner (A prolific writer, O'Conner's unlisted books are generally from $25 to $35, but his novels *Boomtown* and *Conquest* are in the $200 range.)

The Best of Jack O'Conner, Clinton, 1977, limited edition of 1,000, signed, slipcased 275.00
The Big Game Rifle, Borzoi/Knopf, 1952, scarce, fine condition, good dj 150.00
Game in the Desert, Derrydale Press, 1939, limited edition of 950, numbered, fine condition 750.00
Game in the Desert Revisited, Clinton, 1977, limited edition of 1,000, signed, slipcased 350.00
Horse and Buggy West, New York, 1969, scarce, fine condition, dj . . 350.00
Hunting in the Rockies, Borzoi/Knopf, 1947, fine condition, dj 225.00
Hunting in the Southwest, Borzoi/Knopf, 1945, fine condition, dj . . 175.00
The Hunting Rifle, New York, 1970, very fine condition, good dj. . . . 25.00
Jack O'Conner's Big Game Hunts, New York, 1963, first edition
Fine condition, good dj. 85.00
Worn condition, without dj. 35.00
The Rifle Book, Borzoi/Knopf, 1949, third printing, fine condition . . 35.00
The Shotgun Book, New York, 1965, very good condition, good dj . . 35.00

John T. Ordeman

Frank Benson—Master of the Sporting Print
PP, 1983
Limited edition of 50, s/n 500.00
Limited edition of 950 . . . . 75.00
Second printing 75.00
Frank W. Benson's Etchings, Drypoints, and Lithographs, pp, 1994
Limited edition of 200, s/n. 250.00
Limited edition of 1,000 . . . . 100.00
To Keep a Tryst with the Dawn—An Appreciation of Roland Clark, pp, 1988
Limited edition of 150. . . . . 250.00
Limited edition of 1,000 . . . . 100.00

William J. Schaldach: Artist, Author, Sportsman, pp, 1987
 Limited edition of 150, s/n 250.00
 Limited edition of 1,000 . . . . 75.00

C. F. Orvis, and A. N. Cheney

Fishing with the Fly, Boston, good condition
 1883, first edition 275.00
 1886 . . . . 125.00
 1968 facsimile 65.00
 1988 facsimile 25.00

Ray Ovington

How to Take Trout on Wet Flies & Nymphs, Boston, 1952, Ovington's best
 book, very good condition 45.00
Spinning in America, Harrisburg, 1954, fine condition, good dj 15.00
Tactics on Trout, New York, 1969, first edition, very fine condition. . 10.00

John C. Phillips

A Natural History of the Ducks
 1922–1926, four volumes, fine condition. 4,750.00
 Dover reprint 100.00
A Sportsman's Scrapbook, Boston, 1928, fine condition, dj 85.00
A Sportsman's Second Scrapbook, Boston, 1933, rare, very good condition,
 dj 95.00

Bert Popowski

Calling All Game, Harrisburg, 1952, fine condition, fine dj 20.00
Calling All Varmints, Harrisburg, 1952, fine condition, fine dj. 17.50
Crow Shooting, New York, 1946, very good condition, good dj 17.50
Olt's Hunting Handbook, Omaha, 1948, scarce, fine condition 20.00

Edgar M. Queeny

Prairie Wings, New York (Ducks Unlimited), classic, fine condition
 1946 . . . . 300.00
 1947 . . . . 250.00
 1962 . . . . 125.00

Jim Quick

Fishing the Nymph, New York, 1960, very good condition 20.00
Trout Fishing & Trout Flies, New York, 1957, fine condition, dj. 16.00

George Reiger

The Bonefish, New Jersey, 1993, very fine condition
 Limited edition of 100, slipcased 275.00
 Trade edition 50.00

Fishing with McClane, New Jersey, 1975, first edition, fine condition, dj 20.00
The Silver King, New Jersey, 1992, very fine condition
    Limited edition of 100. . . . . 275.00
    Trade edition 50.00
The Undiscovered Zane Grey Fishing Stories, New York, 1984, like new, fine dj. 35.00
Zane Grey: Outdoorsman, New Jersey, 1973, third printing, fine condition 30.00

Louis Rhead

American Trout Stream Insects, New York, 1916, first edition, very good condition 125.00
The Speckled Brook Trout, New York, 1902, fine condition
    Large paper edition 425.00
    Trade edition 195.00

Ray Riling

The Powder Flask Book, New York, 1953, reprinted edition, fine condition 75.00
Rifles and Shotguns, New York, very good condition
    1951, limited edition of 1,500 . . . . 150.00
    1982. . . . . 75.00

Kermit Roosevelt

The Happy Hunting Grounds, New York, 1920, first edition, good condition 50.00
The Long Trail, New York, 1921, very good condition, torn box 35.00

Theodore Roosevelt

African Game Trails, New York, 1910, very good condition
    Scribner's edition, first printing. 75.00
    Syndicate edition 50.00
Hunting Trips of a Ranchman, New York, 1886
    Presidential edition. 35.00
    Very good condition, worn spine. 95.00
Outdoor Pastimes of an American Hunter, New York, fine condition
    1905, first edition 35.00
    Later printing 20.00
Ranch Life and the Hunting Trail, New York, 1906, "Elkhorn" edition 100.00
The Wilderness Hunter, New York, 1893, first edition, very good condition 125.00

Theodore and Kermit Roosevelt

Trailing the Giant Panda, New York, 1929, foldout map, fine condition 75.00

Theodore Roosevelt, et al.

The Deer Family, New York, 1902, first edition, good condition. 50.00
Life Histories of African Game Animals, two volumes, library markings, good condition. 175.00

Robert Ruark (Ruark collectors are interested in his other titles, but they cannot be considered sporting titles. Fans might like *Someone of Value—Robert Ruark* by Hugh Foster.)

Horn of the Hunter, New York, fine condition
  1953, first edition
    Fine dj. 150.00
    Without dj. 100.00
    Later printings . . . . to 25.00
The Old Man and the Boy, New York, fine condition
  1957, first edition, fine dj 75.00
  Reprints . . . . to 25.00
The Old Man's Boy Grows Older, New York, 1961, fine condition, fine dj 85.00
Use Enough Gun, New York, 1966, first edition, fine condition, fine dj 65.00

Leonard Lee Rue, III

Gamebirds of North America, New York, 1973, very good condition 15.00
Sportsman's Guide to Game Animals, New York, 1981, second printing, fine condition. 15.00
The World of the Ruffed Grouse, Philadelphia, 1973, fine condition . . 35.00
The World of the Whitetailed Deer, Philadelphia, 1962, very fine condition, dj 15.00

Jack Russell

Jill and I and the Salmon, Boston, very good condition
  1950, first edition 85.00
  Later printing 75.00
  Facsimile edition 125.00

Archibald Rutledge

From the Hills to the Sea, Indianapolis, 1958, first edition, fine condition 65.00
Home by the River, Indianapolis, very good condition
  Large paper edition, signed 35.00
  1941, first edition 25.00

Hunter's Choice, New York, 1946, fine condition, very good dj 75.00
Old Plantation Days, New York, 1921, first edition, very good condition 85.00

BIBLIOGRAPHIES

Sporting book bibliographies are important and expensive. The "new"
Izaak Walton bibliography by Dr. R. L. Coigney joins Oliver and Horne on
the Waltonian fans' shelves and costs $150, if you can find a copy. This is
a low-to-average price for a sporting bibliography as they are all limited
in number.

Dean Sage

The Restigouche and Its Salmon Fishing, Goshen, 1973, limited edition of
250, slipcased... 850.00
Salmon and Trout, New York, very good condition
1902, first edition 75.00
1904... 50.00
1924... 100.00

Ledyard Sands

The Bird, the Gun, and the Dog, New York, 1939, first edition, very good
condition, good dj 75.00

William J. Schaldach (See Ordman for *William J. Schaldach—Artist,
Author, Sportsman,* a biographical study of this fine artist and his work.)

Carl Rungius—Big Game Painter, New York, 1945, limited edition of 1,250,
fine condition
Slipcased 1,500.00
Without slipcase..................................... 1,200
Coverts and Casts, New York, 1943, limited edition of 160, fine con-
dition 325.00
Currents and Eddies, New York, 1944
Limited edition of 250................................ 275.00
Trade edition 45.00
Fish, Philadelphia, 1937, fine condition
Limited edition of 150, s/n 1,500.00
Limited edition of 1,560 .... 300.00
The Path to Enchantment, New York, 1963, fine condition, fine dj... 35.00
The Wind on Your Cheek, New York, 1972, fine condition
Limited edition of 200................................ 175.00
Trade edition, fine dj 25.00

Ernest Schwiebert

Death of a Riverkeeper, New York, 1980, first edition, fine condition,
 dj 25.00
Matching the Hatch, New York, 1955, fine condition
 First printing. 125.00
 Later printing 75.00
Nymphs, New York, fine condition
 1973, first edition, fine dj 75.00
 1977. . . . . 45.00
A River for Christmas, Lexington, 1988, like new, fine dj 20.00
Salmon of the World, New York, 1970, limited edition of 750, s/n, fine con-
 dition 1,500.00
Trout, New York, 2 volumes
 1978, first edition, 2 volumes, slipcased
 Fine condition 225.00
 Good to very good condition. 125.00
 Revised edition 50.00

Francis E. Sell

Advanced Hunting on Deer & Elk Trails, Harrisburg, 1954, fine condition,
 dj 40.00
The American Deer Hunter, Harrisburg, 1957, first edition, fine con-
 dition 45.00
The Deer Hunters Guide, Harrisburg, 1964, first printing, fine condition,
 dj 15.00

Ernest Seton-Thompson (A prolific writer, Seton-Thompson's myriad
 books are valued from $20 to $50 for fine copies, and his autobiography,
 Trail of an Artist-Naturalist, is $75.)

The Arctic Prairies, New York, fine condition
 1911, first edition 125.00
 1917. . . . . 45.00
Wild Animals I Have Known, New York, very good condition
 1898, first edition 50.00
 Later printing 20.00

Charles Sheldon (Note: These books have been reprinted in several edi-
 tions.)

The Wilderness of Denali, New York, very fine condition
 1930, first edition 325.00
 Later printing 45.00
The Wilderness of the North Pacific Coast Islands, New York, 1912, first edi-
 tion, fine condition. 225.00
The Wilderness of the Upper Yukon, New York, very good condition
 1913, first edition 325.00
 Later printing 45.00

Colonel H. P. Sheldon

Tranquillity, Derrydale Press, 1936, limited edition of 950 . . . . 200.00
Tranquillity and *Tranquillity Revisited*
    Countryman Press, 1945
        Limited edition of 475, boxed set 550.00
        Trade edition 75.00
    Willow Creek Press 65.00
Tranquillity Revisited, Derrydale Press, 1940, limited edition of 485
    Fine condition. 375.00
    Very fine condition 450.00
The Tranquillity Stories, New York, 1974, *Tranquillity* and *Tranquillity*
    Revisited in single volume, fine condition, dj 75.00

William G. Sheldon

The Book of the American Woodcock, Amherst
    First edition, scarce, dj. 75.00
    Second edition, corrected 35.00

Harry Worcester Smith

Life & Sport in Aiken, Derrydale Press, 1935, limited edition of 950, fine
    condition 195.00
A Sporting Family of the Old South, Albany, Georgia, 1936, scarce
    Fine condition. 150.00
    Fair to good condition 85.00

Burton L. Spiller

Firelight, Derrydale Press, 1937, limited edition of 950, fine con-
    dition 425.00
Grouse Feathers, Derrydale Press, fine condition
    1935, limited edition of 950 . . . . 325.00
    1947, trade edition 35.00
    Later printing 20.00
Grouse Feathers and *More Grouse Feathers,* Crown, 1972, limited edition
    set of 750
    Fine condition. 225.00
    Without slipcase 150.00
More Grouse Feathers, Derrydale Press, 1938, limited edition of 950, fine
    condition 325.00
Thoroughbred, Derrydale Press, 1936, limited edition of 950, fine con-
    dition 275.00

H. G. "Tap" Tappley

The Fly Tyer's Handbook, New York, 1949, hard-to-find book, fine condi-
    tion, dj 35.00

A Sportsman's Notebook, New York, fine condition, fine dj
　1964 . . . . 25.00
　Later printing 20.00

John Taylor

African Rifles & Cartridges, Samworth, fine condition
　1948, first edition 175.00
　1977 reprint. 25.00

Robert Traver (John Voelker)

Anatomy of a Fisherman, New York, 1964, fine condition, dj
　Signed 175.00
　Unsigned. 125.00
Trout Madness, New York, 1960, first edition, fine condition, dj. 35.00
Trout Madness and *Trout Magic,* Utah, 1982, two-volume set, like new,
　slipcased 65.00
Trout Magic, New York, 1974, first edition, fine condition 25.00

Ted Trueblood

The Angler's Handbook, New York
　First edition, fair condition. 35.00
　Second edition, fine condition 50.00

Fred F. Van de Water

In Defense of Worms, New York, 1949, first edition, fine condition
　With dj 25.00
　Without dj. 18.00

Theodore S. Van Dyke

The Still Hunter, New York
　1922, first edition, good condition 35.00
　1943
　　Fine condition 45.00
　　Soiled 15.00

Howard T. Walden, II

Big Stoney, Derrydale Press, 1940, fine condition
　Limited edition of 550. . . . . 325.00
　Trade edition 35.00
Familiar Fresh Water Fish, New York, 1964, fine condition, fine dj . . 15.00
The Last Pool, New York, 1972, combines *Big Stoney* and *Upstream and
　Down,* fine condition 25.00
Upstream and Down, Derrydale Press, 1938, very fine condition
　Limited edition of 950. . . . . 250.00
　Trade edition 35.00

IZAAK WALTON

A compleat list of Walton's *Compleat Angler* would be impossible in a volume of this scope. Rather than settle for an 'incompleate' listing of these hundreds of collectibles, they are not listed at all. I respectfully refer you to the sporting book dealers listed in this volume's appendix.

Roland Ward

Roland Ward's Records of Big Game, London, fine condition
  1903, fourth edition 250.00
  1964.. 50.00
  1969.. 45.00

Frederick Watson

Hunting Pie, Derrydale Press, 1931, very fine condition
  Limited edition of 750.................................... 125.00
  Trade edition 50.00

Townshend Whenlan

Hunting Big Game, Harrisburg, 1947, two-volume set
  Fine condition, dj's..................................... 150.00
  Worn condition.. 85.00
The Hunting Rifle, Harrisburg, 1940, first edition, scarce, very good
  condition* 45.00

Stewart Edward White (White wrote many other volumes in addition to the ones listed here. Collectors want all of them.)

African Camp Fires, New York, 1913, first edition, very good condition 50.00
The Forest, New York, 1903, first edition, fine condition.......... 40.00
The Land of Footprints, New York, 1914, first edition, good condi-
  tion.. 45.00
Lions in the Path, New York, 1926, first printing, very good con-
  dition 50.00
The Mountains, New York, 1904, second printing, very good con-
  dition 25.00
The Pass, New York, 1906, first edition, very fine condition........ 35.00
The Rediscovered Country, New York, 1915, first printing
  Fair condition 15.00
  Very good condition..................................... 45.00

Ben Ames Williams

The Happy End, Derrydale Press, 1939, limited edition of 1,250, fine condition 150.00

Bruce S. Wright

Black Duck Spring, New York, 1966, first edition, scarce, fine condition 35.00
High Tide and an East Wind, Harrisburg, 1962, first edition, fine condition, dj 75.00

Lee Wulff

The Atlantic Salmon, New York, 1958, fine condition
    Limited edition of 200, s/n, slipcased 425.00
    Trade edition 25.00
Leaping Silver, New York, 1940, limited edition of 540, s/n, slipcased, fine condition 450.00
Lee Wulff on Flies, Harrisburg, 1980, signed, fine condition, fine dj   35.00
The Sportsman's Companion, New York, 1968, fine condition 15.00
Trout on a Fly, New York, 1986, limited edition of 500, s/n, slipcased, fine condition 150.00

Paul Young

Making and Using the Dry Fly, Michigan, 1934, scarce, fine condition 325.00
Making and Using the Fly and Leader, pp
    First edition... 100.00
    Second edition 85.00

Ed Zern

Are Fishermen People, New York, 1953, scarce, very good condition   25.00
A Fine Kettle of Fish Stories, New York, 1971, fine condition
    Fine dj.. 30.00
    Without dj... 20.00
How to Catch Fishermen, New York, 1951, fine condition
    With dj 25.00
    Without dj... 20.00
How to Tell Fish from Fishermen, New York, 1947, first edition, fine condition, dj 35.00
Hunting and Fishing from A to Zern, New York, 1985, first printing, fine condition
    Signed... 65.00
    Unsigned... 40.00
To Hell with Fishing, New York, fine condition, fine dj
    1945, first edition 35.00
    Later printing 20.00
To Hell with Hunting, New York, 1946, first printing, very good condition 20.00

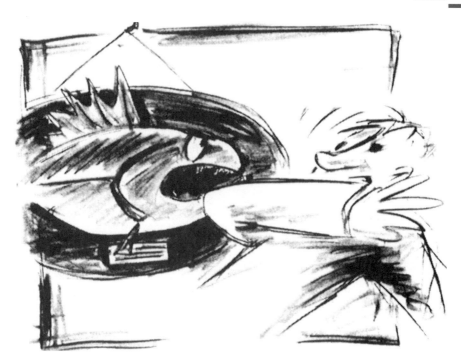

Ed Zern's wonderful zany pictures are as much a part of his books as are his words. This example is from *Are Fishermen People,* and the original hangs on my wall, willed to Ed Zern's godson: my son Chip.

CHAPTER 4

Ephemera

A Winchester trapshooter's scorecard, a cabinet card showing Buffalo Bill Cody, a ticket to the New York Sportsman's Show at the old Grand Central Palace, or a prospectus for Joel Barber's book *Wild Fowl Decoys* from Chicago's famed Von Lengerke and Antoine—each is a reflection of our sporting past and valuable both in its own right and as an adjunct to a given collection. As a case in point: both book and decoy collectors would bid on the V.L.A. prospectus were it offered at auction. The trapshooter's scorecard would sell, if only for the Winchester name; and Western Americana collectors, as well as historians with an interest in guns and gunning, would compete for the Cody photograph. But the early (pre-1950) Sportsman's Show ticket might go begging unless someone remembered that it was then and there that Charles "Shang" Wheeler and Ed Zern first met when Shang was exhibiting his award-winning decoys and Zern was selling Nash motorcars.

Only a scrap of paper? A quick look at some of the prices realized for sporting ephemera may suggest that you go into the "scrap" business or, at least, pay more attention than you have in the past to this often-overlooked area of sporting collectibles.

My dictionary defines ephemera as "anything short-lived or transitory," and I have used the title "Sporting Ephemera" to mean almost anything and everything that would normally have been lost, discarded, or worn out in short order, such as catalogs and flyers, advertising stationery, cards, and envelopes, and other material that might, elsewhere, be a separate chapter entity. I have also taken the liberty of including in this seemingly endless list fishing and hunting licenses, as

The famous paper label used sporadically by Anthony Elmer Crowell and his son, Cleon, from its inception in the 1930s until Cleon's death in 1961, is valued at $150.00. *Illustration courtesy of Joe and Carol Deer.*

well as antique and collectible photographs. Advertising calendars and posters have a chapter of their own, but pins and badges—the little, easily lost collectibles once given away by just about everyone—are included here. It seems to me that they fit the meaning of ephemera to a tee, and, if proof is needed, I have eerily lost the little Remington "Lesmok" pinback I borrowed from my postmaster to photograph for this chapter.

Collecting sporting ephemera is as easy as looking through an old box in your grandmother's attic or as complicated and costly as pursuing a particularly desirable article at an auction that specializes in such things. No one can tell you what to collect or what to pay for what you collect. When I am backed into a corner and asked by someone just which of the myriad ephemeral categories I suggest they pursue, I tell them to buy the best they can afford in their area of interest and everything that is underpriced at auctions, barn sales, and flea markets. I try to follow this advice and so should you.

Consider a recent barn sale where the owner had found several boxes of old, turn-of-the-century catalogs and cards showing farm machinery, fishing tackle, and a few firearms in one form or another. The owner sorted the material, placing the fishing tackle and firearm cards and catalogs in one small box and everything else in another. He priced the box of "sporting" material at $50 and the larger box of "odds and ends," as he called it, at $5. I bought both boxes, kept a few things, and sold everything else to a man who buys and sells nothing but this type of material. Yes, I made a substantial profit; no, I do not know where the next bonanza will be. But that's what makes it fun.

Sporting ephemera turns up just about anywhere and everywhere, and while I cannot direct you to the next bonanza, I can and will steer you on your way. Sales and auctions at older homes are undoubtedly the best bet for finding trunks and/or boxes filled with old sporting ephemera. The trick here is all in the timing. If it's a sale, be the first one on the scene; if it's an auction, be there at the end when they clean up the last of the "stuff" from the attic. This advice does not count at auctions where a catalog and/or absentee bidding is involved, but it can work at those rare good old-fashioned country ones that still actually occur now and again. The best advice I have regarding sporting ephemera after it has left its original site is to look at anything and everything carefully. That big old

This 1909 illustration on a blotter is very collectible as more and more women fish. This somewhat worn example of sporting ephemera set me back $22.00 at a recent auction.

box you walked by at the flea market last summer might have contained a photograph of Annie Oakley or a replacement for my missing Remington pinback.

The following listings are arranged by category. The prices do not reflect the buyer's fee that was added to auction sales.

ADVERTISING PINBACKS, ETC.

Pinback

Ballsite Powder Company, target design in red, white, and blue
    Very good condition 40.00
    Good condition. 30.00
Chittenden County (Vermont) Fish & Game Club, excellent condition 3.00
Colt, familiar logo of rearing colt
    Very good condition. 425.00
    Very rusty 95.00

DuPont

Standing quail, color
    .889″, very good condition. 135.00
    1¼″, very good condition. 65.00
Woodcock, full-color artwork, .889″, very good condition 275.00
Hercules, "Keep 'em Shooting," red, white, and blue
    Light rusting 20.00
    Mint condition 65.00

Peters

Dog retrieving quail jumping through "P," .889″. 550.00
Mallard flying through "P," .889″ 120.00
"Peters Ideal," gold on red, scarce 600.00
"Shoot Peters Referee Shells," purple shotshell, mint condition . . 90.00

Remington

Bear cubs and .22 repeater, .889″. 55.00
Bear with "Lesmok" promotion, .889″. 45.00
"Steel Lined Shells," bear cubs in action, .889″. 75.00

Remington/UMC

"Shoot Remington/UMC Arrow & Nitro Club Shells". 65.00
"Shoot UMC/Remington Arrow & Nitro Club Shells". 75.00

Western Cartridge

"Longest Run of 1907—274 Straight," fine condition 175.00
Topperweins ads, full color 350.00

Rare and wonderful signed cabinet card photograph of "Little Sure Shot,"
Annie Oakley, was auctioned with a group of her paraphernalia for $8,500.00
by Swann Galleries, New York City. *Photograph courtesy of Swann Galleries, N.Y.*

Trapshooters Heil, Crosby, and Gilbert, mint condition 600.00
"The Wonderful Topperweins," full color 500.00
"White Flyer" clay target, very good condition. 325.00

Winchester

"Ask for Winchester Nublack". 75.00
Large red W, blue background, ¾″ 35.00

STUCK

Pinbacks, stickpins, and all related material have been copied and reproduced. Remember, if it's worth something, someone wants to cash in. Know who you are dealing with.

Stickpin

William Mills, smallmouth bass, celluloid. 85.00
Winchester, "The 97.20% Shells," on miniature shotshell 145.00

Whistle, Baker shotguns, shorebird, 1¼″, rare 350.00

BADGES, LICENSES, ETC.

Fishing licenses

California (5), 1923–27, fishing scenes in color, paper 275.00
Pennsylvania (11) 175.00

Guide's license, New Brunswick, 1971, very good condition 40.00

Hunting and fishing license

Montana resident, 1920, paper, fair condition. 20.00
New York resident, 1917, first year 100.00

Hunting badges (3), North Carolina state/county resident, early
1930s. 75.00

Hunting license

California (7), 1919–26, color artwork, paper 250.00
Connecticut resident, excellent condition
   1926 . . . . 50.00
   1931 . . . . 50.00
New Jersey, 1938, bright, excellent condition. 42.50
Wisconsin, 1930, very good condition. 35.00

Hunting/fishing/trapping license, New York

1929 . . . . 12.00
1934 . . . . 8.00

CARDS, ENVELOPES, ETC.

Card, Parker Brothers, hammerless shotgun, excellent condi-
tion 165.00

Envelope

Dead Shot, falling duck, very good condition 65.00
DuPont, multicolored woodcock 250.00
Hazard Powder Company, calling mallard
    Large size 60.00
    Small size 55.00
Hercules Powder Company, Hercules holding club, very fine
    condition 125.00
Ithaca Gun Company, line drawing of shotgun, very good
    condition 150.00
Laflin and Rand Powder Company,
    "Extra Orange" powder 70.00
    Gunner in duck marsh
        Good condition 120.00
        Light soiling 80.00
        Torn and soiled 28.00

**This Hazard duck from the early
1900s is worth about $65.00.** *Author's
collection.*

Parker Brothers, woodcock and shotgun, color, very good condition. 220.00
Peters
   Two hunters at rest
      Poor condition. 40.00
      Very good condition 160.00
   Two setters at work, excellent condition 125.00
Remington
   Flying geese and model 11 shotgun, fine condition. 30.00
   Hawk chasing fleeing ducks, scarce. 250.00
Winchester
   Bear in hunter's camp 120.00
   Hunters in camp with fire, full color. 325.00
   Model 97 shotgun, 1899 postmark 75.00

Factory Invoice, Winchester

Flashlights, 1921. . . . . 15.00
Shells purchase, 1921. . . . . 15.00
.22 cartridges, 1921 . . . . 20.00

Letterhead and envelope, Daisy, 1939, mint condition 35.00

Letterhead, Parker Brothers, 1937 . . . . 25.00

POSTCARDS

Collectors should be aware of the potential value of sporting postcards as well as of others they may encounter. This is a popular collectible that can be worth big bucks.

Postcard
   DuPont
      Quail on rail fence, 1928 postmark, light wear. 55.00
      Shot tower, mint condition 15.00
   Iver Johnson factory, full color, mint condition. 15.00
   Remington, factory and shot tower, very good condition 20.00
   Winchester
      Factory. 20.00
      Shot tower, full color 25.00

Scorecard, Winchester

Junior Rifle Corps shooter's. 20.00
Trapshooter's scorecard, very good condition 45.00

Stationery, Ithaca Gun Company, open gun at top, very good
condition 35.00

Trade card, Remington, two double-barreled shotguns, 1914, very good
condition. 225.00

CATALOGS AND FLYERS

Catalog

Abercrombie & Fitch
 1930s to the 1950s (25) 250.00
 1949, very good condition 60.00
David T. Abercrombie catalog, 1908, minor staining on cover. . . . 20.00
L. L. Bean
 1932, rear cover torn and taped 35.00
 Late 1947 into the early 1960s (5) 55.00

This Abercrombie & Fitch catalog of a decoy exhibition was put together by author/collector Joel Barber in 1931 and has a current value of approximately $50.00. *Author's collection.*

Bristol
  1907, cover art by Oliver Kemp 80.00
  1910, cover art by Oliver Kemp, very good condition 90.00
Crossroads of Sport
  1948–49, cover by Ogden Pleissner 50.00
  1970–71, mint condition. 75.00
Hardy's *Angler's Guide,* very good condition
  1921 . . . . 95.00
  1927 . . . . 85.00
  1937 . . . . 95.00
Heddon
  1950, showing bamboo rods for sale, excellent condition 75.00
  1957, excellent condition 20.00
Leonard Rod Company
  1974, excellent condition 40.00
  Maxwell era, excellent condition 75.00
William Mills and Son
  1938, excellent condition 50.00
  1940, excellent condition 45.00
Old Town Canoe and Boat
  1937, very good condition 105.00
  1956, very good condition 20.00
Pflueger
  Retail catalog, 1940 . . . . 45.00
  Trade catalog, #61, 1940, very good condition 75.00
South Bend
  Bait Company (3), 1947–48–49, excellent condition 100.00
  "Fish and Feel Fit" tackle, 1937 . . . . 40.00
F. E. Thomas, 1935, 1956 price list pasted on back cover 45.00
Edward Vom Hoff
  1933, very good condition 225.00
  1940, very good condition 205.00
Winchester
  Arms
    1892, very good condition. 325.00
    1896, very good condition. 325.00
  Fishing tackle, excellent condition 145.00
  Salesman's, leather bound 275.00

REPRODUCTIONS

Reproductions are a collector's worst nightmare, and, when one collects paper ephemera, the dream never ends. Today's fancy copying machines work wonders. Caveat emptor!

Flyer

Parker Brothers, three shotguns, 1932, fine condition. 65.00
Winchester, model 21 shotgun, late 1940s 55.00
V L & A promotional for Barber's 1932 book *Wild Fowl Decoys* . . 25.00

Price list, Parker Brothers jobber's price list of guns, 1936 . . . . . . 175.00

COMIC BOOKS

Remington

How to Shoot, promotes safety and shooting 18.00

PHOTOGRAPHS, AUTOGRAPHS, ETC.

Cabinet card, portrait of Buffalo Bill Cody, 1890s, light staining. . 450.00

Christmas card,

Drawn, colored, and signed by Charles "Shang" Wheeler
    1944 . . . . 450.00
    1945 . . . . 450.00
Etchings
    Signed by Richard Bishop, excellent condition (2) 290.00
    Signed by Roland Clark (2) 550.00
    Signed by William Schaldach (3) 475.00

Cigarette card

A. H. Bogardus. 125.00
Dr. W. F. Carver 105.00
W. F. Cody. 125.00
Miss Annie Oakley. 235.00

Photograph

Bonefishing, signed by A. J. McClaine, excellent condition. 55.00
Zane Grey with record-size tuna fish. 65.00
Gunner and curly coated retriever with bag of ducks and rabbits,
    early. 85.00
Bert Lahr in lion's suit from *The Wizard of Oz,* from A. J. McClaine
    estate auction 75.00
Shore bird gunner in blind with decoys at water's edge, black and
    white, rare. 275.00
Ed Zern fishing the Test, signed by Zern, glossy. 35.00

This chapter would, if one were to let it, take over the entire project and be a book unto itself. A company's annual calendars and posters and duck stamps issued but for a single year are certainly ephemeral, and who can say that used cartridges and shotshells are not. The so-called line in the sand must be drawn. Calendars and posters as well as duck stamps and all forms of ammunition deserve a place of their own in a book of this kind. Sporting ephemera covers the loose ends, picks up the oddities and the unusual, and, I admit, gives me a way for dealing with all manner of materials. Now if I could only do something with the old Sportsman's Show ticket. . . .

WHAT'S IN A NAME?

Indeed, what is in a name? Why do some collectors go wild over marked items from Abercrombie & Fitch, including that once-famous firm's distinctive boxes? Do L. L. Bean collectors know something you are overlooking? Actually, the answer is also the answer to the growing popularity of all sporting collectibles: A & F and L. L. Bean represent something solid, a piece of the past when quality counted. And people today are willing to pay for it.

CHAPTER 5

Magazines and Periodicals

Today's sportsmen and women, often too intent on hurrying hither or yon', can easily overlook sporting magazines and periodicals as a source of both joy and a modicum of money. These old fishin' and huntin' magazines are a very real part of our sporting heritage and serve as a wealth of editorial and advertising information for collectors.

Consider what I've just noted thumbing through an October 1925 *Hunter, Trader, Trapper:* all the column-heading illustrations are from pencil drawings done by Lynn Bogue Hunt, a Parker Trojan model could be had for the sum of $55 and a "Baby Lefever" in .410 for "only" $29, L. L. Bean's Maine Guide Shoes are postpaid at $7.50 a pair, and Heddon's "New" Baby Game Fisher was at the dealers for just $1.25 each. The classified advertising section offers a pair of "wild" mallard decoys that both fly and call for $2.50 a pair or $12 a dozen, a 60-acre farm in western Pennsylvania was $9,000, and a group of 10 mounted deer heads was $100.

If this is typical of moderately collectible sporting magazines, you begin to understand the appeal of all such publications, including those aimed at the country-club set like *The Field* from Great Britain and our own *The Sportsman.* The former continues to flourish, whereas the latter failed after 10 years of effort. Both magazines are collectible, with early and special copies worth from $20 to $50.

SELLING

Sporting collectors and just about everyone else complain about how little they are offered for collections of old sporting magazines. A magazine that lists here for say $5 probably is not worth more than 10% to 20% of that to a dealer who must wait for months (perhaps years) before he finds a buyer at the retail price.

There is no single reason for collecting sporting magazines and periodicals, but perhaps the most common one is to gain information about another collectible. Many fishing tackle companies existed for only a very short time, and sometimes the only means we have of identifying their lure is a small advertisement in a sporting publication. This is equally true of other short-lived manufacturers, such as this writer's venture with his father into the duck decoy business in the late 1950s.

One collector I used to know set out to put together a complete set of *The American Rifleman*. His project was complicated by the fact that the publication actually began as *The Rifle* in 1885, became *Shooting and Fishing* in 1888, *Arms and the Man* in 1906, and, finally, *The American Rifleman* in 1923. Another collector only buys publications with artwork by Lynn Bogue Hunt, while still another is partial to William Harnden Foster's covers for *National Sportsman*. Some collect Corey Ford's columns, others want Ruark, Zern, or whoever. Sporting magazines and periodicals are both collectible and hard to come by in good condition.

Finding old sporting magazines and periodicals is no easy matter. Backed into a corner and forced to tell you where to seek these elusive publications, I would be candid and tell you that, in order, I would go to estate auctions, flea markets, and out-of-the-way antiques establishments. You never know. And, if all else fails, the dealers listed in the appendix can help.

The following prices for magazines and periodicals in very good or better condition are based on 1995 auctions and catalog offerings. Prices given are for an individual issue. Defects will lower the value; serious defects

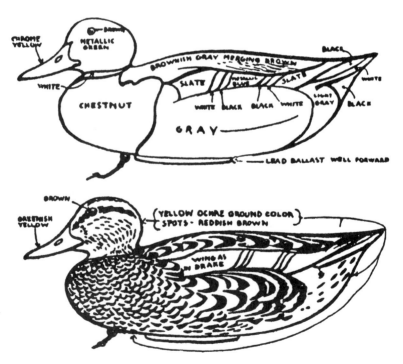

Lynn Bogue Hunt's art and illustrations are just one reason that collectors buy yesterday's publications. These painting diagrams that accompanied Hunt's advice on how to make your own decoys from a 1906 copy of *Outing* Magazine are classic. *Author's collection.*

and/or missing pages and/or covers can render any publication worthless. Caveat emptor.

The American Rifleman

1923–1930	8.00 to 15.00
1931–1939	3.00 to 5.00
1940–present	2.00 to 2.50

Decoy Collector's Guide

January 1963—December 1965, Vol. I, No. 1 to Vol. III, No. 4*	12.00 to 15.00
1966–1967 annual	15.00 to 20.00
1968 annual	15.00 to 20.00
1977 annual	15.00 to 20.00

Decoy (formerly *Decoy World*), 1980–present 3.00

Decoy World (later *Decoy*), 1974–1979 . . . . 3.00

DECOYS

There have been a number of publications about decoys and not all are included in this chapter. *Toller Trader, Ward Foundation News,* and *Decoy Hunter* are three others. There are more, and someone somewhere wants them all.

Field and Stream (monthly). Note: *Field and Stream* covers and art by well-known figures such as Lynn Bogue Hunt, A. L. Ripley, and Edwin Megargee command higher prices.

Prior to 1910	20.00
1910–1930	15.00
1930–WW II	10.00
1945–1959	5.00
1960–date	3.00

Fly Fisherman (six issues per year)

Vol. I, No. 1, May 1969	150.00
August 1969	50.00
October 1969–May 1971	5.00 to 10.00
Vol. III, No. 1—present	3.00 to 5.00

*The 12 quarterly issues were published as a hardcover book. See Sorenson in Chapter 3.

DECOY COLLECTOR'S Guide
VOLUME SIX 1977

Edited By
Harold D. Sorenson

Illustrated By
William J. Koelpin

COVER: Artist Bill Koelpin captures in oils his vision of a decoy carver in the 1930's. Without such industrious and talented carvers, decoy collectors would have little for their shelves except factory-produced birds. Incidentally, the resemblence of the canvasback heads to a Ward Bros. style is truly coincidental.

The editor/publisher's signature on the title page of the last issue of *Decoy Collector's Guide* (1977) adds interest and value. *Author's collection.*

FORTUNE

There may not be a fortune in old magazines, but some issues are worth your undivided attention. Several *Fortune* magazines worth noting are the 1932 issue with the innovative article on decoys by Joel Barber, and the 1946 and 1948 issues with John McDonald's fly fishing articles illustrated by John Atherton. Also of particular interest are the 1952 copies of *Gentry* with a Gentry wet fly attached to the centerfold.

Forest and Stream (This publication was first published weekly, next bimonthly, and lastly on a monthly basis.)

Weekly issues, large, good condition 5.00
Bimonthly issues, good condition 5.00
Monthly issues, colorful. . . . . 5.00 to 20.00

Gray's Sporting Journal, fall 1975–present . . . . 8.00 to 10.00

Gun Digest Note: These prices are for examples in very good or better condition. Flaws will lower the value in proportion to their seriousness.

1944, No. 1
   Original. 150.00
   Reprint 35.00
1946, 1947, and 1949. . . . . 100.00 to 150.00
1951–1956 . . . . 30.00 to 40.00
1957–present. . . . . 7.50 to 10.00

Gun Dog (six issues per year)

Vol. I
   No. 1. . . . . 30.00
   No. 2–No. 6 . . . . to 25.00
Vol. II
   No. 1–No. 6 . . . . to 15.00
   No. 1 and No. 2 . . . . to 10.00
Vol. III, No. 3–Vol. IV, No. 6. . . . . to 7.50
Vol. V, No. 1–present . . . . to 3.00

Gun World, 1960–present . . . . to 3.00

Guns

January 1955, Vol. I, No. 1 . . . . 15.00
Other 1955 copies. 5.00
Others to date. 3.00

Guns & Ammo (monthly). Note: Collectors of Elmer Keith's writing lead all takers for *Guns & Ammo*

Vol. I, No. 1, 1958 . . . . 15.00
Others to date. . . . . 3.00 to 5.00

Hunting & Fishing, one of several outdoor magazines that made a half-hearted run at the "big boys" (*Field and Stream, Outdoor Life,* and *Sports Afield*) between WW I and II, all issues . . . . 3.00 to 5.00

North American Decoy (quarterly)

1967. . . . . 35.00
1968–1971 . . . . 25.00
1972. . . . . 15.00
1973. . . . . 10.00 to 20.00
1974, winter 5.00
1975, spring, summer, and fall. . . . . 10.00 to 20.00
1976. . . . . 20.00
1977. . . . . 3.00
1978
    Spring. 15.00
    Summer, fall, and winter 3.00
1979. . . . . 3.00
1980 . . . . none issued
1981–82. . . . . 9.00
1983 . . . . none issued
1984, annual 9.00

Outdoor Life (monthly)

Prior to 1920. . . . . to 20.00
1920–1930. . . . . to 15.00
1930–WW II . . . . to 10.00
1945–1960. . . . . to 5.00
1960–present . . . . to 3.00

Outdoors, see information under *Hunting & Fishing*

Outer's Recreation, all issues . . . . 3.00 to 5.00

Shooting Times

1960 and 1961. . . . . to 5.00
All others . . . . to 3.00

Sporting Classics (every two months)

Vol. I
- No. 1. . . . . 50.00
- No. 2–No. 6. . . . . 10.00 to 25.00

Vol. II
- No. 1. . . . . 5.00
- No. 2–No. 5 . . . . 10.00

All others 3.00

Sports Afield, this fine monthly publication deserves its own place in the scheme of things, but, like it or not, the information listed under *Field and Stream* and *Outdoor Life* will serve and save space.

The Sportsman (monthly)

- 1927–1937 . . . . 25.00
- Bound volumes, 6 months each volume . . . . 50.00 to 100.00

Stoeger's Shooter's Bible

1931
- Original 60.00
- Reprint 10.00

- 1934–1935 . . . . to 50.00
- 1939, World's Fair issue 75.00
- 1940–1941 . . . . to 40.00
- 1942–1949 . . . . to 30.00
- 1950–1960 . . . . to 10.00
- 1961–present . . . . to 7.50

All lists come to an end and this one ends here, but not without a reminder that there is more to know. Sporting magazines date back to 1820 and the *American Turf Registry and Sporting Magazine,* and include such heretofore unmentioned publications as *Argosy, True,* and Arnold Gingrich's *Esquire.* All are both interesting and collectible, and only you can decide which ones, if any, are worthy of your attention. A word of warning: Old magazines are time consuming, and, if you will excuse me, I think I'll drop a note to that man who is selling the $9,000 farm in Pennsylvania.

BINDERS

Many publications sold binders designed to hold and preserve their fragile outpourings and many sold bound copies of their publications. These binders enhance any given magazine or periodical collection, and, if the originals are not available, you can buy ones that will serve from larger stationery suppliers. Any binder is better than no binder.

CHAPTER 6

Calendars and Posters

It was a time of plenty when, after the Civil War, the ability to print in living color became practical, and a new form of cheap advertising came on the American scene. The use of this new medium was not restricted to sporting manufacturers, but they embraced it lustily. Companies such as DuPont, Union Metallic Cartridge Company, Remington, Winchester, and eventually all the others, were soon providing both calendars and posters to their customers, thereby adding another collectible to the so-called "golden age" of American sport. From the 1880s to the 1940s and the start of World War II, fine art in the form of calendars and posters hung in the homes of sportsmen for little or no cost. Think about it: our parents and grandparents were able to enjoy the art of luminaries such as Lynn Bogue Hunt, Carl Rungius, N. C. Wyeth, and Phillip Goodwin at cost of not more than a buck a pop. And, to top this, the art was replaced each year as new calendars and posters became available. The golden age was indeed a special time, and it is no wonder that these fragile antiquities are costly collectibles today.

Finding old calendars and posters on a hit-and-miss basis can prove to be a disappointing experience. I have been chasing sporting collectibles for a few more years than most of you and, in that time, have only discovered one example of either—an 1898 Union Metallic Cartridge calendar depicting Molly Pitcher at Monmouth that I paid $1 for. So unless your luck runs a good deal better than mine, you will have to deal with dealers, and this leads inevitably to "let the buyer beware," an oft-used but ever-applicable translation of caveat emptor.

Finding and authenticating material can take a bit of doing. Next to authenticity, condition is the most important factor in judging any paper collectible, whether it is a calendar, poster, or advertising envelope. Most early posters and calendars were made with metal bands top and bottom. If these are missing or the material has otherwise been trimmed or altered, value is greatly reduced. Tears, cracks, and heavy creases also can lessen values, as will water or other stains. Badly damaged paper goods are worth next to nothing, and fragments of calendars and posters worth even less. The prices listed are for material in very good or better condition.

One final word before you read on or head out the door with your checkbook—*reproductions*. The field of sporting advertising probably contains more reproductions than even the most suspicious collector imagines, and caution is well advised. Know what you are buying and who you are buying it from. Deal only with people who stand behind what they sell; demand

This approximately 10″ × 10″ counter display for American Powder Mills Dead Shot Powder is valued at about $300 to $500 in fine condition.

written guarantees. It is far better to pass up a possibility than to purchase a "100-year-old piece" that was produced in Hong Kong the previous week.

The following listing of both calendars and posters is organized alphabetically by company name and only touches the tip of the iceberg, for there are hundreds upon hundreds of each that do not appear here. The late Bob

REPRODUCTIONS

Both calendars and posters have been reproduced, and buyers should be aware of this fact. Winchester reproduced its own early calendars in the early 1960s, and others by Peters, Remington, and United States Cartridge have found their way to the market. The tin signs one sees at shows and flea markets are fakes and worthless. Know what you are buying and who you are buying it from unless, of course, you and not the object of your interest want to get hung.

Strauss put together two fine volumes of *American Sporting Advertising* and these, though out of print, are available from rare and used book dealers and should be read by anyone interested in collecting this great artwork. Other books do exist, but the two Strauss volumes are the bibles of this appealing and expensive pursuit.

Bristol Thornton Manufacturing Company, Poster

1909, Oliver Kemp, woman "fighting" bass from birchbark
canoe 300.00
1914, Phillip Goodwin, fisherman landing fish from rocky shore-
line 350.00

Colt Patent Fire Arms Mfg. Co., Poster

1910, cowgirl with drawn Colt revolver
  Variation #1, Colt logo 1,000.00
  Variation #2, no logo 1,000.00
  Variation #3, in Spanish, without logo 1,000.00
  Variation #4, in Spanish, with logo 1,000.00
1921, girl shooting clawing jaguar
  Variation #1, in English 1,000.00
  Variation #2, in Spanish 1,000.00
1928, Texas Ranger by Frank Schoonover
  Variation #1, small type, no logo 800.00
  Variation #2, larger type, no logo 800.00
  Variation #3, logo upper left 800.00
  Variation #4, logo upper right 800.00
  Variation #5, no advertising 800.00
World War I
  "Colts to the Front," three servicemen with drawn colts 300.00
  Troops off to battle, horizontal with bands top and bottom,
    C. Wilson 350.00

DuPont Powder Company

Calendar
  1899 . . . . 750.00
  1900 . . . . 800.00
  1901, Edmund Osthaus 350.00
  1902 . . . . 600.00
  1905, Edmund Osthaus 750.00
  1906 . . . . 800.00
  1907 . . . . 400.00
  1908 . . . . 300.00
  1909 . . . . 300.00
  1910, N. C. Wyeth 300.00
  1911, Edmund Osthaus 300.00
  1913 . . . . 250.00

Poster
  1909, Worth Brehm, two boys hunting in the snow 350.00
  1912, "Broadbills Here They Come," Lynn Bogue Hunt 750.00
  1913
    Lynn Bogue Hunt, covey of bobwhite quail 500.00
    G. Ryder, green-wing teal in flight 600.00
  C. 1918
    Lynn Bogue Hunt, shows series of prints available from
      DuPont 200.00
    Hy S. Watson, woman shooting trap with others 400.00
    N. C. Wyeth, man's arrival at trap field 300.00

Hercules Powder Company

Calendar
  1917, Charles Livingston Bull, black-breasted plover 250.00
  1919, "Bagged in France," Norman Rice, hunter with German hel-
    met 100.00
  1920, "A Surprise Party," Arthur Fuller, returning soldier . . . 100.00
  1921, "Outnumbered," Arthur Fuller, three boys rabbit
    hunting 150.00
  1922 through 1959, fine condition 100.00
Poster
  1914
    Ducks taking off from water 200.00
    Trap shooter breaking target 200.00
  1920, "Don't You Fool Me, Dog," F. M. Seigle, black man and
    dog 450.00
  1923, "I'se Lost De Lunch," F. M. Seigle, black man and boy hunt-
    ing 450.00
  1924, "Dah He Goes," F. M. Seigle, black man and boy
    hunting 450.00
  "The Game Bird of the Future—Chinese Pheasants," Lynn Bogue
    Hunt 250.00

Ithaca Gun Company, Poster

  1909, "Cross Fox," Lewis Agassiz Fuertes, crow escaping from
    fox 450.00
  1910, "Snow Shoe Rabbit," Lewis Agassiz Fuertes 400.00
  1912, "Mallard Ducks," Lewis Agassiz Fuertes 500.00
  1914, "Wood Cock," Lewis Agassiz Fuertes 400.00
  "Extinct Passenger Pigeons," Lewis Agassiz Fuertes, passenger
    pigeons 400.00

Marlin Firearms Company, Poster

  1904, "A Great Shot," two hunters over campfire 400.00
  1905, "A Gun for the Man Who Knows," Phillip Goodwin 500.00

These Lafflin and Rand posters, "Spring" with woodcock and "Summer" snipe, are two from a set of four. Each is valued between $200.00 and $300.00.

1907, "A Gun for the Man Who Knows," Phillip Goodwin, hunter and
guide pushing off a canoe 600.00
1908, G. Muss-Arnolt, two mallards dead in the air 750.00
1909, "Quail Shooting in England," Rosseau. 400.00

Parker Brothers Gun Company

Calendar
1922, Bert Sharkey, squirrels in a tree 1,000.00
1929, "protected" wood ducks with gunners in the back-
ground 1,000.00
1930, "Sacred Birds Protected by Our Indians," C. I. Couse 1,250.00
Poster, 1922, Bert Sharkey, squirrels in a tree. 1,000.00

Peters Cartridge Company

Calendar
1903, "Dawn of a New Era," idyllic setting filled with game . . 500.00
1904, "Protected," bull moose in snowstorm 500.00
1905, "Noon Hour" two gunners with their dogs at noon 500.00
1906, "Coming Out Ahead," hunter packing moose head out of the
woods 500.00

1907, "Sun Up and Dad's Finished Milkin'"—Reckon I'll Get Licked," boy with geese. 1,000.00
1908, Duck shooter being poled by guide in marsh, ducks on boat deck 1,000.00
1911, G. Muss-Arnolt, two setters on point over covey of quail 300.00
1912, "Tempter," gunner in businessman's office 300.00
1913, "Getting Ready," C. Everett Johnson, man checking gear. 300.00
1914, Lynn Bogue Hunt, mallard drake jumping from approaching dog 750.00
1915, Arnolt, pair of setters on point at edge of swale 350.00
1916, Frank Stick, mallards flocking to decoys 300.00
1917, Arnolt, two dogs on point in cornfield. 300.00
1918, hunter telling his setter bitch to stay with her pups. . . . 350.00
1919, "Hurrah! You Got Him!," woman and guide in the mountains. 350.00
1920, Osthaus, two pointers in stubble field. 300.00
1921, Phillip Goodwin, four gunners getting set for a day afield 300.00
1922, "Lest We Forget," C. A. Meurer, relics of World War I   200.00
1923, "Outpointed," Goodwin, hunter, dog, porcupine. 200.00
1924, G. Muss-Arnolt, setters on point in overgrown cover. . . 200.00
1925, Joe Burgess, mallards high over gunner's rig of decoys. 200.00
1926, G. Muss-Arnolt, covey of bobwhite quail 200.00
1927, G. Muss-Arnolt, beagle pack in hot pursuit in stubble field. 200.00
1928, G. Muss-Arnolt, solitary setter on a classic point. 200.00
1929, Lynn Bogue Hunt, five mallards dropping into marsh. . 300.00
1930, Phillip Goodwin, puma eye-to-eye with hunter 200.00
1931, Lynn Bogue Hunt, pair of pheasants in almost Oriental setting. 150.00

Poster
  1903
    Flying mallard in hole of large P 300.00
    Trap shooter being congratulated in hole of large P. 300.00
  1911
    Grizzly bear with two cubs in mountains, Phillip Goodwin. 400.00
    Hunter shooting sharptails in hole of large P 300.00
  Phillip Goodwin
    Bugling elk in high mountain setting. 400.00
    Caribou in typical northern setting 400.00

G. Muss-Arnolt, "Steel Where Steel Belongs," mallards in flight 750.00

Attributed to G. Muss-Arnolt, "Steel Where Steel Belongs," pheasant in flight 500.00

Remington and Remington-UMC (Remington Arms Company and Union Metallic Cartridge Company—UMC—merged in the early 1900s, and much of their advertising overlaps: Remington for firearms and Remington-UMC for shotshells, cartridges, and general advertising. These calendars and posters are listed together here. UMC materials before the merger are listed under the Union Metallic Cartridge Company heading.)

Calendar

1912, "Going In," Phillip Goodwin, hunters at railhead 300.00

1913, Carl Rungius, moose wading in lily pads 400.00

1917, Lynn Bogue Hunt, covey of quail in flight 300.00

1919, Lynn Bogue Hunt, diving hawk attacking flight of Canada Geese as they flee 750.00

1921, attributed to Lynn Bogue Hunt, fox attacking two Canada geese. 750.00

1922, "Game Loads Get Em!," sportsmen with purchase of ammunition 300.00

1923, hunter painting decoys with decoys, shotshells, and 1922 calendar in background 600.00

Robin Hood material is highly collectible as is evidenced by the $450.00 price tag on this 8″ × 12″ poster.

1925, "Let 'Er Rain," old gunner and decoys in boat 500.00
1926, old gunner cleaning gun on deck of gunning camp with decoys
   showing 500.00
1928, "Old Boy! We Have the Winning—," Hy S. Watson, old-timer
   with dog 200.00

BANDS

Early calendars and posters came with metal bands at the top and, in most instances, the bottom as well. If these are missing, the piece cannot be considered original, and values are decreased.

Poster
   1901, F. E. Getty, sassy sportswoman with Remington gun. . . 600.00
   1906, "well-turned-out" gunner with auto-loading shotguns . . . 300.00
   1907, hunter and grizzly meeting on narrow trail 500.00
   1913, Hy Watson, black man directing hunters and their
      dogs 300.00
   N. C. Wyeth, hunters approaching fishing bear. 350.00
   Carl Rungius, moose wading in lily pads (same as 1913 calen-
      dar) 250.00
   Young boy and dog looking over a groundhog's digs 150.00

Savage-Stevens

Calendar
   1904, Carl Rungius, hunter with downed bull elk 500.00
   1921, Charles Livingston Bull, lynx with dead turkey in a live
      oak 500.00
   1947, "There They Are," Richard Bishop, mallards in flight   100.00
Poster
   1906, sportswoman with gun and man showing off pair of wood
      ducks 750.00
   Phillip Goodwin, hunter and guide in canoe with guide calling
      moose 300.00
   Lewis Agassiz Fuertes, mule deer in snowy setting 300.00

Union Metallic Cartridge Company

Calendar
   1889, Annie Oakley type woman loading shotgun. 1,500.00
   1890, "The French in Algeria," produced for French UMC
      agent 1,200.00

Very rare, this 1884 Smith & Wesson calendar is worth up to $750.00.

1891, young girl dressed for the hunt surrounded by hounds 750.00
1892, boy in costume of the day with a gun that is bigger than
    he is 750.00
1893, black guide poling boat as hunter picks up duck from
    water 1,250.00
1896, Indian mounted on horse in desert setting. 600.00
1897, "Saving His Scalp," rider escaping from Indians 600.00
1898, "Molly Pitcher at Monmouth—," Gilbert Gaul. 500.00
1899, soldier and sailor and war scenes of Cuba 400.00
1900, head of bison close-up in grassy setting 500.00
1901, "A Chip Off the Old Block," boy, gun, and bagged game
    birds 600.00
Poster
1905, "In a Tight Place," Everett C. Johnson, charging bear. . 300.00
1906, Everett C. Johnson, mountain lion pursued by hunter and
    hounds 350.00
1907, Lynn Bogue Hunt, pair of blue-wing teal 500.00
1908, covey of quail in flight headed toward the viewer 400.00
Oliver Kemp, "Calling the Moose," also illustrates cartridges for big
    game 300.00

These two 12″ × 8″ counter cards by the Union Metallic Cartridge Company are worth between $100.00 and $300.00 each.

United States Cartridge Company

Calendar
  1917, Alexander Pope, hanging mallards, shells, and gun. . . . 500.00
  1919, "The Black Shells," hunter with bag of ruffed grouse . . 300.00
  1922, bear with wooden case of "Black Shells" 500.00
  1925, H. C. Edwards, shooter in rigged sink-box. 600.00
  1926, William Eaton, old-timer touching up decoys. 400.00
  1927, 8 mallards in flight over marsh and rigged decoys 450.00
  1928, Joe Burgess, gunner sitting with setter puppies and
    bitch 300.00
  1929, William H. Foster, hunter tugging beagle past hidden
    rabbit. 350.00
Poster
  1890, 75 "Popular and Expert Trap Shooters of America" including
    Annie Oakley 750.00
  1911, "The Black Shells," man, dog, and ammunition 400.00
  Joe Burgess
    Canada geese flying through thunderstorm 600.00
    Canada geese huddled in marsh during thunderstorm 500.00
    "The Black Shells," falcon attacking green-wing teal pair 1,750.00

Western Cartridge Company

Calendar
  1920, William Eaton, card-playing hunters in camp. 250.00
  1921, "Devotion," William Eaton, hunter sneaking by church 250.00
  1922–1934. . . . . 150.00
Poster
  By Norman Hall, "Dreams," black man napping and dreaming of
    rabbits. 350.00
  By V. K. Murray, "The Elk Fight". 200.00
  By A. Russell
    "The Unexpected," old black man and a boy smoking out a
      snake 750.00
    "You Can't Shoot Without Shells," black family and dogs   750.00
    "Champions of America," 200-target winners Frank Troeh and Bart
      Lewis at trap field. 250.00

Winchester Arms Company

Calendar
  1887, deer, elk, and turkey shooting in scenes from *Harper's* maga-
    zine. 2,000.00
  1888, moose, bear, and seal shooting in scenes from *Harper's* maga-
    zine. 1,200.00
  1889, A. B. Frost, duck, bear, and deer shooting. 1,200.00

This 13″ × 11″ store display featuring "Woodcock Worthy" shot shells is rare and in good to excellent condition is valued at $250.00.

1919, Robert Amick, farmer plowing and watching waterfowl in
  flight 450.00
1920, father and son in boat returning with bag of ducks 350.00
1921, Arthur Fuller, father and son and setter on point 350.00
1922, E. C. Edwards, cowboy meeting bear on narrow trail . . 400.00
1923, Phillip Goodwin, hunter high above a herd of trophy
  sheep 400.00
1924, G. Ryder, gunner in reeds awaiting approaching ducks 300.00
1925, H. R. Poore, pointers with setters in background 500.00
1926, Phillip Goodwin, hunter facing bear at point-blank
  range 350.00
1927, Frank Stick, hunter on snowshoes approaching deer . . 400.00
1928, P. F. Elwell, hunters in canoe sneaking up on moose . . . 350.00
1929, Lynn Bogue Hunt, dog, gunner, and flushing pheas-
  ants 400.00
1930, hunter holding calendar pages that include some fishing
  scenes 300.00
Store calendars, 1921–1929 . . . . 200.00 to 300.00
Poster
1904, "The Kind that Gets Them," hunter with trophy sheep 800.00
1905, "Cock of the Woods," large turkey in wooded setting 1,000.00
1906, hunter on snowshoes stalking game 850.00
"They Are the Hitters," three mallards in flight 700.00

VALUES

Age, scarcity, and subject matter are important in determining the value of this or that calendar or poster, but nothing is as important as condition. If you view these materials as you would a fine print, the point is quickly made. Few buyers want a tattered and torn piece of artwork, and restoration is very, very expensive.

Women were featured on many firearms posters as is shown here with two by Winchester from far-apart eras. The Annie Oakley-type on the left and the demure sportswoman on the right are valued at $850.00 and $250.00 respectively, proving that age does indeed make a dent in our scheme of things.

PART II
FISHING

CHAPTER 7

Split-Cane Rods

We have come a long way since 1653 and the publication of Izaac Walton's *Compleat Angler* and the advocacy of 18-foot fishing rods to the fine split-cane rods that today's anglers use and collect. A brief history of the development of the fishing rod should benefit angler and collector alike.

Fishing and fishing rods changed very little from the time of Walton and Cotton until after the American Civil War when the popularity of the sport developed at a rapid pace and the need for better "tools" was noted. In the 1840s Sam Philippi made the first split-cane rod, but it remained for Hiram L. Leonard to bring the concept of the six-sided split-cane rod to fruition in his Bangor, Maine, workshop in 1869. Leonard's success was immediate, and in the early 1880s he moved his shop to Central Valley, New York, to be closer to New York City and the majority of his growing number of customers. Leonard rods are the stuff of dreams, as are those made by Eustis Edwards and Edward Payne, who Leonard trained in his Bangor shop.

Rueben Leonard, Bill and Gene Edwards, and Jim Payne all followed in their fathers' fine footsteps, and I think it is safe to say that not only did Hiram Leonard create the split-cane rod we know and use today, but he is also responsible for a chapter in American history as well. And, when you consider the odd fact that such legendary rod makers as Thomas Chubb, Fred Devine, George Varney, Fred Thomas, and the Hawes brothers were all graduates of Leonard's Bangor, Maine, shop, the chapter about Hiram L. Leonard's historic contributions to America's and the world's angling history begins to look more like a book.

A short introduction on the history of split-cane rods cannot hope to tell you much of anything, but I hope I have whet your appetite. Whether you are a seasoned or beginning collector or only a weekend fly-caster, the history of America's rod and reel makers will add to your enjoyment. To this end, a list of suggested reading can be found in the appendix.

One cannot afford to collect split-cane rods made by the men who made them famous unless armed with both knowledge and the wherewithal. Rods by the masters are expensive and, unless you know more than I do, you will do well to deal only with individuals you can trust and who will guarantee what they sell you. Split-cane rods are "big business" and should be approached as you would any other business venture—with both care and an understanding of the product. There are several excellent books on this subject as well as museums and fishing tackle shows where fine rods may be examined. These are listed in the appendix, and I urge you to learn all you can if you plan to compete for the historic split-cane rods that come up for sale in today's marketplace.

As is the case with all sporting collectibles, condition is the single most important consideration in examining a split-cane rod, whether it was made by the men mentioned or recently by a fine modern rod maker like Jon Parker of Ballston Lake, New York. A broken tip, if the rod was supplied by its maker with two tips, might be excused for a price; but a single-tip rod in that condition is worth only a fraction of its counterpart in original condition. Broken parts and other disabling and disfiguring faults are usually enough to render a given split-cane rod worthless, but a properly refinished rod can often be as good as new and promoted and priced accordingly. There is a world of difference between "repaired" and "refinished" and you must know the difference.

STAND UP STRAIGHT

The admonishment we heard as youths to "stand up straight" should be remembered and applied to split-cane rods today. These fine instruments are designed to flex and bend in use but should be stored so as to prevent any movement. In or out of the case, always store your rods in a vertical position to prevent sags and sets that can do serious damage to both the rod and your wallet.

Rod repairs may be as simple as the professional replacement of parts or as severe as clumsy attempts that went awry, but all detract from a rod's worth. Professional revarnishing and fine rewrapping of silks that do not in any way detract from either the rod's action or original characteristics are permissible and often necessary. Remember: know what you are buying and from whom you are buying it. The money is yours. The care and protection of fine rods after one purchases them is not to be overlooked. Split-cane rods should be stored in a vertical position to avoid the possibility of a set or permanent warp developing. Insurance is another consideration. The average homeowner's policy may protect the average rod, but it is not likely to cover a $2,500 Payne or Leonard, and it certainly will not cover a collection of fine split-cane rods. Call your broker and be sure you are protected against loss.

The following listing of fine split-cane rods includes both the collectible work of yesterday and a few of the equally collectible rods being made by today's talented craftsmen. If you are an angler, I urge you to purchase the very best rod you can afford that fits your fist. If you are a collector, I urge you to try your hand at fishing. Both angler and collector appreciate the true craftsmanship of fine split-cane rods, but only on quiet waters in the half-light of dawn or dusk do the rods truly work their wonders. The photographs in this section were provided by South Bay Auctions of East Moriches, New York.

DROUGHT

Split-cane rods are made from bamboo, bamboo is wood, and wood gets thirsty. In other words, with the possible exception of impregnated examples, rods dry out and become brittle. To prevent this, check them periodically and apply a very light coat of fine furniture wax such as that offered by Constantine & Son in the Bronx in New York City.

THE NUMBER CODE

Virtually all catalogers and auctioneers use numerical shortcuts in listing split-cane rods. The 2/1, 2/2, 3/2, etc., you come across tell you first the number of sections in the rod and second the number of tips. In other words, a 3/2 is a three-piece rod with two tips. And, in spite of what else you may have been told, the extra tip is almost always just that—an extra tip providing insurance against breakage.

L. L. Bean

7½' (2/2), built by Bean for Heddon
  Excellent condition 385.00
  Needs refinishing, one tip broken and repaired. 75.00

C. W. Carlson

7½' "Riverton," six-sided, two tips, near mint condition 2,100.00
7'9" "Steamer Special," four-sided, two tips, near mint condi-
  tion 3,500.00
9' four-sided (3/2) salmon rod, light wear 1,250.00

F. D. Devine

8½' (3/2) trout rod, marked "The Devine Rod, Utica, NY," revar-
  nished 200.00
9' (3/2) lancewood trout rod, marked "The Devine Rod, Utica, NY,"
  and "Dec 1st, 1885" patent, rare, very good condition in original
  canvas case 400.00
9' trolling rod, marked "The Devine Rod, Utica, NY," serial #H1932,
  very good condition 150.00
9' (3/2) trout rod, "The Devine Rod, Utica, NY" decal, revar-
  nished 200.00
9½' salmon rod, 1885 patent date, very good condition, missing one
  tip. 195.00

L. L. Dickerson

8' model 801510 (3/2) 4 oz. rod, new condition, one repaired tip masterfully refinished 1,875.00

8' (2/2) trout rod marked "8013-48," loose top guide but otherwise in mint condition 3,200.00

9' two-tip trout rod, showing heavy wear and use 600.00

E. W. Edwards & Son

7½' trout rod with V L & A mark, late 1920s, one ferrule replaced on one tip, excellent condition 725.00

8' (3/2) rod marked "E. W. Edwards Autograph #70 Deluxe 8' Medium," 1930s, very close to original condition.......... 980.00

9' Special with over varnish, needs refinishing 340.00

Eugene Edwards

7' one-tip Quadrate spinning rod, very good condition 110.00

8' (3/2) Edwards Quadrate Model 34, light varnish roughness but otherwise in excellent condition 650.00

8' (2/1) Quadrate salt water spinning rod, new and unused condition.. 250.00

QUADRATE

The Eugene Edwards "Quadrate" rods are, as any first-year Latin student can tell you, four-part split-cane rods. These are out of step with the accepted six-sided rods we are familiar with but have proven very popular with some anglers and are, of course, collectible.

Everett Garrison (Garrison made less than 900 rods during his lifetime. Existing rods are both scarce and expensive.)

7' (2/2) trout rod, refinished "like new".................. 6,000.00

8' (3/2) trout rod, original excellent condition 7,000.00

This 8' Garrison Model 212 (2/1) trout rod in excellent used condition is valued at $1,300.00.

This 8′ H. S. "Pinky" Gillum "Custom Built" (3/2) trout rod sold for $1,300.00.

H. S. "Pinky" Gillum

8′ (3/2) 5¼ oz. trout rod, rare, excellent condition with original bag
and tube 5,250.00
9′ (3/2) salmon rod, two guides rewrapped in original colors, showing
only very slight use 2,000.00

Goodwin Granger

7′ (2/2) 3 oz. trout rod marked "Made by Goodwin Granger, Denver"
Poor condition 200.00
With minor problems 800.00
7′ (2/2) "Aristocrat" trout rod, poor condition with one tip in very poor
condition 200.00
8½′ "Stream & Lake" trout rod, made by Wright & McGill, missing
guide 125.00
8½′ (2/) "Granger Victory" trout rod, made by Wright & McGill, one
tip shortened. 150.00
9′ (2/) "Granger Victory" trout rod, made by Wright & McGill, refin-
ished to original condition 100.00

Although in need of refinishing, this 7′ Goodwin Granger "Aristocrat" (2/2) is still worth $550.00.

GRANGER AND WRIGHT & MCGILL

Goodwin Granger built his rod business in Denver, Colorado, where he prospered until WW II. After the war he sold out to Wright & McGill who made a limited number of "Granger" rods before turning their entire production to glass a few years after acquiring Granger's company.

George Halstead

9′ two-tip 4½ oz. trout rod, marked "G. H. Halstead Rods" on locking ring, very good condition 1,850.00

Hardy

6′8″ single-tip trout rod, new unused condition in carrying case 475.00
7½′ (2/2), new in bag and case 650.00
9′ "Coronation" salmon rod, one of two tips broken. 210.00
9½′ one-tip salmon rod with extension butt, marked "The Reservoir Fly," excellent condition 390.00

H. W. Hawes

8½′ (3/2) trout rod, shipped by Hawes in 1919, refinished by Art Taylor, a fine early rod in "like new" restored condition . . . 1,800.00

Heddon

7½′ (2/2) trout rod, marked "Heddon Featherweight Thoroughbred," minor varnish roughness, in labeled bag and tube 450.00
8½′ (3/2) trout rod, marked "Ed. M. Hunter Approved" one tip split 130.00
8½′ "Black Beauty" trout rod, little if any use, in original bag and tube 450.00

H. L. Leonard

7′ (2/2) pre-fire rod, refinished to excellent condition 1,500.00
7′ (2/2) model 704 "Duracane" trout rod, excellent condition with bag and tube. 575.00
7½′ (3/2) model 38½L "Fairy Catskill" rod, c. 1929, near mint unfished new condition with original bag and tube. 2,250.00
8′ (3/2) pre-fire model 50 DF rod
Fair condition. 280.00
Old professional refinish 700.00
8′ trout rod, serial #614, one of two tips split, otherwise in excellent condition with original bag and tube 500.00
8′ trout rod, one tip missing, otherwise in original condition . . . 325.00
8½′ (2/2), nearly original condition with original bag 870.00

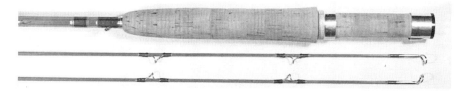

A 7′ G. H. Howell (2/2) serial #4925 trout rod in mint condition is worth $1,000.00.

This fine split-bamboo fly rod is a three-piece, two-tip (3/2) example of the talented Japanese maker Kakuhiro's art. *Author's collection.*

A 7½′ H. L. Leonard (2/2) Model 39 in excellent used condition brought $1,250.00.

9′ (3/2), factory refinished, one tip 1½″ short 360.00
9½′ (3/2) pre-fire salmon rod, excellent condition. 470.00
9½′ trout rod, 1875 and 1878 patents. 150.00
12′ (3/2) low-water salmon rod, c. 1960, very good condition with origi-
    nal bag and tube 525.00
14′ (3/2) two-hand salmon rod, needs minor repairs. 340.00

A 10½′ H. L. Leonard (3/2) salmon rod with extension butt, in fishable condition, $150.00.

GONE TO BLAZES

A disastrous fire destroyed the Leonard factory in the 1960s and marked an end to the kind of work that had gone before. A knowledgeable collector commented that after the fire, the love that had nurtured the company was gone and the product showed this lack of affection. Be that as it may, "pre-fire" Leonards are the rods that matter.

Orvis

5' (2/1) "Mighty Mite," shows only minimal use 550.00
6½' (2/2) "Impregnated Deluxe" trout rod, serial #24,00X, excellent condition 450.00
6½' (3/2) "Rocky Mountain" trout rod, Federation of Fly Fishermen 1969 marks, with original case 600.00
6½' "Battenkill" spinning rod 200.00
7' (2/2) "Superfine" trout rod
    Mint unfished condition with bag and tube 625.00
    Very good condition 400.00
7½' (2/1) "Madison" trout rod, showing use but in very good condition 340.00
8' (2/2) "Battenkill" trout rod
    Excellent condition 300.00
    One tip repaired 175.00
8½' (2/2) "Limestone Special," replaced wrap but otherwise in excellent condition 250.00
9' (2/1) "Battenkill" trout/salmon rod, near mint condition with bag and tube 175.00
9' "Shooting Star" with extension butt, marked "light salmon,"
    (2/1), refinished for salt-water use 250.00
    (2/2), shows very little wear or use, with bag and tube 320.00
Boat rod, c. 1895, in original case 250.00

This 6½' Orvis "Battenkill" (2/1) fly rod with a two-piece handle brought $300.00.

Jon Parker

6'9" (2/2) trout rod, mint condition, original bag and tube 750.00
Identical rod, sold at different location (proving that there are, indeed,
   bargains for those who seek them. 150.00

Edward Payne

9½' (3/2) "E. F. Payne Maker" trout rod, one tip in poor condition otherwise in excellent refinished condition 300.00

Jim Payne

8' (2/2) rod, historically important because it was built for Roy
   Steenrod in the late 1920s, with authentication and Steenrod
   flies 1,500.00
8' (2/2) model 102H trout rod, excellent refinished condition with bag,
   tube, and tag. 1,800.00
8' (3/2) model 201 trout rod, only a few signs of use, with original bag,
   tube, and tag. 2,100.00
8' (2/2) model 103 trout rod, marked "Made for Abercrombie & Fitch,"
   near mint condition with bag, tube, and tag 2,100.00
8' (3/2) model 200 trout rod, marked "Made for Abercrombie & Fitch,"
   excellent condition. 1,300.00
9½' fly rod, marked "Made for Abercrombie & Fitch," complete with
   two tips but needs repair 490.00
10' two-tip Salmon rod, made for A & F, new unused condition with
   original bag, tube, and tag. 1,550.00

PAYNE AND ABERCROMBIE

Jim Payne and Abercrombie & Fitch enjoyed a long and profitable rela-
tionship as maker and seller, and angling historians might note that when
Jim died in 1970 there was a rush to buy his rods at A & F, where the
price for his remaining output doubled overnight from $225 to $450.

Jim Payne's 7½' (3/2) Model 100 with one tip short is valued at $1,000.00.

Jim Payne's 8½' (3/1) Model 200 in good used condition sold for $120.00.

E. F. Thomas

7½' (5/2) pack rod, refinished like new 1,500.00
8' (2/2) "Brownstone," refinished, with original bag and tube in excellent condition 1,000.00

Winchester

7' (2/2) with decal, near mint condition with original bag and tube 1,200.00
8½' (3/2) trout rod, one tip repaired, with bag and tube 110.00

Wright & McGill, see Granger

Paul Young

7½' (2/2) "Perfectionist" trout rod, dated 1959
Like new 2,300.00
Refinished to excellent condition 2,200.00
7½' (2/2) "Martha Marie," refinished like new 2,000.00
8' (2/2) "Para 15" with wet and dry fly tips
Excellent condition 2,100.00
Dated 5/1.57, excellent condition 2,200.00
9½' (2/2) "Florida Special" salt-water rod, excellent condition . . 750.00

This 7½' F. E. Thomas "Special" (2/2) trout rod, a rarity in this size, sold for $1,700.00.

SHORT IS SEXY

Collectors like to display their goodies, and for those of us who live with normal 8′ ceilings, rods of more than about 7½′ cannot be both assembled and displayed in the proper manner. For this reason, and the fact that these small, light wonders are fun to fish with, split-cane rods of less than 8′ command higher prices than do their longer counterparts.

Edward Vom Hoff's 9½′ (3/2) salmon rod with the prerequisite extension butt sold for $175.00.

Fishing Reels

When I think of fishing reels, three examples come immediately to mind: the fine little Hardy St. George my father gave me, the automatic fly reel I thought I just had to have, and the old Bradford-Boston brass reel I bought for a song at a yard sale. I fished with the trusty little Hardy for a number of years and became proficient at fly-fishing, but, as a typical teenager, I just had to have an automatic fly reel. After a frustrating month of poor casts and few fish, I relegated the automatic to the basement and returned to the trusty Hardy, aware for the very first time of its real worth and craftsmanship. The old brass Bradford reel taught me quite another lesson when I sold it for what I later learned was a fraction of its market value.

REEL CARE

How often has someone screwed up a fine old reel with steel wool or harsh polish? Too often. If you remember that the earliest reels were made by watchmakers and jewelers, perhaps you'll think before you leap. The following rules should be of help:

- Never use steel wool or any abrasive.
- Don't try to straighten bent parts.
- Use mild soap and warm water.
- Use only jeweler's or gunsmith's tools.
- Let any fine old patina speak for itself.
- Seek expert advice when in doubt.

We are all entitled to a mistake now and then, but I have learned from mine; and whether you are a fisherman, a collector, or both, I like to think that what I have to say here will prove both interesting and useful. It may also allow you to step around the pitfalls that await today's unsuspecting collectors.

With the exception of the fine products produced by Great Britain's House of Hardy, reels are an American phenomenon, and collectors and would-be collectors should have an understanding of our reel history. For all intents and purposes, the early Kentucky reels and the New York ball-handle reels were developed independently in the years before the Civil

War. Each served the needs of its locale: trout fishermen in the east and bait casters in the west. These early reels were made by watchmakers and other fine artisans, and names to remember include Meek & Milam from Kentucky and Frederick Vom Hoff in the east, to name but a few of these often unsung early craftsmen.

Wars have a way of changing things, and the end of the Civil War saw the beginning of manufactured reels in America. The machine age had dawned and ushered in what has been described as the golden age of American sport. Fishing clubs flourished on trout and salmon waters; bass fishing found new favor; and manufacturers, such as Leonard, Milam, Meisselbach, Orvis, Talbot, and Vom Hoff, answered the growing demand with the reels collectors would clamor for more than a century later. This so-called golden age struggled through World War I and the Roaring Twenties only to crash with the market in 1929. Fine handmade reels continued to be made, as they are today; but for the collector of early and historically important reels, the period from 1850 until 1930—a mere 80 years—was the time of plenty. Learn as much as you can about these bygone years—read books, invest in fishing tackle auction catalogs, and seek the advice of other collectors. It is impossible to learn too much.

Knowing as much as you can about collectible fishing reels is one thing, finding them quite

Billinghurst's patent "birdcage" trout reel was America's first commercially patented fly reel. This one, with a fixed handle and the "Rochester, NY–1859" marking, has age patina, brass construction, and is in excellent condition. This rare and historic reel sold for $1,400.00. *Photograph courtesy of Bob Lang, Raymond, Maine.*

REPLACED PARTS

How much "restoration" can a reel undergo and still be the real thing? There is no precise answer. From an antiquarian's point of view—which is the serious collector's view, too—repairs of more than a minor nature render the reel valueless. Someone who is buying a fine old reel to use might be more liberal and ignore replaced handles, feet, or pillars, unless the work was badly done. The final decision is yours. Remember, you get what you pay for and restoration reduces value.

another. Reels such as the Bradford example do indeed turn up from time to time at odd yard sales and flea markets; but they are few and far between, and in 10 years of gleaning, I have only picked up about a dozen collectible reels in this manner.

Auctions and estate sales offer the reel collector myriad opportunities and have the advantage of often being advertised in advance, thereby saving wasted trips. If you have questions, you can often call the auctioneer or seller before the event, but it is imperative that you view the item or items before the sale. Unscrupulous individuals often "load" a sale with tackle they could not sell elsewhere or—and this is more often the scenario—tackle that have been stored under less than ideal conditions and show the ravages of both time and weather. Let me say it again: it is up to you to inspect what you are thinking of buying before you buy it. A bargain is no bargain at all if it is broken or otherwise faulty. Obviously, not everyone has the time it takes to pursue reels at sales or flea markets, and, if this is your situation, you must turn to fine tackle dealers and specialty auctions for your acquisitions.

Buying collectible reels from tackle dealers and at specialty auctions has both its advantages and disadvantages. On the plus side is the fact that not only do you know what you are buying, but who you are buying it from as well. You will, of course, pay for these advantages, and therein lies the only drawback. Most collectors consider the cost and buy or bid accordingly as their budgets allow. Some collectors say they miss the yard-sale and flea-market "game," but most say they are actually saving by buying at auctions and from trusted dealers. If you choose this route to amassing a respectable collection of reels, you will find a listing of both dealers and auction houses in the appendix at the end of this book. I know and recommend these individuals but caution you that it is your money and "caveat emptor" is never out of style.

ORCA

No, it's not a whale; it's the Old Reel Collectors' Association. You can learn more about this nonprofit organization by writing to Michael E. Nogay at PO Box 2540, Weirton, WV 26062.

If you have read the initial preface and the introductions to other chapters in this book, you will know that I cannot separate the history and romance of sporting collectibles from their monetary worth for fear of losing the special values inherent in our past. Take time to smell the roses. If you buy a fine trout reel, consider using it as least once before you relegate it to the shelf. The joy of collecting takes a back seat to the excitement of playing a trout on a reel that speaks to you of yesterdays if you listen. Enjoy.

Abbey & Imbrey

Early bait casting reel, A & I logo in a circle, fair condition. 50.00
Multiplying bait casting reel made for A & I by Julius Vom Hoff, rare
   2/0 size, very good condition. 245.00
Trout reel, early latch-stop and the A & I logo, nickel plated
   Excellent condition 185.00
   Fair condition. 60.00

Abercrombie & Fitch

Stan Bogen multiplying salmon reel made for A & F
   Marked "AF-200-M"
      Light wear, in need of cleaning. 750.00
      Like new, with sought-after green A & F box. 1,800.00
   Marked "AF-300-M" on the foot, rare, has never seen the water,
      excellent condition 1,850.00
Julius Vom Hoff German silver and hard rubber, size 3 trout reel,
   perforated rims, made for A & F in 1913, rare, excellent condi-
   tion. 900.00
William H. Talbot 2″ German silver reel, both Talbot and A & F mark-
   ings, good condition although wear and pitting 465.00

WHO MADE WHAT

Many reels are marked with the name of the company that sold the reel and not that of the maker, although most quality examples carry both maker and seller identification. Abercrombie & Fitch, Abbey & Imbrey, R. H. Macy, Sears & Roebuck, and Bradfords of Boston are but a few of many that sold the work of others under their own trade names. Look for the maker's identification—it was and is the craftsman who creates the value.

T. H. Bate & Co. (Note: Many unmarked "New York State" ball-handle reels are correctly and incorrectly attributed to Bate; but with no markings to go by, one can only guess.)

Brass fresh-water reel, ball handle, c. 1850, excellent condition   175.00
Brass multiplying reel, classic ball handle, 1860s, size 3
   Good condition. 150.00
   Fair condition. 100.00
Blue Grass (see **Horton** and **Meek**)

BLUE GRASS

There is too much confusion about "blue grass" reels. The name, of course, refers to the blue grass of Kentucky and was often used by Kentucky reelsmiths as part of their company's promotions. B. F. Meek & Sons used the name blue grass extensively, as did the later partnership of Meek & Milam to a lesser degree. The confusion arises when novices discover Horton Manufacturing Co. reels with the blue grass designation. Horton bought out Meek, moved the operation north, and continued to make quality reels with both the Meek and blue grass assignations.

Stan Bogden

Size 00 single action reel, problems in its drag system, Ed Zern collection. 575.00
Size 2 salmon reel set for a right-hand wind, functionally excellent with signs of wear on rim, Ed Zern collection. 750.00
Size 100 handmade reel set for a right-hand wind, functionally excellent with signs of wear on rim, Ed Zern collection. 800.00
Size 300 gold-finished salmon reel marketed by Abercrombie & Fitch, marked "64-35" on its foot, excellent condition. 925.00

Bradford

Early German silver trout reel, marked "Bradford-Boston"
   Excellent condition 475.00
   Pitted and worn 85.00
Early unpolished brass latch-stop reel, marked "Bradford-Boston," very good condition 360.00

Conroy

Brass crank-handle trout reel, marked "Conroy-Makers-NY," 1850s
   Bent foot but otherwise in very good condition 300.00
   Excellent condition 500.00
Multiplying bait reel, rim drag button and S handle, early, retains 98% of its original nickel finish, excellent condition. 250.00

G. W. Gayle & Son, German silver 2″ bait casting reel, marked "Geo. W. Gayle & Son, Frankfort, KY-NO 3," scarce

Click and drag switches, very good condition 975.00
Removable bearing caps 900.00
Worn screw slots 975.00

Hardy (Note: Many Hardy reels are worth more than those listed here. These include the rare Bougle and Cascapedia salmon reels, the Jock

Antique "Conroy Makers" brass trout reel with raised back plate click housing and ivory handle is a classic pre-Civil War reminder of our angling heritage. This reel with only minor foot-end filing sold for $500.00. *Photograph courtesy of Bob Lang, Raymond, Maine.*

Scott bait casting reel, and the Tobique River and Zane Grey models pictured.)

Birmingham style 2½" brass trout reel, oval Hardy identification, 1890s, worn. 150.00

Hardy 3⅞" fly rod, extra spool, very good condition 150.00

Hardy Featherweight, wear to finish but otherwise in excellent condition. 135.00

Hardy Flyweight, spare spool, excellent condition. 170.00

Hardy Husky salmon reel, silent drag and dual prong line guide, excellent condition 160.00

Hardy LHR Lightweight trout reel, with original box. 145.00

Hardy Perfect, ivory knob, c. 1921

    Good condition. 320.00

    Worn original finish, in fine working order 425.00

Hardy Princess 3¼" trout reel, moderate wear. 125.00

Hardy St. George 3¾" salmon reel

    Excellent condition, with case. 225.00

    Built-up spool, low #41 serial number, excellent condition . . . 320.00

Hardy St. John, 1970s, near mint condition. 125.00

This rare Hardy Cascapedia salmon reel from Ed Zern's collection is marked "The Tobique" rather than the usual "The Cascapedia" and is quite probably one of a kind. This wonderful reel from sporting artist/author Ed Zern's estate was sold for **$5,000.00.** *Photograph courtesy of Bob Lang, Raymond, Maine.*

Hardy Uniqua 4″ salmon reel, drag click and perforated spool, worn. 200.00
St. Andrew 4″ salmon reel, adjustable drag and reversible line guide, excellent condition 175.00
Zenith salmon reel, adjustable drag, marked "Made by Hardy Bros. England for Abercrombie & Fitch Co.," line guide missing, very good condition 90.00

Heddon

Marked "James Heddon's Sons, Dowagiac Mich"
    "3–15" casting reel, click switch, very good condition. 95.00
    "3–25" German silver bait casting reel, good condition 100.00
    "3–35"
        German silver casting, minor pitting but otherwise in very good condition 75.00
        Wooden arbor tournament spool and balanced handle, near excellent condition. 160.00
Model 3200 free spool reel, new condition 25.00
35th Anniversary Heritage model bait reel, c. 1962, replaced handle 40.00

Horton Mfg. Co.

Blue Grass (Horton)
 No. 3, bait casting reel
  Excellent condition 150.00
  Fair condition 60.00
 No. 33, Simplex, take-apart bait casting reel, very good condi-
  tion 125.00
 No. 34, Simplex, take-apart bait casting reel, very good cond-
  ition. 75.00
Kosmic
 Hard rubber and nickel steel bay reel, click switch and steel bearing
  Very good condition 55.00
  Reportedly made by Julius Vom Hoff. 325.00
Meek (Horton), German silver bait casting reel
 No. 2, screw slot wear 300.00
 No. 3, tournament handle, spool, and removable handle, excellent
  condition. 175.00
 No. 4, jeweled, like new. 450.00

Arthur Kovalovsky

Size 6/0 deep-sea reel, rare size, hard rubber, aluminum, and chromed
 brass, light wear 625.00
Size 9/0 big-game reel, patent #1958919
 Anodized aluminum, worn chrome but otherwise in good condi-
  tion 600.00
 Chrome over brass, worn chrome in places. 375.00

H. L. Leonard

Marked "H.L. Leonard—Pat No 191813" raised pillar trout reel,
 German silver and bronze, 2⅛", rare, excellent condi-
 tion . . . . 1,100.00 to 1,500.00
Marked "H.L. Leonard—Pat June 12, 1877" raised pillar trout reel,
 German silver and bronze, strong click and altered foot, excellent
 condition 900.00
Marked "Leonard-Mills" model 50 trout reel, counterbalanced handle
 and take-up screw, early, 3⅛", excellent condition 775.00
Marked "Leonard-Mills" model 47 Fairy trout reel, hard rubber and
 German silver, made to fit the Leonard Fairy fly rods, very scarce,
 excellent condition. 1,500.00
Marked "Leonard-Mills" model 50A large diameter trout reel, rubber
 and German silver, 3", very good condition. 400.00

This scarce "H. L. Leonard," marbleized trout reel is, with the exception of the handle, identical to the famous Philbrook & Paine model. A German silver reel with orange and black marbleized front and back plates, it sold for $4,000.00. *Photograph courtesy of Bob Lang, Raymond, Maine.*

OIL NOT GREASE

Many reels require lubrication to keep them in good working order; and, in fact, many have removable bearing caps for just that purpose. Use only the finest oils for this occasional, but necessary, upkeep. Heavy oils and grease will, as they say, gum up the works.

B. F. Meek & Sons

Marked "B. F. Meet & Sons, Louisville, KY. No. 3"
Marked "Blue Grass No. 4," click and drag switches German silver, fine condition 350.00
Marked with owner's name, broken drag, original leather case 210.00
Marked with patent date (Nov 26, 01), free-spool reel, made before acquisition by Horton 600.00

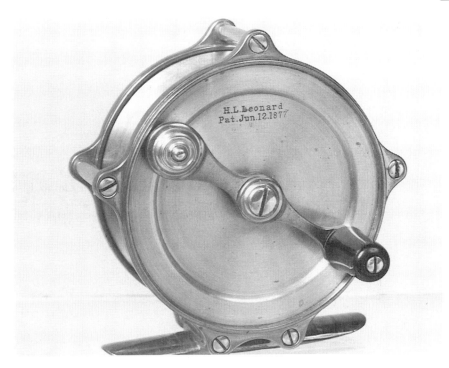

This rare trout reel is marked "H. L. Leonard—Pat June 12, 1877." It has a narrow spool and balanced handle and is made from a combination of bronze and German silver with a brass handle-cross-bar. This handsome interplay of metals in a fine working reel with only screw-slot wear resulted in a sale price of $3,000.00. *Photograph courtesy of Bob Lang, Raymond, Maine.*

An early "Malloch's Patent" spinning reel, made of brass and aluminum, has the Gibbs Patent lever mechanism and click switch. Rated as excellent, it sold for $150.00. *Photograph courtesy of Bob Lang, Raymond, Maine.*

This early Meek & Milam German silver bait casting reel is marked "Meek & Milam, Frankfort, KY = No. 2." It has its original (slightly bent) handle with ivory knob, is in very good condition, and sold for $950.00. *Photograph courtesy of Bob Lang, Raymond, Maine.*

Meek & Milam, marked "Meek & Milam, Frankfort, KY"

"No 3"
Oversize handle, a few minor flaws. 405.00
Screw slot wear but otherwise in excellent condition 1,100.00
"No. 4," replaced handle knob 850.00

Meisselbach

Rainbow model 621 trout reel, most of paint worn to the brass, good
working order 35.00
Tri-part bast casting reel
Model 580, free-spool, very good condition 50.00
Model 581, good, uncleaned condition 40.00

Milam, marked "B. C. Milam, Frankfort, Ky"

"No. 2" bait casting reel, German silver, original counterbalanced
handle
Excellent condition, with VL & A case 450.00
Near mint condition. 760.00
"No. 4," near mint condition. 650.00

Ocean City, model 25 trout reel, non-click drag

Excellent condition. 20.00
Fair condition 15.00

Orvis

CFO reel, excellent condition 150.00
CFO IV reel, early, shows wear 85.00
Madison model 8, like new 35.00

Marked "C. F. Orvis Maker, Manchester, Vt, Patented May 12, 1874"
  Commemorative rod, 1974, limited edition of 250, new in
    box 250.00
  Fair condition 225.00
  Very condition with wear 275.00
  With wrong handle 210.00
Marked "Orvis Lord II Made in Sweden," multiplying salmon reel, from
  Ed Zern collection. 300.00
Orvis SSS adjustable salmon or salt-water reel, shows rim wear 160.00

Peerless

No. 2 trout reel, few nicks on rim, excellent condition, with
  case 270.00
No. 5 salmon reel, "S" handle, black side plates, anodized aluminum,
  new 440.00

Pflueger

Delite trout reel, counterbalanced handle, fine nickel finish 180.00
Model 1492 Medalist, 1950s
  Excellent condition 50.00
  Good condition. 40.00
  With extra spool. 55.00
Model 1494 Medalist, very good condition 180.00
Model 1495AK, made in China, excellent condition. 40.00
Model 1495CJ, excellent condition 25.00
No. 2955 surf casting reel, like new, with box dated 1934 . . . . . . 200.00
Summit level-wind bait casting reel, excellent condition 40.00

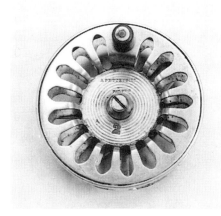

This Pettingill side-mounted trout reel has "Pat Pnd Z" marking and is in excellent condition with a strong click and all of its nickel-plated finish intact. A 2½" reel, it sold for $400.00. *Photograph courtesy of Bob Lang, Raymond, Maine.*

Supreme bait casting reel
>   Minor blemishes 75.00
>   Very good condition 40.00

Shakespeare

Marked "Marhoff" bait casting reel, early "S" handle, very good condi-
tion 35.00
Marked "Tournament Free-Spool 1744 Shakespeare" bait casting reel,
2″, replaced handle knob, uncleaned 200.00
Model HE "Miller Autocrat" ocean reel, adjusting handle brake, excel-
lent condition 200.00
Model 1740 free-spool bait casting reel, tiny, excellent, with case 50.00

South Bend

Level-wind bait casting reel, like new, with worn original box. . . . 20.00
Model 300 anti-backlash bait casting reel, with original box 35.00

Talbot (see also Abercrombie & Fitch)

Marked "Talbot Reel & Mfg. Co., K.C. Mo., USA—Special"
>   "Comet" model, unpolished. 350.00
>   "Niangua" model, German silver, early, excellent working condi-
>   tion 325.00
>   Tournament bait casting reel, aluminum, mint condition 700.00
"Star" model bait casting reel, wear to screw slots. 240.00

Edward Vom Hoff

Marked "Edw. Vom Hoff, Fulton St., NY, " "Pasque," German silver and
hard rubber, size 2/0, shows wear 235.00
Model 355 Peerless trout reel, German silver and hard rubber, almost
new condition. 2,000.00
Model 360 Perfection, #3 size, adjustable drag, completely restored,
like new condition 3,200.00
Model 423 International salmon reel, all parts shiny and
bright 1,150.00
Model 504 multiplying salmon reel, 7-position drag, on-off click shows
only careful use and wear 1,500.00
Model 550 "Star" surf casting reel, size 2/0, excellent condition 275.00
Model 621 "Universal Star" reel, German silver and hard rubber
>   Size 1/0, rare, near mint condition 750.00
>   Size 2/0, with marked leather case
>>   Excellent condition 350.00
>>   Shows wear 250.00
Model 722 "Commander Ross"
>   Size 10/0, with original case 750.00
>   Size 12/0
>>   With left-hand wind. 750.00

A scarce Talbot "Ben Hur" trout reel, this example is marked "Wm. H. Talbot Reel Co., Nevada, Mo.—Pat. Jan. 22, 1901" and "A & F." Other than minor pitting on the spool ends, this handmade German silver reel is in excellent condition; a fact that is reflected in the $3,200.00 selling price. *Photograph courtesy of Bob Lang, Raymond, Maine.*

VOM HOFF, VOM HOFF, VOM HOFF

The Vom Hoff family played an extensive role in American angling, and reels made by them are treasures. The father, Frederick, made fine reels at the time of the Civil War, and his sons, Edward and Julius, learned from him. Both anglers and collectors prize their work.

> With original case. 1,000.00
> Model 800 "Matecumbe," 2¾″ miniature version of Vom Hoff's big-
> game reels, excellent condition 350.00

Frederick Vom Hoff

Marked "F. Vom Hoff & Son, Maker," brass ball-handled reel, early
Heavily pitted 165.00
Unpolished condition. 350.00

A rare Model 360 Edward Vom Hoff "Perfection" trout reel in No. I size has the 1896 patent date and a marked and original case. This reel, which set the standard for others to follow, has only minor dings to the handle-crossbar and sold for $3,100.00. *Photograph courtesy of Bob Lang, Raymond, Maine.*

Marked "November 26, 1867" (patent date), rare reel sets the standard for modern trout and salmon reels 1900.00

Julius Vom Hoff

Big-game reel, marked with 1885, '89 and '11 patent dates together with "Thos. J. Conroy" on bearing cover, screw slot wear but otherwise in excellent condition 350.00

Marked "Abbey & Imbrey," German silver and hard rubber, perforated rim, minor repair. 700.00

Marked "Julius Vom Hoff"
"Brooklyn, NY, Pat. Nov. 17 '85" bait casting reel, German silver, hard rubber 95.00

"Brooklyn, NY, Pat. Nov. 17 '85" and "Pat. Oct 8, 1889," aluminum and hard rubber, size 3/0 .... 125.00

"Pat. Oct 8, 89," all-metal perforated-rim trout reel, rare, excellent condition. 800.00

Raised pillar trout reel, German silver and hard rubber, very good condition
Size 1 .... 300.00
Size 3 .... 300.00

A. L. Walker

Midge trout reel, 2¼", like new. 1,400.00
TR-2 trout reel, excellent condition 600.00
TR-4 steelhead reel, like new. 800.00

Winchester

No. 1235 raised pillar trout reel, excellent condition 110.00
No. 4256 jeweled take-apart, click broken but otherwise in good condition 75.00
No. 4328 non-level wind bait casting reel, broken click 85.00

Otto Zwarg

Lightweight 2/0 multiplying salmon reel, "S" handle screws off, excellent condition

With case. 1,450.00

Without case 1,400.00

Model 400 "Laurentian" multiplying salmon reel, German silver, hard rubber and aluminum, excellent condition 650.00

GERMAN SILVER

German silver is not silver at all. It is an alloy composed of varying amounts of copper, zinc, and nickel. Silver-white in color and very hard and resistant to corrosion, this alloy was discovered by German industrial chemist E. A. Geitner in the early 1800s.

The words "F. Willman, Maker—Stillwater, Minn" are engraved on this one-of-a-kind silver Kentucky-style bait casting reel. An owner's marking area on the back is blank leading to the assumption that this heretofore unknown maker decided to keep this rarity for himself. This reel has only minor flaws, was classified as near mint, and sold for $3,750.00. *Photograph courtesy of Bob Lang, Raymond, Maine.*

This handmade German silver bait casting reel by C. H. Wisner of Flint, Michigan, has name and address together with patent pending markings. Only a few of these free-spool, c. 1899 reels are known to exist, and this one, with the exception of reel foot filing, was termed near mint and sold for **$2,050.00.** *Photograph courtesy of Bob Lang, Raymond, Maine.*

CHAPTER 9

Hand-Tied Flies

I s $20 too much to pay for a fine steelhead fly tied by the late Ed Haas of northern California fame? How about $150 for a "Martinez Special" salmon fly by Belarmino Martinez himself? Are authenticated trout flies by Catskill legends Theodore Gordon and Roy Steenrod really worth up to $2,000 apiece? Only you can answer these questions, but these are today's prices for yesterday's flies. If the cost of these bits of fluff and feather scare you, so be it. But if you are interested, remember that it is much easier to catch a sucker than a trout or salmon. As the popularity of these scarce collectibles increases, the chances for charlatans to hook a live one increase proportionately, for they know all there is to know about sucker bait. Know who you are dealing with and demand written documentation. Quality hand-tied flies from yesterday's and today's tiers make up a wonderful collection that will increase in value in the years to come. Remember, it is one thing to get hooked on flies and quite another to get hooked by them. Buyer beware!

Hand-tied flies come in all sizes and shapes, from the tiniest aquatic and terrestrial imitations to the opulent full-dressed salmon flies that have become so popular with collectors. All trout and salmon flies, as well as bass

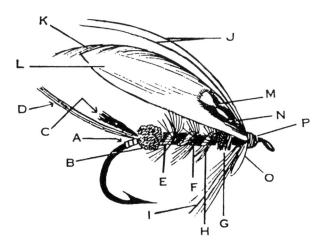

Counting the hook, there are 17 parts to a full dressed fly. They are: **(A)** tip, **(B)** ruff, **(C)** tag, **(D)** tail, **(E)** ribbing, **(F)** body, **(G)** joint, **(H)** body hackle, **(I)** hackle, **(J)** horns, **(K)** topping, **(L)** wing, **(M)** shoulder, **(N)** cheek, **(O)** throat, and **(P)** head.

and salt-water varieties, can be the basis for a fine collection. No one can tell you what to collect, but I will suggest that you specialize right from the very beginning. All too many would-be collectors buy anything and everything and then discover that a number of the flies have no real value in and unto themselves. Decide at the outset what you want to collect and build your collection one or two flies at a time at a pace you can afford. Buy the best you can afford, be certain of the authenticity of your purchases, and let the collection take care of itself. You will find that your collection will grow faster than you might imagine and you will be assured of lasting enjoyment and an almost certain increase in worth. The only time to change your buying habits is when you are able to purchase authenticated flies at bargain prices. Buy these bargains even though they do not fall within the perimeters of your interest, and trade them with other fly collectors for items you seek. Many flies change hands in this time-honored way.

Collecting fine flies is one thing and caring for them another. These bits of feather and fluff are subject to the ravages of moisture, sunlight, and—most importantly—insect infestation. The following suggestions should prove useful.

Flies can be attractively framed for display, with or without the addition of a sporting etching or print, but properly done, this can run into big bucks. An alternative is to stitch the flies to a piece of acid-free mat board and assemble with other mats in such a way that the end result is thick enough to accommodate the flies' depth without their touching the glass when they are framed. Plain or fancy, always use acid-free materials and add a pinch of paradichlorobezine or camphor to the assemblage before sealing the back with paper. An ounce of prevention and a pinch of insect repellent will protect your investment. Finally, never hang the framed flies where they will get damp or be in direct sunlight—both are enemies of these tiny treasures.

PARADICHLOROBENZENE

It's a mouthful, but a little paradichlorobenzene goes a long way. You should use it to separate your artificial "bugs" from the real ones that will eat your collection if given the chance. Put a pinch in all storage containers and frames.

The rules that apply to framed flies apply equally to those you store in fly chests made just for that purpose or in some lesser accommodation, such as the glass-and-plastic-topped display boxes advertised in virtually all antiques and collectibles magazines and papers. Add some silica gel to keep your collection dry and a few flakes of paradichlorobezine or camphor to keep the bugs at bay, and avoid sunlight and harsh lighting. With care your collection will be preserved.

INSURANCE

Home fire and theft insurance will not cover a collection of fine flies unless your rider so states. Check with your agent for full-value coverage and document each and every item in your collection, preferably with photographs and receipts. No insurance company will pay you for a $2,000 loss of a tiny bit of fluff and feathers unless you can prove your original expenditures.

Restoring tired old flies to their former glory is a tricky and heartbreaking undertaking, but I would be remiss if I failed to tell you that it can sometimes be accomplished. Some people will tell you that steaming old flies will bring them back to their former brilliance, and others insist that steam will cause irreparable damage. Both are right. I prefer to start with a high-speed hair dryer and only resort to steam if the fly resists fluffing from hot air. And if I do use steam, I use the hair dryer to thoroughly dry the fly afterwards. An old fly that is allowed to remain moist will be quickly ruined.

Light machine oil will protect old hooks but discolor the fluff and feathers, so it must be applied with great care. Silicone also works well, but the same precautions must be observed. And, as a case of last resorts, old flies can be treated with feather dressing that is available from fly-tying suppliers. My rule for treating fine old flies is to handle them as little as possible and take only those steps necessary to prevent further deterioration.

At this point in these chapter introductions, I usually suggest you use this or that collectible a time or two to get the "feel" of the past, but I can't say that here. No matter. If you can conjure up yesterdays just by holding a fine old fly in the palm of your hand, we are fishing the same stream anyway.

The following list of collectible fly tiers includes present-day tiers as well as many from our angling past. Amateurs as well as commercial makers are listed, and a bit about them is added as "qualification" for their inclusion here. This list is only a beginning. There are myriad collectible tiers in every area of the world and the following is only a place to start. (Prices are given when information on recent sales was available.)

LOCAL TIERS

Any area where fly fishing is popular has its own local group of fly tiers. Find out who they are and get examples of their work if it pleases you. Who knows—one of them may be the next Lee Wulff or Harry Darbee.

Clovis Arsenault—Clovis' salmon flies often spelled the difference for anglers in Canadian waters.

"Green Highlander" salmon flies (3) 90.00
Salmon flies (14) 70.00

John Atherton—Artist and author of *The Fly and the Fish* and a sometime fly tier.

Joseph Bates—No introduction should be needed. His books, flies, and many contributions to angling history are legend.

Low-water salmon fly 95.00
Full-dressed salmon flies (4) 350.00
Salmon fly, matted and framed, proceeds to American Museum of Fly
    Fishing . . . . 375.00 to 400.00

Ray Bergman—His book *Trout* is an all-time classic, and his Catskill shop's angling products and flies are historic.

Hendrickson, original glassine envelope marked "Bergman" . . . 500.00
March Brown trout fly, original glassine envelope marked
    "Bergman". 450.00

William Blades—Author of *Fishing Flies and Fly Tying* and the innovator of many patterns.

Megan Boyd—A world-class salmon fly tier, her "Irish Hairy Mary" is a classic. All her work is pricey.

Blue Charm salmon fly on treble hook 185.00
Garry Dog salmon fly on double hook 85.00
Irish Hairy Mary on double hook 100.00
March Brown salmon fly on double hook. 85.00

Edgar Burke—Dr. Burke was an artist and author of the rare Derrydale book *American Dry Flies.*

Dry fly mounted on driftwood, encased in glass dome, documenta-
    tion. 300.00
Light Cahill trout fly, documentation. 300.00

Rube Cross—A Catskill legend and author of *Tying American Trout Lures* and *Fur, Feather, and Steel.*

Elsie and Harry Darbee—The Darbees are a part of Catskill history, and their flies are most collectible.

#10 March Brown. 100.00
#12 Hendrickson. 125.00
Black-Nosed Dace streamer fly 150.00
Dun Super Spyder 200.00
Others . . . . 100.00 to 200.00

Charles DeFeo—Considered by some to be the dean of North American fly tiers, he is also know for his paintings.

Muskers Fancy salmon fly 75.00
Salmon flies (3) . . . . 210.00 to 235.00

Winnie and Walt Dette—Another couple who filled page after page in the angling journals with their Catskill patterns.

Catskill dry fly patterns (5), marked and in original pack-
aging . . . . 135.00 to 165.00

Art Flick—No serious angler can be without his *Streamside Guide,* nor is a collection complete without his flies.

Black-Nosed Dace 125.00
Dry flies (10) as shown in Flick's *Streamside Guide,* documenta-
tion 1,800.00
Hendrickson dry fly 125.00
Red Quill dry fly, provenance and documentation 120.00

Keith Fulsher—A innovator and author whose flies are important to the collector.

Syd Glasso—A West Coast fly tier of fine steelhead patterns who pos-
sesses a special talent.

Gold Rush salmon fly on Glasso's card 850.00
Jockie double salmon fly on Glasso's card 850.00

Theodore Gordon—Needs no introduction to the fly fisherman, his flies are rare and very collectible.

Bumblepuppy wet fly, with authentication and in-family prove-
nance 1,800.00
#10 Quill, with authentication and in-family provenance 2,000.00
#14 Quill Gordon, authentication and in-family provenance . . . 2,000.00

George Grant—An innovator of large western nymphs and flies, his work should grace every collection.

Montana nymphs (6), large, with original labeled box 175.00
Montana trout flies (4), together with Grant's book on the
subject 125.00
Western trout flies (9) 135.00

Elizabeth Greig—Elizabeth's wet flies are just about as fine as wet flies get and are very collectible.

Ed Haas—A West Coast fly tier whose steelhead patterns are among the most collectible of such examples.

Steelhead flies (6), sizes 4 to 8, with original labeled box 145.00
No. 4 Kispiox Special steelhead fly 25.00

FAKES

When any collectible becomes expensive, facsimiles and fakes are never far behind. Fine old flies are easily faked and you must know what you are buying and who you are buying it from. Caveat emptor—let the buyer beware—is a Latin phrase to learn and remember.

Edward Hewitt—Yet another Catskill mountain man who seemed to turn all he touched to golden collectibles.

    Yellow nymph, unusual, proper documentation 650.00

Preston Jennings—Author of the Derrydale book *A Book of Trout Flies,* his flies are scarce and collectible.

Poul Jorgensen—Another author of books on flies and fly fishing and one whose work is eagerly sought.

    Flies by this innovative author and fly tier . . . . 20.00 to 50.00

Lefty Kreh—Author of several innovative fly fishing books and tier of equally inventive salt-water imitations.

Charles Krom—Krom's wet flies and nymphs are among the very finest ever tied and are hard to come by.

Gary La Fontaine—Author of *Caddisflies* and other books, both Gary's lore and his flies are worthwhile.

James Leisenring—His *The Art of Tying the Wet Fly* is a modern classic, and his flies are equally worthy.

    Chalkstream flies (3), picture of Leisenring and documenta-
    tion. 750.00
    "Favorite Flies" framed set, from the famed Hotel Rapids in
    Pennsylvania 6,000.00

Mary Orvis Marbury—Author of the 1800s book *Favorite Flies and Their Histories,* a fly by this early nimrod would be a find.

Vincent Marinaro—His books *A Modern Dry Fly Code* and *In the Ring of the Rise* and his rare flies are classics.

Belarmino Martinez—A Spaniard, Martinez's streamer and salmon flies are among the finest in the world.

    Baron salmon fly. 140.00
    Blue Doctor salmon fly
        Large (5/0). 195.00
        Small. 150.00
    Others by Martinez. . . . . 125.00 to 195.00

Ted Niemeyer—His nymphs are classic, but he is best known as a trusted expert on identifying collectible flies.

T. E. Pryce-Tennatt—Author of *How to Dress Salmon Flies,* Pryce-Tennatt's flies are few and hard to find.

Blue Doctor salmon fly, encased in glass dome, documentation 1,200.00
Bonne Bouche salmon fly, authentication. 500.00

Lois Rhead—Rhead's book *American Trout Stream Insects* is the basis for this innovator's unusual flies.

Alfred Ronalds—His book *The Fly Fisher's Entomology,* complete with actual trout flies, is a rarity.

Polly Rosborough—His book on fuzzy nymphs is considered a classic, and his flies are very collectible.

Peter Schwab—A very accomplished West Coast fly tier, his steelhead flies are important.

Ernest Schwiebert—Book and fly collectors alike vie for Ernie's innovative contributions to angling history.

Helen Shaw—Author of two books on fly tying, Helen's work is eagerly sought by collectors.

Ora Smith—Old-time New Hampshire tier of note, his trolling flies are becoming expensive.

Frances Stearnes—Maine fly tier who worked with L. L. Bean, her flies are eagerly collected.

Hackle flies collection, signed 300.00
Irish salmon flies collection, signed 480.00
Salmon flies, framed set of 24 . . . . 1,300.00
Streamer flies, framed set of 32 . . . . 750.00

Roy Steenrod—Another Catskill legend whose flies are scarce and very expensive.

#10 Hendrickson, the fly Steenrod originated, provenance and documentation 2,000.00
#12 Black Quill, provenance and documentation. 1,500.00

Carrie Stevens—There are those who say that Carrie Stevens "made" Upper Dam, Maine, with her matchless streamer flies.

The Judge streamer fly, original card from Mrs. Stevens 240.00
Queen of the Waters streamer fly, original card from Mrs. Stevens 225.00
Other streamer flies on Stevens's cards . . . . 200.00 to 300.00

CARRIE STEVENS DAY

If anyone should doubt the importance of Mrs. Carrie Stevens's contribution to our angling history and to the state of Maine, they will do well to remember that in the governor officially proclaimed August 15th as "Carrie Stevens Day" in recognition of her legendary and lasting impact on both.

Ted Trueblood—Another author whose flies are worthy of inclusion in any collection.

Matthew Vinciguerra—Tier and photographer, his work is important and has had an influence on today's tiers.

Charles Wetzel—Wetzel's book *Practical Fly Fishing* is rare and expensive, and so are his flies.

Dave Whitlock—Yet another author/angler whose flies are important and collectible.

Innovative "Sculpin" fly, with Whitlock's signature 150.00

Lee Wulff—Lee's contributions to angling and angling history are the stuff of legend, and his flies are too.

Royal Wulff, on card signed by this famous innovator of this
  style. 250.00
Threadless Black Streamer, documentation 125.00
Other Wulff patterns . . . . 150.00 to 250.00

FINE TUNING

Lee Wulff once said, "I think of my flies as piano keys. Each is a little different. "And," he added, "I want to play a melody with my flies." He did. From tiny little black beetles to colorful salmon and salt-water varieties, Lee left a legacy of music for the ages.

CHAPTER 10

Lures

My introduction to fishing lures dates back half a century to a time in Montana when a dyed-in-the-cloth bass-fishing minister from Michigan shared his equipment, expertise, and enthusiasm with a 16-year-old boy from Connecticut. The good reverend's tackle boxes were chockablock with the stuff today's collectors dream about. In those halcyon post-war times, the fish judged the values of our lures and, I am happy to report, lunker bass bought everything we offered them.

Times change. Uneducated fish are few and far between, and the lures that our fathers and grandfathers fished with are rare collectibles that bring hundreds, and even thousands, of dollars in the marketplace. A number of things fuel the various sporting collectible markets: scarcity, condition, historical, or geographical significance and, I like to think, at least a modicum of sentimentality. And now, as I write "scarce" or "rare" or "hard to find," the pleasant chill of remembered Montana twilight intrudes and the echoed splash of bass on a darkening lake makes it all worthwhile. But enough of sentimentality. You came here to learn about lures and their values, so let's get on with it.

Call them lures, baits, spoons, plugs, or what you will, the history of these man-made aquatic temptations is murky at best. Earliest man made hooks of stone and bone and fashioned crude spinners from a variety of materials. Metal lures in fishlike forms were being used in Europe before

This multicolored oddball musky lure from Michigan's upper peninsula is 7" long and in excellent condition. As much folk art as fishing lure, this contraption sold for $800.00.

LITTLE THINGS

The hardware on a given lure is often the only clue to its identification. A serious collector can tell at a glance the differences between a wide variety of lures just by their hook hangers, spinners, and/or other hardware. Learning these little details can mean the difference between small change and big bucks.

Columbus discovered the new world, and both Walton's *Compleat Angler* and Dame Berner's *Fishing with a Hook* tell of these early accomplishments. It has been said that the Devon minnow, introduced about 1810, was the only significant advance in lures until the 1890s, but that has since been proven wrong. A number of New York state metal lures and spinners date from the 1850s, as does the now-famous Haskell minnow which was made by Riley Haskell of Painesville, Ohio, and carries a September 20, 1859, patent date. The 1890s are, however, a good estimate for the start of the wooden-lure craze that swept the nation from that time, until WW II and plastics combined to change so many things.

James Heddon carved his first frog lures in about 1898, and in a few years he and hundreds of other known and unknown makers had created a new industry. Shakespeare patented the unusual "Revolution" bait in 1900 and its rubber minnow-look-alike, the "Evolution," in 1902. Pflueger, who had been in the business of making metal spinners since the 1800s, introduced the now rare and collectible "Neverfail" and "Competitor" minnows to what was seemingly an insatiable market of fishermen. Americans had discovered pond and lake fishing, and a new industry was born to serve their needs. Factories flourished, and basement and garage workshops burned the midnight oil to meet the demand.

THE TERRIBLE TREBLE

As anyone who has ever had a fish hook imbedded in their anatomy can attest, it's no picnic. Single hooks are one thing, but trebles are a triple threat. Use care and cover the points and barbs with plastic or tape. It is one thing to be hooked on a hobby and quite another to be caught by it.

You might think that the lures that were produced in quantity during the early part of this century would be easy to find, but this is not the case. The years have taken their toll, and well-meaning mothers and grandmoth-

Hand-carved frog attributed to James Heddon but lacking authentication sold for $325.00. *Photograph courtesy of South Bay Auctions, East Moriches, N.Y.*

ers "cleaned out those dirty old things" for too many generations. Twenty years ago only a handful of people collected fishing lures. Today thousands do, and you should too. Take a quick look at the list of values I have assembled here. Many of these little darlings command big bucks, and whether you collect them yourself or pick them up to sell or trade, they deserve your attention. They can and do turn up in the strangest places, including the yards of the mothers and grandmothers who still can't wait to clean them out. It's true; I met some of them just last summer.

The sign said "Moving Sale" and pointed down a rutted dirt road. After more than two miles of twisting and turning and avoiding potholes, I came to an old house situated on the edge of a lake where another "Moving Sale" sign announced that I had arrived. I was greeted by two charming women who informed me that everything in both the barn and the house was for sale. They and other family members had already taken the things they wanted that morning, and I was the first "outsider" to come to the sale. I could drag this story out and tell you about all the wonderful antiques I bought, but, in truth, everything was broken or worthless with the exception of one grand old wooden tackle box that contained five early Chapman and Son metal baits which I took away with me for a song. If there is a moral to all this, it is that the early bird does indeed prosper and four-figure collectibles can still be found for a pittance.

Antiques shops and malls and flea markets are excellent sources of supplies for collectors. Few dealers know much about the old lures they sell, and many price all of them the same way. Near where I sit and write this there is an antiques center with a dealer who prices all of his many lures at

Florida Shinner by F. L. B. Flood in its original box with papers brought a winning $625.00 bid. *Photograph courtesy of South Bay Auctions, East Moriches, N.Y.*

$20 each. Most are not worth anything. But now and again a $20 expenditure turns me a tidy profit and proves that the more you know, the more you can make. Beginning collectors should learn all they can about their subject. Read the books listed in the appendix, get the fishing-tackle auction catalogs put out by Bob Lang and South Bay Auctions, and join the National Fishing Lure Collector's Club. Collecting fishing lures is time consuming and costly. The more you know, the better your chances are in this competitive climate.

The following list of makers and manufacturers is far from complete and should be looked upon as indicative of the prices asked and received in the mid-1990s for a variety of metal and wooden lures, baits, plugs, spoons, spinners, etc. Prices are from catalogs and auctions and do not include the 10% buyer's premium that has become common at most auctions.

WHO'S WHO

It is sometimes confusing to collectors to find on lures and other sporting collectibles the name of a store, such as Abercrombie & Fitch or Sears & Roebuck, instead of that of the actual maker. Makers such as Heddon, South Bend, and others made and marked lures for a variety of companies, as you will discover in old catalogs. Many are worth more than those marked only with the maker's name.

Abbey & Imbrey

Glowbody glass-bodied lure. 75.00
Spiral aluminum torpedo-type lure, A & I and Geo. Jennings, Newark,
    NJ, markings
    2¼″ 150.00
    3″ 175.00

Fred Arbogast

Fly rod Hula Popper
    Cork-bodied lure
        Frog finish. 35.00
        Red and white, without skirt. 20.00
    Wood, red and white finish, without skirt 45.00
Tin Liz
    Twin, red and white blended finish, very good condition 55.00
    Snakes (7), framed in display without metal tails, mint condi-
        tion. 2,200.00
    Sunfish
        Excellent condition 150.00
        Worn finish 110.00
    Walleye, rare, excellent condition. 275.00

Bailey & Company

Manitou minnow, patented 9/26/05, with original box, take-down
    instructions, and brass wrench, near mint condition 1,100.00

J. T. Buel

#3 Arrowhead trolling spoon, silver/copper finish, early "T"
    markings. 40.00
#6 kidney-shaped casting spoon, fixed hood, good paint 20.00
Size 4/0 hollow arrowhead spinner, 10″ overall length, good
    feathers 155.00
1852 patent 3″ spinner, 4″ overall length, good condition. 325.00
Display card
    Graduated arrowhead spinners, sizes 1/0 to 4/0, one of original 6
        missing 80.00
    Later (Watertown) arrowhead spinners, one of original 12
        missing 100.00

J. T. BUEL

Perhaps the easiest way to separate the early (and more valuable) J. T. Buel spinners and spoons from the later ones is to think "Christmas." Early lures carry the maker's name and address in a two-line treelike form.

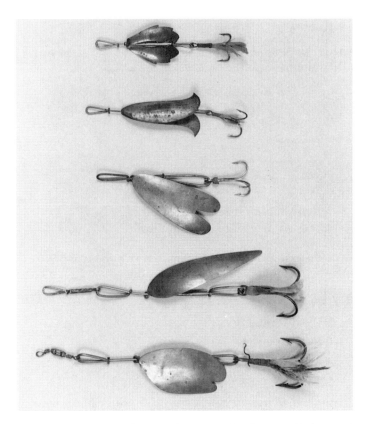

Chapman metal baits continue to rise in popularity and price. These (top to bottom) are the 1½" "Allure" ($130.00), 1870 "Minnow Propeller" ($130.00), "Chapman" marked 1870 spinner ($105.00), 1/0 "Willow Leaf" ($100.00), and an unusually shaped spinner ($70.00).

W. D. Chapman/Chapman & Son

Chapman & Son bait
 Marked "Allure," patented 1883
  1/0 marking.. 225.00
  3⅜", excellent condition 250.00
 Marked "Minnow Propeller," very good condition 190.00
 Marked "W. D. Chapman—Theressa, NY" lure, "The Boss" stamping, early, 3" 675.00

Charmer

Underwater minnow
 3⅛", red head and stripe on white body, chipped 165.00
 3⅜", green with gold stripe, old repair 130.00
 3½", gold with red spiral stripe 325.00

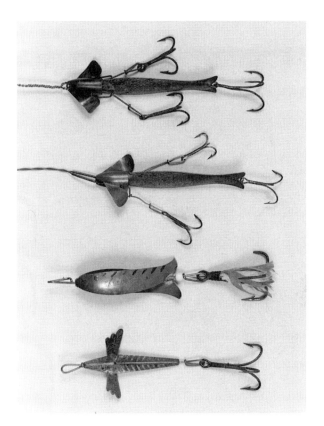

Rare Chapman & Son, Theresa, N.Y., metal lures include (top to bottom) a 4″ marked "Water Nymph" ($750.00), another "Water Nymph" ($700.00), a combination minnow-propeller with a damaged feathered treble hook ($550.00), and a diamond-shaped "Helgramite" with light corrosion ($625.00). These four Chapman lures and others depicted on these pages were found in upstate New York in an old tackle box.

Chippewa

3″

All white, very good condition. 275.00
Green and yellow, good condition. 250.00
Green and white, good condition 160.00
Red and silver, chipped 170.00

Harry Comstock (Note: Comstock's lures have been copied and/or reproduced. Collectors are urged to heed the oft repeated "caveat emptor." Such a fake or possibly early effort by Comstock was offered and sold at auction in 1994 for $275.)

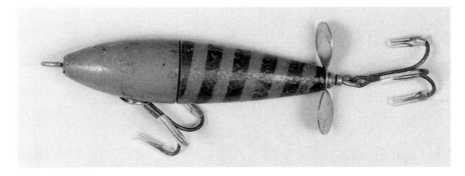

Charmer "Topwater" bait in orange with a green spiral stripe was rated in good condition and sold for $450.00.

Flying Helgramite
    Type I, 1883 patent, good condition 2,250.00
    Type II, very good condition. 5,000.00

Creek Chubb Bait Company

Baby Injured Minnow, #1600
    Dace Scale finish 30.00
    Red head, white body 28.00
    White, early and rare, excellent condition 150.00
Beetle, #3850, red head and white body, bead eyes, very good
    condition 225.00
Beetles, various finishes and condition
    5 pieces. 220.00
    10 pieces. 650.00
Crawdad, #300
    Crab finish 20.00
    Red, white and black finish, without feelers. 40.00
    Tan crab finish 20.00
Deluxe Wagtail Chubb, #800
    Natural chubb finish, very good condition 50.00
    Perch finish 35.00

Shiner finish, good condition 45.00
Wee Dees (3), frog, red/white, and yellow/green finishes, wire leaders
    intact, excellent condition. 625.00
Weed Bugs (2), frog and red/red finishes
    Good condition. 275.00
    Without leaders but otherwise in very good condition 625.00
Wigglefish, #2400, Silver Shiner finish, very good condition 35.00

EMPTY BOXES

It goes without saying that a lure in its original box is worth more than one without such a container, but just how much is an empty box worth? If it's old enough and rare enough, an empty box in fine condition can often sell for more than the lure that came in it. An empty Creek Chubb dealer box recently sold for $400, a fine empty Heddon wood box for a Dowagiac minnow brought $475, and a black-and-white Shakespeare box for a Revolution bait was also knocked down for $475.

Ans. B. Decker

Surface Water casting bait lure, marked with maker's name, with box
    Near mint 355.00
    White, with cracking 35.00
    Yellow, with single hooks 75.00

Detroit Bait Company

3¼″ heavy glass bait holder, company name and address on front
    Good condition. 450.00
    Soiled 300.00

Detroit Glass Minnow Tube Company

3½″ North Channel minnow, c. 1907, rare
    Damaged 220.00
    Good condition. 425.00
ABC minnow, red-painted back, early, chipped, poor condition   120.00

Donaly

Dealer carton with 6 lures, slightly worn, fine condition. 2,200.00
Redfin Floater, red and white, early, minor paint flaking. 90.00
Wow, black and gold, 3″, minor wear and chipping 85.00

Dunk's

Bestever, all black
    Chipped 15.00
    Fine condition, with original box 80.00

Expert Minnows (These were originally designed by Franklin Woods and were marked "Holzworth." In 1914 the patent was sold to Fred Keeling, who then also sold these sought-after lures. J. L. Clark also marketed "Expert" minnows beginning in 1908. The original Woods patent dates from 1903. All are collectible.)

5-hook minnow, very good condition
    Marked "Expert Minnow" . . . . 225.00 to 245.00
    Marked "Holzworth" 550.00
    Marked "Keeling" 175.00

Al Foss

Fan Dancer, #18, nickel with red and white hackle, near mint condition, with box. 40.00
Minnie-the-Moocher, nickel with red and white hackle, excellent condition 95.00
Oriental Wiggler, #3, glass eyes, red and white finish, near mint condition, with box 25.00

Heddon

Baby Crab Wiggler, #1900, "L" rigging, very good condition
    All white finish, rare 95.00
    Perch finish 70.00
Baby Tadpolly, #5000, "L" rigging
    Green scale finish 50.00
    Rainbow finish 35.00
    Shiner scale finish 75.00

Samuel Friend "Kent Frog Floater," c. 1900, is 2½" long and has a frog finish with only minor flaws. It sold for $950.00.

A rare C. R. Harris "Cork Frog" in excellent condition, this 3″ example dates from the late 1800s and sold for $500.00.

Considered the most important of all fishing lures, the Haskell minnow set the all-time high for fishing tackle when one was sold for $22,000.00 in the 1980s. The 3¼″ example pictured here has the 1859 patent and all the right stuff and sold for $8,800.00.

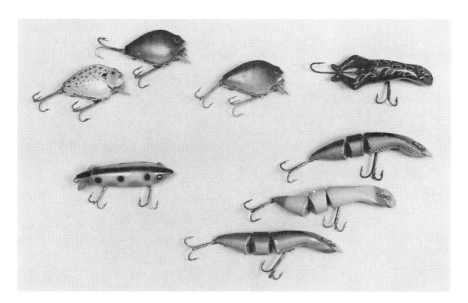

Heddon lures include (upper left) three Punkinseeds that sold as a lot for $210.00, a #3500 Luny Frog (upper right) that went for $80.00, a yellow and red Crab Wiggler for $60.00, and a group of three Gamefishers sold as a lot for $70.00.

Baby Vampire, #7400, "L" rigging
    Pike scale finish, very good condition 30.00
    Strawberry finish, fine condition 45.00
Crab Wiggler, #1800, "L" rigging
    Frog finish, minor flaking 85.00
    Green scale finish 45.00
Crazy Crawler, #2100, 2-piece rigging
    Frog finish 30.00
    Green "glowworm" finish 45.00
    Silver shore minnow finish 25.00
Dowagiac minnow
    #100
        Cup rigging, very good condition
            Crackleback finish 140.00
            Rainbow finish. 115.00
            Red and black finish 145.00
            Two-tone silver finish 365.00
        "L" rigging, very good condition
            Crackleback finish 135.00
            Dark green finish 145.00
    #150, "L" rigging
        All white finish, good condition 185.00
        Crackleback finish, very good condition 175.00
        Rainbow finish, worn condition 125.00

Heddon #702 4½″ Musky Minnow in white with red eyes is in near mint condition and in its original box. It sold for $775.00.

Dowagiac Swimming minnow
  #800
    Strawberry finish, very scarce, very good condition 385.00
    White and green finish 195.00
  #900, 4½″
    Crackleback finish, good condition 135.00
    Yellow with green and black spots 225.00
Flaptail, #7000, 2-piece rigging, very good condition
  Gray mouse finish 50.00
  Pike scale finish 45.00
Flaptail Jr., #7110, 2-piece rigging, very good condition
  Perch scale finish 55.00
  Red and white finish 35.00
  Shiner scale finish 55.00
Heddon Basser, #8500, "L" rigging, very good condition
  Rainbow finish 75.00
  Red scale finish 95.00
  Strawberry finish 40.00
Jointed Vampire, #7300, "L" rigging, pike scale finish, very good condi-
  tion 30.00
Little Luny Frog, #3400
  Meadow frog finish 80.00
  Pyraline open leg model, "toilet-seat" rigging 110.00
Lucky-13, #2500
  "L" rigging, perch scale finish 60.00

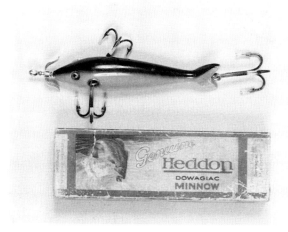

**Heddon #1300 Black Sucker in a Heddon box is a
rare lure in any condition and this one, rated near
perfect, sold for $1,250.00.**

Heddon Minnow with three-pin collar and original box sold for $75.00. *Photograph courtesy of South Bay Auctions, East Moriches, N.Y.*

No eyes, cup-rigging
  Red and white finish 75.00
  Red scale finish 65.00
  Strawberry finish, very good condition 65.00
Luny Frog, #3500, "toilet-seat" rigging 75.00
Meadow Mouse
  #4000, "S" rigging, soiled
    Brown flocked mouse finish 40.00
    Gray flocked finish 35.00
    White with black stripes, early, very good condition. 70.00
  #9800
    Gray flocked finish 40.00
    White flocked finish 40.00
Midget Crab Wiggler, #1950, "L" rigging
  Crackleback finish 60.00
  Red and white finish 45.00
  Shiner scale finish 50.00
Musky Crazy Crawler, #2150, "toilet-seat" rigging, gray mouse
  finish 85.00
Musky Flaptail, #7050, "toilet-seat" rigging, 5/0 size, shiner scale
  finish 125.00
Punkinseed #730, 2-piece rigging
  Bluegill finish
    Paint flaking. 65.00
    Very good condition 85.00
  Sunfish finish, very good condition. 85.00
  Yellow shore minnow finish, very good condition 95.00
River Runt, #110, 2-piece rigging, near mint condition
  Pike scale finish 85.00
  Shiner scale finish 80.00

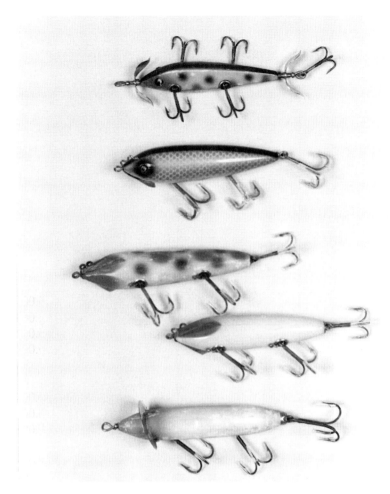

Heddon lures are (top to bottom) #00 minnow in original box (not depicted) and in very good condition ($140.00), a #1700 "Near Surface Wiggler" with age lines in the paint ($170.00), two #1600 "Deep Diving Wigglers" at $125.00 for the pair, and a #200 Surface lure in so-so shape for $25.00.

S.O.S. Wounded minnow, #140, "S" rigging
    Red and white, very good condition, with box 40.00
    Silver glitter finish, very good condition
        With box 35.00
        Without box. 25.00
Surface Bait, #200, white body, 3-pin collar
    Blue head 165.00
    Red head. 125.00

Triple Teazer, #1000, metal
  Red and white hackle, very good condition 30.00
  Red hackle, excellent condition 40.00
Vampire, #7500, "L" rigging, very good condition
  Pike scale finish 40.00
  Rainbow finish 45.00
Zaragossa, #6500, "S" rigging
  Blue shore minnow finish
      Chipped 35.00
      Near mint condition 60.00
  Red and silver finish, excellent condition 50.00

Jamison

Chicago Wobbler, red and white, some soiling and chips 75.00
Struggling Mouse, frog finish, near mint condition 145.00
Weedless Mascot, #1, 4″
  Red and white finish, heavy chipping 85.00
  Red scale finish with slight rust, excellent condition 175.00
Wig-Wag bait, silver and black, near mint condition 110.00

Keeling (see also Expert)

Flapper, yellow with black back and spots, scarce, rusty
  hooks 110.00
Tom Thumb surface lure, excellent condition, with original
  box 165.00

E. J. Lockhart

Baby Wiggler, 2½″, all red with yellow holes, very good condi-
  tion 110.00

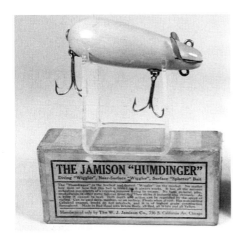

Jamison Humdinger in its original box is rare and sold at auction for $125.00. *Photograph courtesy of South Bay Auctions, East Moriches, N.Y.*

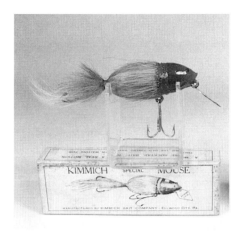

Kimmich deerhair mouse in its original box is a rare find that sold at auction for $175.00. *Photograph courtesy of South Bay Auctions, East Moriches, N.Y.*

Wagtail Witch, 3¾"
    White with red holes, very good condition. 85.00
    Yellow with red holes, near mint condition 95.00
Wiggler, 4", all white with red holes
    Heavily worn 40.00
    Very good condition 85.00

FUR AND FEATHER

Lures that have feathers, fur, and the like need special care. These natural additives are subject to insect infestation and should be treated with a few flakes of camphor or paradichlorobenzene.

Martin's Lizzard is an unusual lure and with its original box brought a tidy bid of $85.00. *Photograph courtesy of South Bay Auctions, East Moriches, N.Y.*

This fine example of Miller's 4¼" Reversible Minnow in white with red and green spots and "pat applied for" marking is in near excellent condition and sold for $3,600.00 at Lang's 1995 spring fishing tackle auction. *Photograph courtesy of Bob Lang, Raymond, Maine.*

Moonlight

Baby Bass Seeker, blue scale finish, some wear to finish but in very
    good condition 35.00
Baby Pike minnow, green and black with gold spots, 3¼", light
    soiling 25.00
Bass bait, #300, 3¾", white and red, black eye rings
    Chipped and rusty 15.00
    Very good condition 40.00
Musky Little Wonder, black and green, white belly, 4¾", rare, very
    good condition 375.00

Paw Paw Bait Company

Baby Wottafrog, green splatter finish with plain trebles, 3"
    Excellent condition 75.00
    Very good condition 65.00
Bass Wobbler, rainbow trout finish, scarce, very good condition   65.00
Bullhead, bullhead finish, scarce, few chips and light soiling 85.00
Croaker, covered with real frog skin, 3", very good condition. . . . 90.00
Hair Mouse, gray head and hair body, very good condition 85.00
Injured minnow, brown back, ribs with gold finish, very good condi-
    tion 30.00
Lucky Seven spoon, red and natural nickel finish, very good condi-
    tion 15.00
Minnie Mouse
    Gray finish, very good condition. 30.00
    Gray fuzzy finish with black back stripe, near mint condi-
        tion 40.00
Pike minnow, rainbow trout finish, 4¼", rare, near mint condition 75.00
Weedless Wow, green spatter finish, rubber legs, 1¾", scarce . . . 70.00

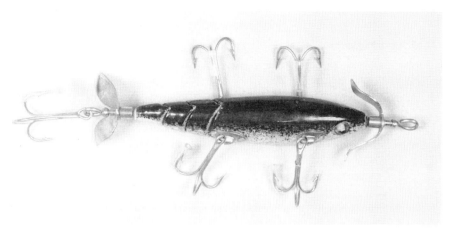

Michigan "Life Like" five-hook minnow patented by Jacob Houston of
Muskegan, Michigan, in 1908 is in excellent condition and sold for $1,100.00.

Wottafrog
    Fly rod, green splatter finish, mint condition 40.00
    3¾", yellow splatter finish
        Near mint condition hair trebles 95.00
        Plain trebles
            Good condition 65.00
            Near mint condition 85.00

Joseph E. Pepper

    Baby Devil 2-hook spinner, red, rusty 12.00
    Red Devil 2-hook spinner, red
        Rusty 12.00
        Very good condition 20.00

Pflueger

    All-in-one minnow, rainbow finish, early, very good condition . . . 195.00
    Fan-Tail squid, red and white finish, celluloid, very good condition
        2½" 50.00
        3½" 60.00
    Four Brothers, #4, marked, fluted bait feathered treble, very good con-
        dition 30.00
    Globe 2-hook model
        2¾", yellow with gold spots, early 30.00
        3⅝", red and white 30.00
    Indian Bead spinner, hammered red/nickel/luminous finish, feather
        treble
        #3 . . . . 90.00

#6, very good condition 110.00
McMurray, #4/0 spinner
   Nickel finish, excellent condition 30.00
   Silver and copper finish, very good condition 18.00
Neverfail
   3-hook minnow, Strawberry finish, minor chipping otherwise in very
      good condition 70.00
   5-hook, rainbow finish, very good condition. 85.00
   Early see-through wire rigging, green crackle finish
      Good condition 120.00
      Light chipping 85.00
Pal-O-Mine minnow
   3¼″, yellow with frog scale finish, near mint condition 70.00
   4¼″
      Red and white 30.00
      Yellow with frog scale finish 55.00
      White and black, scarce 95.00
Wizard fly rod, rainbow finish, no flasher model, scarce, excellent con-
   dition 50.00

Louis Rhead

Frog fly rod, 1¼″, minor wear at nose otherwise in excellent condi-
   tion. 750.00
Grasshopper, 2″, chipped on one side but very collectible 225.00
Yarn, fiber and paint minnow, 3¼″, Shiner finish, near fine condi-
   tion. 125.00

Roberts

Mud Puppy, 7″, natural finish
   Good condition. 25.00
   Near mint condition. 40.00
   With replaced hooks 30.00

J. K. Rush

Rush Tango minnow
   4″, white body with red lip. 25.00
   5″
      White body with red lip. 25.00
      White/green, yellow finish, minor chipping 40.00

Shakespeare

Egyptian Wobbler
   Green and red finish, excellent condition. 35.00
   Rainbow finish, scarce, excellent condition 50.00
Evolution, rubber minnow, green and silver finish, 4″
   Hardened rubber 100.00

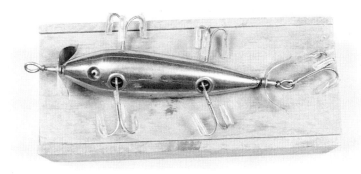

Shakespeare "Gold Plated" #44SG minnow in its original wooden box has some dings that resulted in its low selling price of $450.00.

Hook rust otherwise very good condition 180.00
Five-Hook wooden minnow, early see-through hardware hangers
    Heavily worn 70.00
    Very good condition. 165.00
Jim Dandy Crippled minnow, red and white finish, light hook rust oth-
    erwise in very good condition 45.00
Revolution
    3¼", hollow aluminum, 1901 patent
        Excellent condition 200.00
        Very good condition 175.00
        Empty box for 1901 lures 475.00
    3¾", cork capped with aluminum, rare, worn paint 1,100.00
Swimming mouse, 3"
    Black finish, near to excellent condition. 35.00
    Gray finish
        Fair condition 18.00
        Near to excellent condition. 45.00

Excellent-condition Shakespeare "Revolution" lure in its original good-condition box sold for $900.00.

Wankazoo surface spinner, red and white, considerable wear . . . 75.00
Weedless Flutter Fly, excellent condition
    All black finish 40.00
    Red/white/blue finish 45.00

South Bend

Baby Surf-Oreno, black and red
    Heavily chipped 15.00
    Very good condition 85.00
Bass-Oreno, very good condition
    Glass eyes
        Green scale finish 20.00
        Red/silver finish 30.00
    No-eye
        Frog finish 20.00
        Strawberry finish 20.00
Big Pike-Oreno, #958, red and white finish, very good condition with
    original box 90.00
Jointed Big Pike-Oreno, #960, 6″, red and white finish, near fine condi-
    tion with box 65.00
King Bass-Oreno, red and white finish
    Excellent condition 25.00
    Very good condition 20.00
Min-Oreno
    #926
        Perch finish, excellent condition 40.00
        Red and white finish, very good condition 25.00
    #927, red and white finish, 4″ 35.00
Perch-Oreno
    2½″, metal, rainbow finish, light soiling 35.00
    3¼″, chrome, excellent condition 45.00
    4⅞″, #505, red and white, single treble hook, rare, very good condi-
        tion 90.00
Pike-Oreno, #975
    Early no-eye frog finish, hook rust and chipping 25.00
    Perch finish 15.00
Surf-Oreno fly rod, excellent condition
    Black and red finish, shows no wear 110.00
    Green scale finish 60.00
    Rainbow finish, scarce 60.00
Tarp-Oreno, red and white with black eye rings, single hooks, near
    mint condition 85.00
Whirl-Oreno, #935, excellent condition
    Butterfly finish, rare 135.00
    Frog finish 95.00

South Bend lures include (top to bottom) a rare "Truck-Oreno" 8½" overall and in very good used condition ($825.00), a "Surface Minnow" ($50.00), and a "Plug-Oreno" complete with weed guard and pork rind clip ($100.00).

SIGHT UNSEEN

All too often people buy things sight unseen only to regret their actions. When buying by mail be sure that you have the right of return and time to examine and exercise that right. When buying at auction it is best to have someone act as your agent if you cannot be present. An agent's fee is a worthwhile investment for the absentee bidder.

Bud Stewart

Bloody-Eyed killer spoon, red and white finish, 3½", signed 60.00
Crippled Wiggler
    1¼" fly rod, red and white lure with black scales, very good condition 110.00
    1½" fly rod, red and white lure with black scales, very good condition 110.00
    4¼", very good condition
        Gold with black spots 40.00
        Red/white/green finish 35.00
Pad Hopper, red with frog finish, 2", near mint condition 85.00

True-Temper

Hellcat metal lure, #27, red and white hackle
  Near mint condition. 60.00
  Sparse hackle. 35.00

Winchester

Multi-Wobbler, #9206
  Green/gold finish, good condition 195.00
  Rainbow finish, few minor hook marks, very good plus condi-
    tion 325.00
Spinner Bait, #9625, nickel/gold/red finish, hook missing 30.00
Willow Leaf spinner, #9784, nickel and red finish with red and white
    treble, very good condition 70.00
3-hook minnow
  #9011, green/gold/yellow, new with papers and original
    box. 1,150.00
  #9014, bright red, new unfished condition 700.00

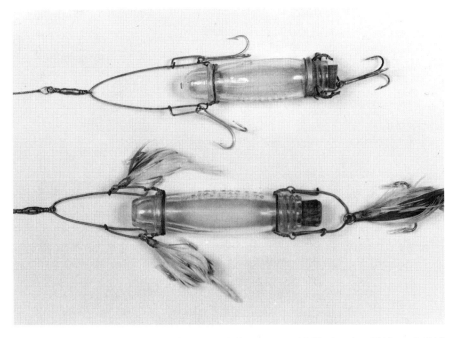

Glass minnow tubes from Welch and Graves, c. 1893, in the 3¾″ and 4½″ sizes sold for $500.00 and $700.00, respectively. These lures are scarce due to their very fragile construction.

This c. 1913 Clinton Wilt "Champion" bait in white with a red spiral stripe is in fine condition and sold for $800.00.

WINCHESTER

The Winchester Arms Company and the Winchester Bait Company should not be confused. The arms company and the one whose baits are listed here is *the* one! Lures by the Indiana concern are also of interest but cannot hold a candle to the magic of everything produced by the gun company.

Five-Hook Winchester #9214 new-in-the-box minnow in unfished mint condition, this gem sold at Lang's spring 1995 fishing tackle auction for $1,650.00.
Photograph courtesy of Bob Lang, Raymond, Maine.

Wright & McGill

Baby Flapper Crab, 2″
   Gray and black, feelers missing but otherwise in mint condition 90.00
   Natural finish, feelers missing but otherwise in mint condition 90.00
Crawfish, 2¾″, without whiskers
   Greenish pink finish 85.00
   Greenish silver finish................................. 90.00
Flapper Crab, natural crab finish, mint with original box
   2¼″ 110.00
   2½″ 110.00

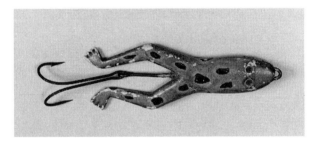

This 3¼″ aluminum frog lure by an unknown maker had worn paint but was otherwise in good condition. It sold for $200.00.

CHAPTER 11

Accessories

Fishermen and fishing accessories go together like kittens and catnip. In each case the attraction is overwhelming, and I have heard it said that the only difference between these addicted examples is that kittens grow up. Be that as it may, anglers do indeed amass all manner of things and have done so since the sport had its beginnings hundreds of years ago. We have covered the rods and the reels, the flies and the lures, and the related angling art and books elsewhere in this book. This chapter covers the other things today's nimrods and collectors covet.

Fishing accessories are, by their very definition, things that add completeness, convenience, or attractiveness to one's basic outfit, and if that doesn't open up an enormous can of worms, nothing can. There are those who collect only marked Abercrombie & Fitch or Hardy items. Others seek only bait boxes with stenciled decoration; while another group is interested in early photos. I recently wrote an article saying that if it any way, shape, or form relates to fishing, someone somewhere wants it. And that, dear reader, is good advice.

Collectible fishing accessories have yet to attain the financial heights reached by the components of the aforementioned "basic outfit," and a careful buyer can still find a bargain along the way. Flea markets, garage sales, and country auctions are all good places to "discover" a keeper. Remember, if it has to do with fishing, someone wants it. If the price is right, buy it to trade for something you really want. Many fine collections have been built upon this time-honored tradition.

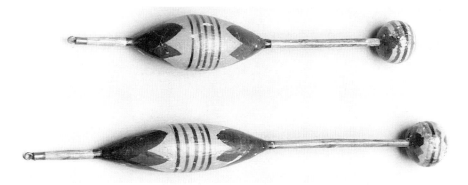

Two early and colorfully painted fish bobbers in wonderful condition sold as a pair for $225.00.

No one can predict future prices, nor can anyone tell someone else what to buy. But as an individual who has trolled these waters for more than half a century and kept an eye on the collectibles market for a decade of strikes and misses, I'm going to stick my neck out and say that fishing accessories are among the best buys in today's confused marketplace.

As with anything else, you must know what you are buying and have full trust in the seller. Condition is—and always will be—of primary consideration. A so-so example of a given item is worth only a fraction of the same item in factory-new condition. Provenance, or source of origin, is of real importance when dealing with a collectible for which value is directly related to who owned the item or where it came from. An example of this would be the creel owned by the late Ed Zern that sold recently for more than $500. Without the association of this well-known sportsman, the item might have brought no more than $75 to $100—all it is worth without documentation regarding its source of origin and place and price of sale. If you purchase or own association items, be sure that your paperwork is in order. This advice applies to any and all antiques and collectibles, both sporting and nonsporting alike.

A final consideration for any fishing accessory is its real worth to you; not its monetary value, but its appeal as a collectible. Is it something you will use or display with joy? If you have doubts, perhaps it would be better to look elsewhere for something that strikes your fancy. I have discovered that the things that I really enjoy "talk" to me of yesterdays, while others are only mute reminders of how much they cost.

Split-willow creel, bound in leather and with leather pouch on front, marked "The George Lawrence Company, Portland, Oregon—Established 1857," is in very good condition and sold at auction for $400.00.

The following listing of fishing accessories covers all kinds of collectibles, from tiny gut cutters to full-size canoes. A number of entries cover fish baskets, or creels, as these have become hot items in the past several years and a comparison of various types should be useful. This is a fascinating area of interest with seemingly something for everyone, and I hope you have as much fun reading it as I did putting it together.

PHOTO CREDITS

Virtually all the illustrations in this chapter were made available by Bob Lang of Lang's Fishing Tackle Auctions in Raymond, Maine. Lang holds three tackle auctions each year that are worthy of your serious consideration. (See the appendix for more information on Lang's.)

Angler's or shooter's box, Abercrombie & Fitch, leather-covered oak, brass hardware and owner's nameplate 700.00

Bag, trout, "Carry all," Hardy, canvas with storage pockets and net front, 1930s 200.00

The "rarest of all trout baskets," this two-part Hardy "Carry-All" has storage space together with a lower basket for fish, has brass hardware, is in excellent condition, and sold for $1,200.00.

Boat

"Kalamazoo," folding canvas, early, very good condition 400.00
Lake, Old Town, wood and canvas, restored, with trailer 1,050.00

Canoe

Birch bark, by "Alb't McLain & Son," Passadumkeag, Maine, 18′, very
    good condition 1,600.00
Courting, "Bergman Charles River," bearing original name "Edith,"
    restored 1,300.00
Old cedar and canvas, in need of a home 125.00

Carving

Northern pike, by unknown Maine carver, 36″ 275.00
Trout
    Antique, framed under bowed glass in shadow box, 20″ 375.00
    On birch-bark panel, 19″, worn and scratched 175.00

Creel

Camp or canoe, willow, four legs, very good condition 75.00
"Saddle creels" (pair), used by Indians to haul loads of salmon in the
    northwest 200.00
Trout, half-moon, wood and original black paint, 19th century . . 200.00

A Hardy "Perfect" creel or fish basket made of brown wicker with a lift-out compartment and side opening for fish also has a woven net bag for additional gear. This rare example with a few minor flaws sold for $800.00.

Collectible fish baskets are pictured from left to right: fine-weave center-hole creel with original latch, $85.00; unusual small center-hole willow basket, $125.00; splint-weave center-hole creel, $95.00; leather-bound split-willow basket in great condition, $85.00.

Collectible fish baskets are illustrated (left to right): a fine split-willow creel with replaced hinges, $105.00; early splint creel with a wooden top decorated with a painted trout, $130.00; unusual willow fish basket with a fitted wrap-around top in excellent condition, $310.00.

Collectible fish baskets are shown (left to right): willow creel with leather binding and pouch, $125.00; tiny child's fish basket of split willow, $125.00; fine split-willow creel with replaced hinges and missing latch, $105.00; and Adirondack-style basket with classic lines, $200.00.

Cricket bait container, woven willow, sliding lid latch and original strap 65.00

Cricket box, pewter, two compartments and original hanging strap 125.00

Fireplace andirons, cast iron, leaping 12″ trout, signed, excellent condition 800.00

Early walnut collector's cabinet has 22 drawers with double knobs, brass hardware, and carrying handle. This rare piece was priced at $1,200.00.

Fly box

Hardy "Neroda," filled with old salmon flies 150.00
Wheatley, Abercrombie & Fitch decal, aluminum, owner's name 175.00

Fly-tying vise, portable for travelers, with assorted material 200.00

Gaff

Brass, collapsible, extends from 13″ to 23″ 110.00
Hardy, collapsible, extends from 18″ to 42″, excellent condition 120.00
Marbles, spring-loaded
    Hand-held, minor rusting 70.00
    Lightly worn 125.00

Hat, adorned with flies, licenses, and such, from Ed Zern collection 375.00

MARBLES

The Marbles Company of Gladstone, Michigan, made all manner of sporting collectibles from match safes to knives and axes, and all are collectible. Marbles catalogs have been reproduced and are of value to identify their products.

ASSOCIATION VALUES

If something you purchase has added value because it came from someone's estate or collection, be sure you keep all paperwork related to that acquisition. Association values are only as good as their pedigrees.

Knife

Fish
Russell (Green River), stainless less with wood handle, missing
  sheath 65.00
  "Safety Folding Knife," Marbles, with stag handle, lightly
  used 250.00
  With descaler and folding gaff, worn and rusted 35.00
Fly fishing, Case "XX," stainless steel
  Considerably worn and rusted 55.00
  Near mint condition. 125.00
Trout
  Ka-Bar, small with leather sheath, unused. 135.00
  Marbles, in original sheath, mint condition 300.00

Knife/priest/scale, angler's, Puma, like new with original package 120.00

Leader and fly box, Hardy "On View," parchment pages and celluloid
  pockets. 95.00

Letter

From Everett Garrison to Jim Payne, excellent condition 50.00
From James Henshall
  Discusses his *Book of the Black Bass,* excellent condition. . . . 275.00
  To Hall Line Company, on Dr. Henshall's stationery. 475.00
From Paul Young to Jim Payne, 1931, 2 letters 70.00

License

Angler's, Pennsylvania, 1934, button, excellent condition 10.00
Fishing
  California, 1923–27, paper with colorful angling scenes, 5
  licenses. 275.00
  New York State non-resident, 1929, button, excellent condi-
  tion 20.00
Hunting, fishing, and trapping, New York State resident, 1929, button,
  excellent condition 8.00

Line dryer

Hardy, folding, collapses for carrying ease. 100.00
Wood and metal, old green paint, 1889 patent date 400.00

Minnow trap, glass

Marked "C. F. Orvis Maker, Manchester VT," original
lid. . . . . 85.00 to 95.00
Unmarked. 40.00

Net

Boat, Abercrombie & Fitch, turned handle, excellent condition . . 90.00
Trout
From Ed Zern collection, well used but still in good usable condi-
tion 335.00
Old laminated wood, made by Ed Cummins of Flint, Michigan,
excellent condition. 85.00

Priest or billy club

Ebony with leaded head. 45.00
L. L. Bean marking, aluminum opens to knife 85.00

Salmon tailer, Hardy, brass, 31″ long with wrapped twine grip. . . 125.00

Sportsman's case, leather, divided compartments and inside tackle
pouches 275.00

Steel sculpture, 18″ trout mounted on sculpted steel base 325.00

Steuben glass sculpture, 8″ leading trout, in original velvet-lined
chest 1,000.00

Tackle box

Eagle Tackle Company, leather covered, two lift-out trays, replaced
handle. 125.00
Leather-trimmed wood, contains 20-odd lures 175.00
Oil-skin covered, double-decker "knickerbocker," very good condi-
tion 100.00
Tole with hand-painted fishing scene, 1880s, rare. 1,200.00

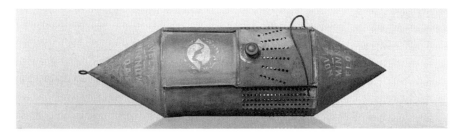

Submarine-style "Novelty Minnow Float," designed to be towed behind a
boat, retains much of its green paint and stenciling. This desirable collectible
sold for $250.00.

Wading staff, Hardy Bros., steel tip, from Ed Zern collection, good condition 250.00

And the list goes on. I don't suppose the bluefish I have stuffed and baked for tonight's repast qualifies as a fishing accessory, but the old fish shears I used to cut it do and offer proof positive that these piscatorial pleasures are everywhere and waiting to be collected. Bon appétit.

SPIT AND POLISH

Old fishing accessories tend to have "age" that should not be polished away. Mild soap and water rarely hurts, but severe polishing can and will reduce an item's appeal and value. When it doubt, leave it alone.

PART III
HUNTING AND SHOOTING

CHAPTER 12

Antique American Firearms

Gun enthusiasts will not be happy with this section of the book. There are no handguns, no automatic weapons, and not even any modern rifles or shotguns. There are, of course, reasons for these exclusions and they are valid. Americans own too many firearms, and, were I to list them all, there would be nothing else in this limited volume. Add to this the fact that I personally have little or no use for handguns and my publisher's parent company has little or no use for guns of any kind. After serious discussions and consideration, we agreed to draw a line between antique and modern firearms that would both keep our noses clean and serve collectors' interests. This is that chapter. And don't let gun enthusiasts get in the way of these words and prices that deal with the finest American firearms ever made. These are the guns that tamed the frontier, won the West, and made America what it is today.

LOCK `EM UP

We had a large locked gun closet in my boyhood home where firearms of all sorts were safely stored. When I came of an age when I respected firearms, I was privy to the key's location and free to open the closet. In those days, locked gun closets and cabinets were uncommon, but I learned from the trust and use. Today things are different and I wonder sometimes if the trust is gone. Times they are a changin', so always lock up your firearms. You and your offspring will benefit and your insurance will be valid as well.

Sporting firearms fall into two general categories and each of these divides further into many more. Basically, there are either breech-loading or muzzle-loading firearms. Each then is classified as a shotgun or fowling piece, or a small-bore or large-bore rifle. Add to this the five types of ignition that have been used over the years, from matchlock and wheel-lock to today's self-contained cartridges and shot shells, and you begin to see what a vast number of possibilities are available to the beginning collector. Let's begin with the famous American Kentucky rifle: A sporting firearm that goes hand in hand with our nation's history from our earliest Colonial days to the years just before the Civil War.

The finest Kentucky rifles were not made in Kentucky but in Pennsylvania, and the name derives from their use on the then-frontier of Kentucky and Tennessee. A classic Kentucky rifle will be a flintlock, full-stocked in fancy tiger or curly maple with fine brass fittings, including a fancy brass patchbox in the stock. The cost for an example such as this can run to six figures but goes down quickly for those that have been converted from flintlock to percussion and have less than full-length stocks. The Kentucky-style rifle of the mid-1800s is often called a plains rifle because these were the guns that went West with the early settlers. Examples of these later firearms are far less costly than early-type Kentucky rifles, but they still command top dollar, particularly if attributable to a famous maker or if they have historic significance.

The development of the breech-loading rifle and shotgun and the coming of the Civil War combined to change firearms forever. The war issued in mass-produced American firearms, and the breech-loader opened the way for all that followed, including the lever action, pump or slide action, and the semiautomatics we know and use today.

It goes without saying that these developments also opened up an entire field of sporting firearms for today's collectors. Names like A. H. Fox, Baker, Ballard, Lefever, and L. C. Smith competed for attention in a time of plenty, and American sporting firearms were plentiful and available at prices to fit all pocketbooks. It is fair to say that these and other American and European firearms makers set the table that we savor to this day. Prices are up and the pickings increasingly meager, but the table is far from bare and it is still possible to pick up a fine morsel if you persevere.

Collecting sporting firearms is a costly proposition and no one should approach it lightly. Before you purchase even one gun, learn all you can about whatever it is you have elected to collect. Read one or more of the many fine books on gun collecting in general, and everything you can find about your specific area of interest. Talk to other collectors and go to gun shows. Visit a gun collection in a museum if possible, and arm yourself for competition in every way you can.

Unlike other chapters, you will note that a range of prices is provided for each entry. Antique firearms come in all kinds of conditions from priceless to worthless, and without actually handling a given firearm, a real value is impossible to determine. My prices reflect the National Rifle Association's "good" to "fine" conditions and give readers a guideline to work with. Buyers and potential buyers should know and understand the NRA standards before collecting. Caveat emptor.

MAKING THE GRADE

There are always questions about the condition of a given firearm. While not detailed, the following simplification of the NRA's standards should prove useful.

Factory new	Just that—100% in every respect.
Excellent	80% original finish with all original parts.
Fine	30% original finish with all original parts.
Very good	All original parts with finish well worn
Good	Minor replacement parts with poor finish.
Fair	Major parts replaced with flawed finish.
Poor	Generally not worth collecting.

The following firearms are listed by maker and generalized for lesser-known individuals and companies in the final few pages. Enjoy. Antique American firearms are a joy to collect and endow their owners with a small segment of our nation as it once was.

Colt Firearms

Colt-Berdan single-shot, trap-door breech rifle and carbine
models, made for Russia . . . . 500.00 to 7,500.00
Colt-Burgess lever-action rifle: 1883–85, made in both rifle and carbine,
.44–.40 caliber. . . . . 750.00 to 5,000.00
Colt-Franklin military rifle, Breech-loader with gravity-feed box magazine, rare . . . . 3,500.00 to 7,500.00
Colt-Laidley military rifle, single-shot breech-loading rifle, only a few
made . . . . 1,500.00 to 2,500.00
Double-barrel rifle, exposed hammers, .45-.70 caliber variations,
rare. . . . . 10,000.00 to 20,000.00
Lightening model slide-action rifle
Large frame (various models) . . . . 750.00 to 7,500.00
Medium frame (various models) . . . . 350.00 to 3,500.00
Small frame .22 caliber. 250.00 to 750.00

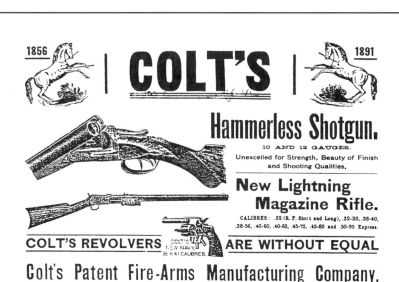

Model 1839
  Carbine, 1838–42, four variations, all scarce . . . 5,000.00 to 30,000.00
  Shotgun, 1839–41, six-shot revolving 16-gauge
    cylinder . . . . 3,500.00 to 8,500.00
Model 1855
  Carbine and musket, 1856–64, revolving five-shot cylinders, made in
    half-and full-stock models . . . . 2,000.00 to 6,500.00
  Revolving shotgun, 1860–64, 10- and 20-gauge five-shot
    cylinders . . . . 1,500.00 to 5,000.00
  Sporting rifle, 1856–64, made in half- and full-stock
    models . . . . 2,000.00 to 6,500.00
Model 1861 special musket, 1861–65, 58-caliber single-shot for govern-
  ment . . . . 750.00 to 2,500.00
Model 1878 double-barrel shotgun, 10- and 20-gauge, exposed ham-
  mers . . . . 500.00 to 3,500.00
Model 1883 double-barrel shotgun, hammerless, 10 and 20 gauges,
  Damascus barrels . . . . 500.00 to 3500.00
Ring-lever rifle
  First model, 1837–38, eight-shot revolving rifle in various
    calibers . . . . 6,000.00 to 12,000.00
  Second model, 1838–42, not as rare as first
    model . . . . 5,000.00 to 12,000.00

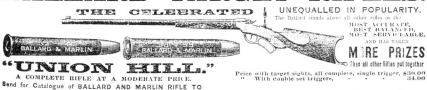

Marlin Firearms

Ballard

No. 1 hunter's rifle, made by John M. Marlin	500.00 to 1,000.00
No. 1½ hunter's rifle	500.00 to 1,250.00
No. 1¾ Far West hunter's rifle	250.00 to 750.00
No. 2 sporting rifle	350.00 to 750.00
No. 3 gallery rifle	350.00 to 750.00
No. 3F gallery rifle	750.00 to 1,250.00
No. 3½ target rifle	500.00 to 1,250.00
No. 4 Perfection rifle	500.00 to 1,000.00
No. 4½ mid-range rifle	750.00 to 1,500.00
No. 4½ A-1	1,000.00 to 3,500.00
No. 5 Pacific rifle	2,000.00 to 4,000.00
No. 6 Schuetzen	
Off-hand rifle	1,000.00 to 3,000.00
Premium grade	1,500.00 to 3,500.00
No. 6½	
Mid-range	750.00 to 2,500.00
Off-hand rifle	1,500.00 to 3,500.00
Rigy barrel	1,500.00 to 3,500.00
No. 7	
Creedmore A-1	1,500.00 to 5,000.00
Extra-long range	2,500.00 to 5,000.00
Long-range rifle	1,500.00 to 4,000.00
No. 8 Union Hill rifle	750.00 to 2,000.00
No. 9 Union Hill rifle	600.00 to 1,500.00
No. 10 Schuetzen junior rifle	750.00 to 2,500.00

Model 1881 lever-action rifle

Early 1881 models	750.00 to 2,000.00
Lightweight model	350.00 to 1,200.00
Standard model	350.00 to 1,000.00
Model 1888 lever-action rifle	750.00 to 1,500.00

Model 1889

Carbine	500.00 to 1,000.00
Lever-action rifle	250.00 to 750.00
Musket	2,500.00 to 5,000.00

Model 1892 lever-action rifle
  .22-caliber model . . . . 150.00 to 500.00
  .32-caliber model . . . . 125.00 to 500.00
Model 1893
  Lever-action rifle . . . . 200.00.00 to 600.00
  Lightweight model . . . . 350.00 to 1,000.00
  Musket . . . . 2,500.00 to 4,500.00
Model 1894 lever-action rifle
  Baby carbine . . . . 500.00 to 1,250.00
  Carbine . . . . 300.00 to 750.00
  Musket . . . . 1,500.00 to 3,500.00
  Standard . . . . 200.00 to 500.00
Model 1895 lever-action rifle
  Carbine . . . . 750.00 to 3,500.00
  Lightweight model . . . . 300.00 to 1,000.00
  Standard model . . . . 500.00 to 1,500.00
Model 1897
  Lever-action rifle
  Bicycle rifle . . . . 500.00 to 1,500.00
  Standard model . . . . 150.00 to 500.00
  Slide-action shotgun
    Riot gun . . . . 150.00 to 400.00
    Standard model . . . . 100.00 to 350.00
Model 1991 lever-action rifle
  .22-caliber short-magazine model . . . . 350.00 to 1,000.00
  .22- and .32-caliber full-magazine model . . . . 200.00 to 500.00

Remington Arms Company

Civil War musket conversions . . . . 250.00 to 1,250.00
Model 1867 Cadet rolling-block rifle . . . . 500.00 to 1,250.00
Model 1883 double-barrel hammer shotgun . . . . 250.00 to 750.00
Model 1885 double-barrel hammer shotgun . . . . 250.00 to 750.00
Model 1887 double-barrel hammer shotgun . . . . 250.00 to 750.00
Model 1889 double-barrel hammer shotgun . . . . 250.00 to 750.00
Model 1894 hammerless shotgun . . . . 250.00 to 750.00
Model 1900 hammerless shotgun . . . . 250.00 to 750.00
No. 1 rolling-block
  Shotgun . . . . 150.00 to 500.00
  Sporting rifle
    Black Hills rifle . . . . 750.00 to 1,500.00
    Light "Baby" carbine . . . . 500.00 to 1,200.00
    Long-range "Creedmore" rifle . . . . 750.00 to 1,750.00
    Mid-range target rifle . . . . 1,250.00 to 2,500.00
    Short-range rifle . . . . 750.00 to 1,500.00
No. 1½ sporting rifle . . . . 250.00 to 750.00
No. 2 sporting rifle . . . . 200.00 to 500.00

No. 4 rolling-block rifle. . . . . 150.00 to 300.00
No. 4-S Military Model rolling-block rifle . . . . 500.00 to 750.00
No. 5 rolling-block rifles/carbines
    Model 1897
        Carbine. . . . . 300.00 to 600.00
        Military rifle. . . . . 150.00 to 500.00
    Sporting and target rifle . . . . 750.00 to 2,500.00
No. 6 rolling-block
    Rifle. . . . . 75.00 to 200.00
    Shotgun . . . . 75.00 to 200.00
No. 7 rolling-block action rifle . . . . 1,000.00 to 3,000.00
N.Y. State contract rifles and carbines. . . . . 250.00 to 750.00
Percussion contract rifle. . . . . 1,000.00 to 2,000.00
Remington-Beals single-shot rifle . . . . 200.00 to 400.00
Remington-Hepburn No. 3 rifles
    Long-range Creedmore . . . . 1,750.00 to 5,000.00
    Match rifle. . . . . 750.00 to 2,000.00
    Military rifle . . . . 1,250.00 to 5,000.00
    Schuetzen match rifle. 7,500.00 to 15,000.00
    Sporting and target model . . . . 750.00 to 2,000.00
Remington-Keene bolt-action rifle
    Carbine model . . . . 1,000.00 to 2,500.00
    Frontier model . . . . 1,500.00 to 3,500.00
    Sporting rifle . . . . 500.00 to 1,000.00
Remington-Lee bolt-action rifles
    Military rifle . . . . 250.00 to 750.00
    Model 1879 by Sharps . . . . 1,500.00 to 3,500.00
    Model 1882 . . . . 500.00 to 1,250.00
    Model 1885 . . . . 500.00 to 1,000.00
    Sporting rifle . . . . 500.00 to 1,000.00
    U.S. Navy Model . . . . 500.00 to 1,250.00
Remington-Whitmore 1874 double-barrel
    Hammer rifle/shotgun combination . . . . 2,000.00 to 5,000.00
    Hammer shotgun. . . . . 350.00 to 750.00
Revolving percussion rifle
    .36-caliber percussion model . . . . 1,000.00 to 3,000.00
    .44-caliber
        Converted to metallic cartridge . . . . 750.00 to 2,500.00
        Percussion model. . . . . 1,250.00 to 3,500.00
Rolling-block military rifle and carbines . . . . 150.00 to 250.00
Single-barrel muzzle-loading shotgun . . . . 200.00 to 400.00
Single-shot
    Bolt-action rifle . . . . 750.00 to 1,500.00
    Breech-loading carbine
        Type I . . . . 500.00 to 1,500.00
        Type II. . . . . 600.00 to 2,000.00
U.S. Navy rolling-block carbine. . . . . 500.00 to 1,250.00

Sharps Firearms

Model 1849 rifle . . . . 2,500.00 to 7,500.00
Model 1850 rifle . . . . 2,500.00 to 5,000.00
Model 1851
    Carbine . . . . 2,500.00 to 5,000
    Rifle. . . . . 1,250.00 to 2,500.00
Model 1852 slanting breech
    Military models. . . . . 2,000.00 to 5,000.00
    Shotgun . . . . 500.00 to 1,000.00
    Sporting rifle . . . . 750.00 to 1,500.00
    Standard carbine . . . . 750.00 to 2,000.00
Model 1853 "John Brown" slanting breech
    Military model. . . . . 1,500.00 to 3,500
    Shotgun . . . . 350.00 to 1,000.00
    Sporting rifle . . . . 500.00 to 1,500.00
    Standard model . . . . 750.00 to 2,000.00
Model 1855 U.S. carbine
    Sporting rifle. . . . . 1,500.00 to 3,500.00
    Standard model. . . . . 1,000.00 to 3,500.00
    U.S. Navy rifle. . . . . 2,000.00 to 4,000.00
Model 1859, new model
    Carbine . . . . 500.00 to 2,500.00
    Rifle . . . . 750.00 to 2,000.00
Model 1863, new model
    Carbine . . . . 500.00 to 2,500.00
    Rifle . . . . 750.00 to 2,000.00
Model 1965, new model
    Carbine . . . . 750.00 to 1,750.00
    Rifle . . . . 750.00 to 2,500.00
Model 1869, new model
    Carbine . . . . 1,000.00 to 1,500.00
    Military rifle . . . . 1,250.00 to 2,500.00
    Sporting rifle. . . . . 1,500.00 to 2,500.00
Model 1870
    Springfield Armory trial carbine, rare . . . . 2,500.00 to 5,000.00
    Type I, percussion conversion . . . . 750.00 to 2,000.00
    Type II, early 1874-style action . . . . 1,000.00 to 2,500.00
Model 1874 rifle
    "A" series sporting rifles . . . . 1,250.00 to 2,500.00
    Business rifle . . . . 1,500.00 to 3,500.00
    Creedmore models. . . . . 2,500.00 to 8,500.00
    Express rifle . . . . 2,500.00 to 5,000.00
    Hunter's rifle. . . . . 1,250.00 to 2,500.00
    Long-range rifles. . . . . 2,500.00 to 9,000.00
    Mid-range models. . . . . 2,500.00 to 7,000.00

Military carbine	1,000.00 to 2,500.00
Military rifle	750.00 to 2,000.00
Officer's rifle	1,500.00 to 2,500.00
Sporting rifle	1,250.00 to 3,500.00
Model 1877 "English" rifle	5,000.00 to 12,500.00
New model conversions to metallic cartridge	500.00 to 1,500.00
New model sporting rifles	1,000.00 to 2,500.00

IS IT LEGAL?

Local, state, and federal laws all can get in the way of an honest firearms collector's rights. Check them *before* buying. Generally speaking, firearms manufactured before 1898 are legal under federal law, but you should know of other possible restrictions before buying. The antique firearms listed here are, for the most part, cleared by the feds.

Sharps-Borchardt Model 1878 rifle

Business rifle	750.00 to 1,750.00
Carbine	750.00 to 2,000.00
Express rifle	2,500.00 to 5,000.00
Hunter's rifle	850.00 to 2,000.00
Long-range rifle	2,500.00 to 6,000.00
Mid-range rifle	1,500.00 to 3,500.00
Military rifle	750.00 to 1,500.00
Officer's rifle	1,500.00 to 2,500.00
Short-range rifle	1,500.00 to 3,000.00
Sporting rifle	1,250.00 to 2,500.00

Stevens Arms Company

Hunter's Pet pocket rifle

No. 34*	350.00 to 600.00
No. 34½	400.00 to 750.00
Ideal rifle No. 44	200.00 to 500.00
Model 42 pocket rifle*	400.00 to 600.00

New model

Pocket rifle No. 40*	300.00 to 500.00
Pocket shotgun No. 39*	300.00 to 500.00
Old model pocket rifle*	350.00 to 500.00
Removable sideplate ideal riffle	750.00 to 2,000.00
Stevens-Vernier pocket rifle*	400.00 to 600.00

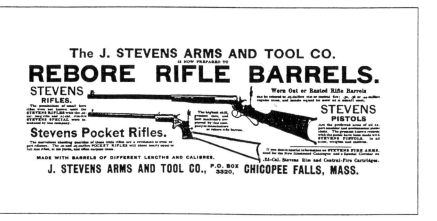

Tip-up rifles
  Ladies
    No. 11 . . . . 350.00 to 750.00
    No. 12 . . . . 400.00 to 800.00
    No. 13 . . . . 500.00 to 1,000.00
    No. 14 . . . . 750.00 to 1,250.00
  With forends . . . . 300.00 to 500.00
  Without forends . . . . 200.00 to 400.00
Tip-up shotgun . . . . 100.00 to 200.00

Frank Wesson Firearms

Large frame 1870 pocket rifle* . . . . 500.00 to 1,000.00
Model 1862 tip-up pocket rifle* . . . . 250.00 to 500.00
Model 1870
  Pocket rifle* . . . . 250.00 to 500.00
  Pocket shotgun . . . . 400.00 to 600.00
Two-trigger rifle
  First-type
    Military carbine . . . . 300.00 to 500.00
    Sporter . . . . 200.00 to 350.00
  Second type . . . . 150.00 to 300.00
  Third type . . . . 150.00 to 350.00
  Fourth type . . . . 500.00 to 750.00
  Fifth type . . . . 250.00 to 500.00
Under-lever rolling-block rifles
  No. 1
    Long-range . . . . 2,500.00 to 6,500.00
    Mid-range . . . . 2,000.00 to 6,000.00

*Prices are for complete pistols with detachable stocks.

No. 2

    Hunting . . . . 1,500.00 to 5,000.00

    Long-range . . . . 1,500.00 to 5,000

    Mid-range. . . . . 1,500.00 to 5,000.00

Whitney Arms Company

1798 contract muskets

    Converted to percussion . . . . 500.00 to 1,000.00

    Flintlock . . . . 1,000.00 to 10,000.00

1812 contract musket

    Converted to percussion . . . . 500.00 to 900.00

    Flintlock. . . . . 500.00 to 2,500.00

1822 contract musket

    Converted to percussion . . . . 300.00 to 500.00

    Flintlock. . . . . 750.00 to 1,250.00

1841 U.S. percussion rifle. . . . . 1,000.00 to 3,000.00

1861

    Contract(s) rifle musket . . . . 500.00 to 2,500.00

    Navy percussion rifle. . . . . 750.00 to 2,500.00

Double-barrel shotgun . . . . 250.00 to 500.00

Excelsior single-shot top-loader . . . . 500.00 to 1,000.00

"Good and Serviceable Arms" (made by Whitney from condemned and foreign parts from 1857 to 1864)

    Enfield type . . . . 600.00 to 1,250.00

    Maynard Tape primer. . . . . 600.00 to 2,000.00

    "Mississippi"-style rifle . . . . 750.00 to 1,500.00

    Musket. . . . . 600.00 to 1,250.00

    Richmond Humback-lock type . . . . 600.00 to 2,000.00

Percussion shotguns

    Double-barrel. . . . . 250.00 to 500.00

    Single-barrel. . . . . 250.00 to 600.00

Whitney-Burgess-Morse lever-action

    Carbine. . . . . 1,000.00 to 2,750.00

    Military rifle . . . . 1,000.00 to 2,500.00

    Sporting rifle . . . . 500.00 to 1,250.00

Whitney-Cochran carbine . . . . 750.00 to 1,500.00

Whitney-Howard lever-action single-shot . . . . 250.00 to 500.00

Whitney-Kennedy lever-action repeater

    Carbine. . . . . 1,000.00 to 2,500.00

    Military rifle . . . . 1,000.00 to 2,500.00

    Sporting rifle . . . . 300.00 to 1,200.00

Whitney-Laidley rolling block

    Carbine. . . . . 400.00 to 800.00

    Creedmore rifle. . . . . 750.00 to 3,500.00

    Gallery rifle. . . . . 250.00 to 700.00

Military rifle . . . . 450.00 to 900.00
Sporting rifle. . . . . 250.00 to 750.00
Whitney-Phoenix breech-loader
    Carbine . . . . 750.00 to 1,750.00
    Gallery rifle. . . . . 350.00 to 750.00
    Military rifle. . . . . 750.00 to 1,500.00
    Rifle. . . . . 250.00 to 750.00
    Scheutzen rifle. . . . . 750.00 to 1,500.00
Whitney-Remington rolling block
    Carbine . . . . 400.00 to 800.00
    Lightweight sporting rifle . . . . 500.00 to 1,000.00
    Shotgun . . . . 150.00 to 350.00
    Sporting rifle. . . . . 250.00 to 750.00
Whitney-Scharf lever-action repeater
    Carbine . . . . 1,500.00 to 3,500.00
    Military rifle . . . . 1,500.00 to 4,500.00
    Sporting rifle . . . . 500.00 to 1,250.00
Whitney swing-breech carbine. . . . . 1,500.00 to 2,500.00

Winchester Firearms

Double-barrel shotgun . . . . 1,000.00 to 3,500.00
Model 53 rifle. . . . . 500.00 to 1,000.00
Model 65 rifle. . . . . 500.00 to 1,000.00
Model 71 rifle. . . . . 500.00 to 1,500.00
Model 1866 rifle
    First model
        Carbine. . . . . 2,500.00 to 10,000.00
        Rifle. . . . . 7,500.00 to 20,000.00
    Second model
        Carbine. . . . . 1,250.00 to 3,500.00
        Rifle. . . . . 1,500.00 to 5,000.00
    Third model
        Carbine. . . . . 1,000.00 to 3,500.00
        Musket. . . . . 1,000.00 to 3,000.00
        Rifle. . . . . 1,250.00 to 5,000.00
    Fourth model
        Carbine. . . . . 1,000.00 to 3,500.00
        Musket . . . . 1,000.00 to 3,500.00
        Rifle. . . . . 1,250.00 to 5,000.00
Model 1873
    Carbine . . . . 750.00 to 3,500.00
    Musket. . . . . 750.00 to 3,500.00
    Rifle . . . . 500.00 to 3,500.00
    .22 rimfire rifle. . . . . 750.00 to 1,500.00
Model 1876
    Carbine . . . . 800.00 to 3,500.00

Musket	2,500.00 to 5,000.00
Rifle	650.00 to 2,500.00
Model 1886	
Carbine	1,750.00 to 5,000.00
Full-stock carbine	2,500.00 to 7,000.00
Lightweight rifle	500.00 to 1,000.00
Musket	3,000.00 to 8,500.00
Rifle	750.00 to 2,000.00
Take-down rifle	600.00 to 1,200.00
Model 1887 lever-action shotgun	400.00 to 1,000.00
Model 1890 slide-action rifle	
First model	1,000.00 to 3,000.00
Second and third models	250.00 to 750.00
Model 1892 rifle	
Carbine	500.00 to 2,000.00
Musket	3,500.00 to 7,500.00
Rifle	350.00 to 750.00
Take-down model	500.00 to 1,000.00
Model 1893 slide-action shotgun	250.00 to 750.00
Model 1894 carbine	250.00 to 2,500.00

Model 1895 rifle
    Carbine .... 500.00 to 3,500.00
    Flat-side musket .... 4,000.00 to 10,000.00
    Rifle .... 350.00 to 750.00
    Standard musket(s) .... 500.00 to 2,000.00
    Take-down model .... 500.00 to 1,250.00
Model 1897 slide-action shotgun
    Pigeon gun .... 450.00 to 900.00
    Riot gun .... 250.00 to 500.00
    Standard grade .... 200.00 to 400.00
    Trap gun .... 350.00 to 750.00
    Trench gun .... 300.00 to 600.00
Model 1901 lever-action shotgun .... 400.00 to 1,000.00
Single-shot rifle
    High-wall/thick-wall express .... 1,000.00 to 2,500.00
    High-wall .22 musket .... 250.00 to 450.00
    Take-down .22 high-wall .... 450.00 to 900.00
    Three models, various calibers, barrel lengths, and
        weights .... 250.00 to 10,000.00
Winchester-Hotchkiss bolt-action
    Army and Navy models .... 500.00 to 1,500.00
    Carbine .... 400.00 to 800.00
    Musket .... 400.00 to 800.00
    Sporting rifle .... 350.00 to 750.00
Winchester-Lee rifle .... 500.00 to 1,000.00

This ends this more-or-less complete listing of better-known early American collectible firearms. Much more in the way of detail, description, and dating is necessary for any potentially serious collector, and, as you will note, even more is needed if you plan to collect the many rarities that follow. I strongly recommend that you read more before you even think about collecting, and, just as strongly, I recommend Norm Flayderman's *Guide to Antique American Firearms* as the place to begin. This large, lavishly illustrated book is on sale wherever collectibles books are sold or it can be ordered by your local bookseller.

MAKING A POINT

Never point a firearm at anything you are not prepared to shoot. If you remember the "all firearms are always loaded" rule, this follows naturally.

Rarities

Damascus Barrel Shotguns

Baker Gun Company
   Regular . . . . 100.00 to 500.00
   Three-barrel drilling . . . . 300.00 to 750.00
Charles Day, imported . . . . 250.00 to 750.00
Fox Gun Company . . . . 100.00 to 350.00
Hollenbeck Gun Company, three-barrel gun valves   350.00 to 1,000.00
Lefever Arms . . . . 200.00 to 500.00
Parker Brothers
   Early models . . . . 350.00 to 1,250.00
   Others . . . . 350.00 to 10,000.00
L. C. Smith . . . . 350.00 to 1,500.00
Spencer Arms . . . . 200.00 to 400.00
Young Repeating Arms . . . . 400.00 to 800.00

BLOWN BARRELS

Firearms with Damascus or twist-steel barrels may be lovely to behold, but they can cost you an eye or your life. Modern ammunition is far too powerful for yesterday's gun barrels. If you are hell-bent on shooting your old twist-steel barreled gun, have it thoroughly checked by an able gunsmith and then, *and only then,* use low power loads such as those sold by New England Arms of Kittery, Maine.

Lefever Hammerless Guns.

The best trap and field Gun made. It will cut-shoot all others; is simpler
in construction and more durable.

THE
L. C. Smith Hammerless Gun

THE CELEBRATED

"L. C. SMITH"

Hammerless and Hammer Guns,

AS PRIZE WINNERS, HAVE NO EQUAL.

Descriptive Catalogues Mailed Upon
Application.

CORRESPONDENCE SOLICITED.

L. C. SMITH,

Manufacturer of Fine Guns, - SYRACUSE, N. Y.

Kentucky Rifles

Heavy "Match" rifles . . . . 250.00 to 2,500.00
Heavy "Match" rifles converted to percussion . . . . . 250.00 to 10,000.00
Transition-era rifles. . . . . 500.00 to 25,000.00+
1780–1830 models. . . . . 500.00 to 10,000.00+

Lever and Slide Actions

Bullard sporting rifle . . . . 500.00 to 5,000.00
Burgess rifles and shotguns . . . . 350.00 to 2,000.00
Evans lever-action rifles. . . . . 500.00 to 1,500.00
Henry lever-action rifles . . . . 3,500.00 to 25,000.00+
Jennings rifles. . . . . 500.00 to 2500.00
Robinson rifles. . . . . 750.00 to 1,250.00
Savage lever-action rifles. . . . . 500.00 to 3,500.00
Smith-Jennings rifles. . . . . 2,500.00 to 5,000.00
Volcanic rifles. . . . . 1,000.00 to 10,000.00+

Percussion Rifles

Bench-rest models. . . . . 750.00 to 5,000.00
Breech-loading rifles . . . . 500.00 to 1,500.00
Half-stock models . . . . 250.00 to 7,500.00
Plains rifles. . . . . 250.00 to 7,500.00
Schuetzen rifles . . . . 750.00 to 3,500.00

Shotguns

Double-barrel
    Flintlocks . . . . 1,000.00 to 2,500.00
    Flintlocks converted to percussion . . . . 250.00 to 750.00+
    Percussion shotguns . . . . 250.00 to 750.00
Single-barrel
    Flintlocks . . . . 500.00 to 1,000.00+
    Percussion shotguns . . . . 200.00 to 750.00

Single-Shot Rifles

Buck rifle. . . . . 250.00 to 750.00
Bullard rifles. . . . . 500.00 to 3,500.00
Farrow Arms . . . . 1,500.00 to 5,000.00
Holden rifles. . . . . 500.00 to 2,500.00
Hopkins & Allen. . . . . 250.00 to 1,500.00
Howard rifles. . . . . 250.00 to 500.00
Lee rifle . . . . 250.00 to 500.00
Maynard patent rifles. . . . . 500.00 to 3,500.00
Peabody/Peabody-Martini . . . . 1,250.00 to 5,000.00
Wurfflein tip-up rifles. . . . . 250.00 to 2,500.00

ALWAYS LOADED

I was brought up to believe that all guns are always loaded and should be handled appropriately. There are countless cases where an "empty" rifle or shotgun killed its owner or an innocent bystander. Such events will continue unless everyone treats each and every firearm as the deadly tool it is.

CHAPTER 13

Gunning and Shooting Accessories

ccessories may not be just the right word for the wide variety of "stuff" that gunners and shooters collect, but it will serve to introduce the reader to the vast array of these collectibles. Some of these things are—or were—necessities that are part of the particular pursuit, some are trophies, and still others are a reminder of another time or place. I do not necessarily consider native-American bird and arrow points sporting collectibles, but the one I picked up on the shores of the Chesapeake Bay when my father took me gunning there talks to me of other times, and sometimes I feel that is what collecting is all about.

Many sporting collectibles that might well have found their way into this section have chapters of their own, and there is no doubt some of the things listed here deserve greater attention. However, a book of this size and scope has limitations. I have tried to be selective in judging the merit of the gunning and shooting odds and ends one finds in today's marketplace, and I have listed the ones I feel will interest readers. There are, of course, many, many worthwhile collectibles, and I respectfully refer you to the listings in the appendix for further reading and information.

Andirons (or fireplace log holders)

Dog, retrievers, cast iron. 1,050.00
Duck decoys, cast iron, c. 1890. . . . . 5,050.00

A gunning skiff from the Havre de Grace, Maryland, tidewaters, this 75-year old canvas-covered boat was sold at auction for $500.00. *Photograph courtesy of Richard Oliver & The Ward Foundation, Salisbury, Maryland.*

Flying ducks, cast iron, old repair 3,750.00
Leaping salmon, cast iron, 20″ 2,600.00

Ashtray, brass, signed by maker

Flying ducks 575.00
Flying pheasants. 420.00

Baskets

Clam-style, used to carry decoys, Mackey collection stamp, good condi-
    tion. 225.00
Live decoy carrier made with ash splints
    Old repaired hinges. 375.00
        Poor condition 110.00

Bookends

Mallard hen and drake, carved wood, original paint 170.00
Setter, painted cast iron, worn condition
    Black-and-white 70.00
    Gilded. 35.00

Boxes, etc. (Note: Paper shotshell boxes are listed separately)

Dovetailed carton, very fine condition
    Peters shotshells 85.00
    Remington shotshells 45.00
    Western air rifle shot. 25.00
    Winchester shotshells. 65.00
Early shooter's box
    Fired brass shells, 24. . . . . 280.00
    Loaded brass shells, 97 of a possible 100 . . . . 775.00
Handmade box, 23 Parker Brothers brass shotshells 475.00
Wooden carton, for 10 Model 94 Winchester rifles, faded condi-
    tion 30.00

Calls and Whistles

Crow call by Charles Perdew of Henry, Illinois
    Fair condition. 175.00
    Fine condition, signed 300.00
Duck call, checkered, owner's initials and Perdew's signa-
    ture 3,050.00
Duck, goose and quail calls (11), from the collection of Jack Mitchell of
    Remington Arms. 250.00
Herter's, with original box
    Duck call 35.00
    Goose call. 30.00
Lohman calls (2) and Sure Shot calls (2), with original boxes. . . 175.00

Hand-carved and painted duck call by decoy and call maker Charles Perdew of Henry, Illinois, came in its original box and was sold for $4,400.00. *Photograph courtesy of Guyette/Schmidt, West Farmington, Maine.*

Olt
    Duck calls (6) and goose calls (3) 250.00
    "Turkey Hooter Owl Call," with original cardboard box 35.00

Carved ears of wooden corn

Hand-carved, from Maryland's eastern shore, worn paint
    One 400.00
    Two 600.00
Painted cottonwood ears (7), carved, with applied husks from real
    corn 325.00

Counter felt (for store counters)

Dead Shot Powder "Kill Your Bird Not Your Shoulder," multicolored
    on black
    Mint condition 225.00
    Trimmed 90.00
Harrington & Richardson "Shot Gun & Revolvers," gold print on
    maroon felt 100.00
UMC "UMC Cartridges for Game and Gallery" 75.00
Winchester "Shoot Where You Aim" 175.00
Others . . . . 50.00 to 350.00

Set of two calls (duck and goose) made by Kent S. Freeman of Cape Girardeau, Missouri, feature detailed waterfowl scenes on the barrels and sold (as a pair) for $800.00. *Photograph courtesy of Guyette/Schmidt, West Farmington, Maine.*

Decoy collars (box of 12), used to secure live decoys to stakes

Good condition 450.00
Mint condition 600.00

WHAT'S IN A NAME?

Colt, Parker, Winchester, and other gunning and shooting companies made all manner of things, and collectors want them all, be they lawn mowers by Winchester or old washing machines by Savage Arms. Be on the lookout for these oddball collectibles, and, if you don't want them, rest assured that someone does.

Doorstop, cast iron

Decoy-shaped 110.00
Standing duckling-shaped 55.00

Duck calls (and goose calls, too) have become hot collector items. Those pictured here are (left to right): "Glodo style" checkered step call by Murry Worthen of Murphysboro, Illinois ($650.00), a goose call by Skippy Barto of Illinois ($850.00), and a duck call by Charles Grubbs of Bureau, Illinois ($675.00). *Photograph courtesy of Guyette/Schmidt, West Farmington, Maine.*

Electric outlet, Colt 50.00

Footscraper, cast iron, decoy-shaped 35.00

Glass target balls

    Amber (10) 365.00
    Basketweave, with shooting figure
        Green 185.00
        Purple 210.00

Three collectible duck calls are (left to right): a laminated example by A. M. Bowles of Little Rock, Arkansas ($200.00), a checkered "Glodo style" call by Jerry Reed of Elkville, Illinois, that has a small crack ($700.00), and a "Flapping Bill" duck call by the Natural Duck Call Company of St. Paul, Minnesota ($700.00). *Photograph courtesy of Guyette/Schmidt, West Farmington, Maine.*

Bogardus
    Amber..255.00
    Green...380.00
Cobalt blue, gridded, unmarked ....110.00 to 175.00
Deep purple 225.00
Three-piece mold
    Amber...65.00
    Lavender..255.00
Others ....50.00 to 4,000.00

Shorebird whistles (calls) include a group of three (at left) that sold for $400.00, a sterling silver whistle by the R. Woodman Company of Boston, Massachusetts ($375.00), and two sterling whistles by the Willard Manufacturing Company of Melrose, Massachusetts, that went for $200.00 and $275.00, respectively. *Photograph courtesy of Guyette/Schmidt, West Farmington, Maine.*

Gun oil bottle and cans

Glass oil bottle
    Keen Kutter 45.00
    Remington 55.00
    Winchester 65.00
Nitro solvent tin, Marbles, rare 245.00
Oil can
    Remington, yellow and blue lithographed 35.00
    Winchester
        Green
            Fair condition 45.00
            Very good condition 95.00

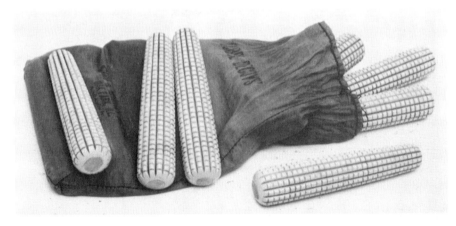

Wooden ears of corn were used after baiting was outlawed by the Federal government. This set of 12 ears in their original cloth bag was manufactured by Cobbe Decoys of Illinois in the 1930s and sold at auction for $4,000.00. *Photograph courtesy of Guyette/Schmidt, West Farmington, Maine.*

Three glass target balls (left to right): an amber example produced by Gurd & Son of London, Ontario and so marked, and a rare gridded green ball together with an oversized black glass ball that sold as a lot for $325.00. *Photograph courtesy of Guyette/Schmidt, West Farmington, Maine.*

"New Gun Oil"...................................35.00

"Not New Gun Oil"...............................45.00

Red, fair condition..............................45.00

Gun rack, for two guns, marked "Winchester" on the single crossbar, fine promotional item.......................................45.00

Heads, hides and horns (Note: Many game animals and birds are protected under the endangered species laws, and buyers should be aware of possible fines and confiscation.)

Alaskan wolf head, fine condition 350.00

Black bear

   Rug, felt backing, very good condition, original skull and

      teeth 550.00

   Standing, fine condition..............................900.00

Buffalo (bison) head, mounted........................2,000.00

Deer

   Head, mounted.............................65.00 to 450.00

   Horns, mounted............................20.00 to 300.00

Elk

   Head, mounted..900.00

   Horns, mounted on plaque 275.00

Game birds, mounted.........................50.00 to 150.00

Grizzly bear, standing, honey color, fine condition 5,750.00

Moose

   Head, mounted on shield panel

      Good condition...................................1,500.00

      Very large, fine condition.........................1,800.00

Horns, mounted
  Large 425.00
  Small 175.00
Polar bear rug, head and claws, average wear 2,750.00
Waterfowl, mounted . . . . 50.00 to 150.00
Zebra
  Head, mounted on walnut panel 225.00
  Rug (made out of skin) 350.00

Ink stand

One well, hunting dog, cowboy hat, shooting bag, etc., worn silver
  plate 425.00
Two wells
  Dogs chasing stag (deer) over fence, worn painted cast iron   225.00
  Signed by Jacob Petit, fine porcelain dog and detail 3,400.00

Parker Brothers

Alarm clock, broken 95.00
Coffee grinder, marked "Parker Bros." 110.00
Paperweight, bear-shaped, cast iron
  Marked "Parker" and "Meridan" 145.00
  "P" on cap and "Parker Vises" on coveralls 285.00
Powder & shot measure, nickel plated 90.00
Wad starter for reloading old brass shotshells, nickel plated 50.00

Powder flasks and horns (Note: Metal powder and shot flasks have been reproduced in a multitude of designs and patterns.)

Flask
  Copper, embossed with setter and game birds 60.00
  Tin
    Hazard Powder Company, painted green, paper label 85.00
    Pewter cap, 1860s 55.00
Powder horn
  Engraved (carved)
    Battle scenes, dated 1777 . . . . 2,000.00
    Cross hatching 100.00
    Fighting men, signed and dated 1775 . . . . 8,500.00
    Hunting and fishing scenes 2,600.00
    Pewter fittings (pair), from Scotland 150.00
Soldier's priming horn, small, dating to the American Revolu-
  tion 450.00

Stickpin

"Dead Shot," falling duck, gold 275.00
DuPont, setter, gold 125.00

Hopkins and Allen, pistol, silver 115.00
Savage Arms, Indian head
    Copper finish 75.00
    Silver. 95.00
Winchester, "25 Year" pin, silver. 110.00

Toy guns (Note: Cap guns and the like are not sporting collectibles and are not listed here, nor are air and BB guns.)

Daisy, "Red Ryder Training Rifle," shoots corks 85.00
Fox
    Paper target with center bell, marked "Fox" and "Philadelphia,"
        excellent condition. 225.00
    Shotgun, double-barrel, very good condition with light wear   200.00
    Shotshells for shotgun, each. 85.00
Marx, "Hunter and Target Set," with windup rabbit, shotgun, and original box. 145.00

Trap

Glass target balls tossing, no brand markings 700.00
Hand (for tossing clay pigeons)
    Remington 45.00
    Western 40.00
    Winchester. 95.00

Trivet, made by Colt Firearms, cast iron 85.00

Watch fob

Colt Firearms, leather strap. 75.00
Dead Shot
    Porcelain insert with falling duck 185.00
    Silver plated 110.00
DuPont, shows trap shooter, silver 175.00
National Sportsman
    Copper 25.00
    Silver. 65.00
Smith and Wesson, silver plated 35.00

Weather vane

Decoy, handcrafted copper, greened old patina. 1,100.00
Flying goose, by Elmer Crowell, old "in-use" repaint. 985.00

Whirligig, original paint

Canada goose 55.00
Flying mallard. 55.00

Fly fisherman weather vane with fish and rod is 50″ tall and has traces of its original paint together with the expected rust of time. This folk art piece sold for $1,000.00.

REPRODUCTIONS

If it's valuable or simple to make, you can bet that someone somewhere has thought about reproducing it—if they haven't already done so. In fact, many of the objects that one sees at flea markets and "iffy" shops never were produced by the companies they project and are the work of today's "artists" and "artisans." Caveat emptor and then some!

CHAPTER 14

Cartridges, Shotshells, and Powder Cans and Kegs

artridges have been in vogue since the time women on the frontier were urged to "save the last shot for yourself" in the long-ago days of Indian raids. A serious collector has thousands and thousands of varieties to search for, and if we add brass and paper shotshells to the list, it becomes mind-boggling. I know one collector who has five dentist's cases filled to overflowing with his collection, and there are thousands he still lacks. These loaded and unloaded collectibles are not my bag, but I must admit I do enjoy the way the morning sun shines on the handful of old brass shotshells I have in the window. There is a touch of a new day and a trace of better yesterdays gleaming there, and, in my opinion, that is what sporting collectibles are all about.

EXPLOSIVE

Cartridges and shotshells are dangerous and should be handled with great care. Many people have been hurt through careless handling that also endangers those around them. Just as guns are treated as always loaded, ammunition should be treated as though it was *always live* and kept under lock and key.

Cartridges, shotshells, and the boxes they came in all interest collectors. If we add the powder cans and kegs that predate factory loads, today's list of possibilities is limited only by the cost of these rarities. Cartridges and the like can be found almost anywhere, but the best place for a beginner to start is at one or more of the many gun shows that are held in all areas with regularity. Go to a show or two and talk to the dealers and collectors. You will learn more than I can tell you here, and chances are you'll get a bang out of the experience.

The following lists of cartridges, shotshells, shotshell boxes, and powder cans and kegs are designed to introduce you to these collectibles. They are only the tip of a very large iceberg that you may wish to learn more about. If you do, the list of sources in the appendix will prove helpful. Good hunting.

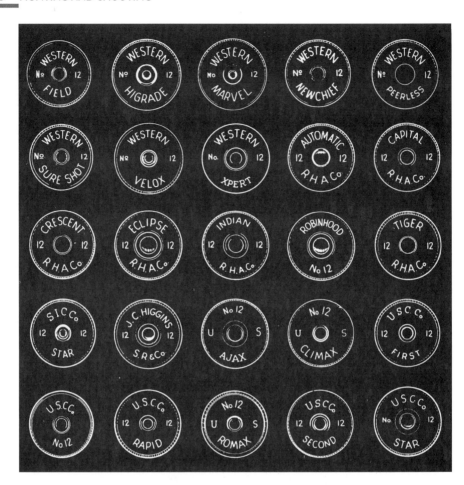

Shotshell headstamps are what separate the men from the boys in this specialized pursuit, and readers should note the six Robin Hood shotshells in the center line of the illustration. These 12-guage examples are shown approximately actual size.

Cartridges

.31 Crispin, rare 1,274.00
.32 Long Rimfire Merwin's cone base 110.00
.36 Theur's Patent for Colt pocket model 220.00
.40 Logan & Hart 206.00
.40–60 Colt 160.00
.40–70 Remington Reloadable 200.00
.40–90 Peabody Martini "What Cheer" 298.00
.41 Roper Revolving Rifle
     Brass. 175.00
     Steel 185.00

.42 Russian Gattling 500.00
.43–77 Hollow Bullet—Brass Dummy 315.00
.44 Henry flat rimfire 178.00
.45
    Adams Patent (1852), Eley headstamp 275.00
    Van Choate 150.00
.46 Short Ethan Allen Rimfire 120.00
.50
    Ball Carbine (rimfire) 242.00
    Crispin Short 551.00
    Maynard Model 1865 Logan & Hart 850.00
    Remington Pistol 260.00
    Warner Rimfire 302.00
    3¾″ Sharps paper patched bullet 205.00
.50–70 Rodman-Crispin Patent 115.00
.50–70 with Orcott primer 165.00
.50–140 Winchester Express 521.00
.54
    Burnside tinned case 193.00
    Star Rimfire 200.00
.56–46 Long Spencer Sporting Cartridge 200.00
.58
    Danderfield & LeFever 260.00
    Morse tinned case 420.00
    Musket Rimfire 125.00
    Rimfire 155.00
.307 Triangular, rare 1,687.00

For Those of You Who Feel Cartridge Collecting Is Only for Loaded
    Collectors . . .
.25
    Short Stevens Rimfire 50
    Stevens 60
.30
    Cup Fire 5.00
    Long 3.50
    Short Blank 1.25
.32
    Extra Short 2.50
    Winchester Special 1.25
.32–20 W.C.F. 1.50
.32–35 Stevens 4.50
.32–40 Ballard & Marlin 7.50
.35 Whelen 1.50
.41
    Long 1.00

Short Rimfire 1.00
Swiss Rimfire 2.50
.42
    Cup Fire 10.00
    Forehand & Wadsworth #64 . . . . 3.50
.44
    Extra Long 10.00
    Henry Flat, long case 5.00
    Long 2.50
    Short 1.00
.46 Carbine 5.00
.50
    Remington Army 7.50
    Remington Navy 30.00
.50–70 U.S. Government 10.00
.56–46 Spencer 8.50
.56–56 Spencer 4.50
.56–50 Spencer 3.50
.58 Musket (short case) 17.50
.310 Remington (shot) 1.50
.338 Winchester 2.00
.340 Weatherby 3.00

Shotshells (Note: The following shotshells are identified by their head-stamps.)

.410–12mm Climax brass shot shell 35.00
A. C. Co. 12-gauge
    Alert, brown paper 15.00
    Bang, red paper shotshell 34.00
    Crack Shot, brown paper 125.00
    Invincible, red paper 75.00
    Rust color paper 4.00

SHIPPING

The rules for shipping collectible ammunition have been relaxed by UPS and other carriers, but check them out before sending or receiving ammunition.

A. L. Howard no. 10 New Haven, Ct., brown paper shotshell 20.00
Austin
    10-gauge Ct'ge Co., blue paper 43.00
    12-gauge Ct'ge Co., brown paper 55.00

C.A. Co. no 10, gray paper 31.00
Capital 12–12 R.H.A. Co., brown paper 20.00
Cassidy no. 10, gray paper shotshell 187.00
C.C.C. no. 10, Mandan blue paper 15.00
Eley's no. 8, Ejector London-brass shotshell. 48.00
Everlasting no. 12 brass shotshell, rare 250.00
Federal Hi Power no. 12. . . . . 45.00
Gambles no. 12 Tiger. 45.00
Hudson's Bay no. 12, company brown lacquered paper shell 90.00
Kynoch Perfect, cutaway brass shotshell 14.00
Liberty Bulk no. 12, red paper. 15.00
Mallard C.C. Co. 12-gauge, duck on side 127.00
No. 10
    U.S. Climax, green paper. 45.00
    U.S. New Climax, black paper. 20.00
No. 16 U.S. Rapid, black paper 50.00
No. 28 U.S. New Rapid, black paper 50.00
Patent—Zund no. 20 "H" brass 20-gauge shotshell 25.00
P.C. Co.
    Prize 12-gauge brown paper shotshell 10.00
    Quick Shot 16, purple paper, 16-gauge shotshell. 8.00
    12-gauge Victor, red-and-white striped 157.00
Peters
    League no. 20
        Brown paper 3.00
        Red paper. 4.00
    Premier
        No. 12, orange paper. 50.00
        No. 16, orange paper. 60.00
    Target no. 12, red paper 3.00
    Victor 16-gauge, black paper. 25.00
J. Purdy & Sons 12 brass shotshell 32.00
Red Devil no. 12, red paper shotshell, devil on side 181.00
Remington-UMC
    No. 4 brass shotshell 75.00
    No. 20 Nitro club, tan paper, "SKEET". 30.00
Robin Hood
    No. 10, red paper 20.00
    No. 12, 1903, red paper 24.00
    12–12 R.H.P. Co. 24.00
UMC Club no. 10, brass. 6.00
UMC Co.
    Bridgeport, Ct., nickel-plated brass shotshell. 20.00
    No. 2, paper yacht cannon shell 275.00
    No. 4
        Black paper, reloaded 40.00

Brown paper shotshell 35.00
Metal-lined green paper shotshell 180.00
Red paper shotshell. 188.00
No. 8
   Brass 16.00
   Trap green paper shotshell. 21.00
No. 16 Walstrobe, purple paper. 75.00
U.S
   No. 32–14mm Climax, black paper 15.00
   Second Quality no. 10, black paper shotshell. 4.00
V.L. & A. no. 10 Chicago, orange paper 25.00
Western Field no. 20, red paper 4.00
Winchester
   No. 8, black paper 20.00
   No. 10, gray paper 8.00
   Pigeon no. 10, green paper 8.00
W.R.A. Co. no. 10 brass shotshell 84.00

Shotshell Boxes

10-Gauge
   Peters
      Referee 2-piece box, empty, good condition 78.00
      Target, empty, excellent condition 108.00
   Remington-UMC Nitro Club, full, good condition 72.00
   UMC
      Arrow, full, stained label 36.00
      Nitro Club, full, excellent condition 68.00
   USC Co. 1-piece box with gunner, empty. 54.00
   Winchester
      Leader, full, good condition 64.00
      New Rival, full 72.00
12-Gauge
   Henry G. Squires, empty, with flaws. 67.00
   Mallard Sportload 1-piece box, empty 21.00
   Mercury
      "New trap load" 1-piece box 11.00
      Victoria, 1-piece box 11.00
   Meridan 2-piece Pointer, empty, minor flaw. 39.00
   Mullerite 1-piece box with gunner on label 30.00
   Peters 1-piece Victor Trap shell box. 3.00
   Remington-UMC
      Arrow Express, mixed contents, flaw. 24.00
      Long Range Game Load 30.00
      Nitro Club, full. 60.00
   Robin Hood Eclipse 2-piece box, excellent condition. 333.00

UMC
    Extra Quality Smokeless 47.00
    Nitro Club
        With duck in flight, empty 75.00
        Later than above 42.00
Western Super-X, empty 3.00
Winchester
    Brass shells, 2-piece box, full 47.00
    Leader, near mint condition 91.00
    Repeater
        Fair condition 20.00
        Full box 21.00
16-Gauge
American Cartridge Co. American Eagle 1-piece box 21.00
Meridan Fire Arms Pointer 2-piece box, stained 60.00
Remington
    Arrow Express shells 37.00
    Kleanbore Shur Shot 1-piece box 12.00
Winchester, Repeater
    Full sealed box 47.00
    Mixed shells in open box 21.00
    10-round box 7.00
20-Gauge
Montgomery Ward Red Head 1-piece box with duck 25.00
Peters
    High Gun 2-piece box with shorebird 84.00
    Victor Trap 17.00
Remington
    "Arrow," poor condition 16.00
    Nitro Club Game Loads, with quail, mint condition 104.00
    Shur Shot Shells
        Full box 35.00
        Near mint condition 37.00
USC Co.
    Ajax 2-piece box, full 80.00
    Climax Heavies 1-piece box with gunner 44.00
    Defiance, with setter and hunter, empty 35.00
Western Field 2-piece box
    Full 31.00
    Partial contents 13.00
Western Super-X
    Full sealed box 55.00
    Partial contents 11.00
Winchester
    Leader 2-piece box 20.00

Repeater
  Full box 56.00
  10-round box 25.00
28-Gauge
  UMC Nitro Club, mixed shells 55.00
  USC Co., Climax, empty 20.00
32-Gauge, Winchester 2-piece box, empty 30.00
9mm, Winchester, 9mm Long Shot, red label, box of 50 . . . . 43.00
100-Round
  Dominion 16-gauge, 33 shells 21.00
  Peters League 12-gauge, full 100.00
  Remington-UMC
    12-gauge Nitro Club Grade, full 78.00
    16-gauge Nitro Club, full 54.00
    .410 cartridge cases, full, soiling. 100.00
  UMC Union, 12-gauge 85.00
  Winchester
    12-gauge
      Leader, empty 35.00
      New Rival, full 80.00
      Repeater, full 72.00
    16-gauge
      Blue Rival, full, soiled label 60.00
      Repeater shotshells, full 72.00
.410
  Red Head 2-piece, duck on box, empty. 78.00
  USC Co., 2-piece box
    Empty. 42.00
    Sealed. 90.00

BLACK POWDER

Black powder that predates today's modern smokeless varieties is extremely unstable and ammunition with this ingredient should be handled with extra care.

Powder Cans and Kegs

American Powder Mills
  ½-pound can
    Dead Shot Rifle Powder, pink label 75.00
    Red can, Dead Shot multicolor lithography 75.00

1-pound can
  Green Dead Shot. 106.00
  Red Dead Shot. 92.00
6½-pound keg, "Triple Refined" Dead Shot, fair condition 42.00
25-pound keg, Black with green and black label 61.00
American "E. C." & Schultze Gunpowder Company, 1-pound can
  Gold and dark green lithographed 56.00
  Orange lithographed
    Fine condition 55.00
    Scratched. 10.00
American Wood Powder Company, 1-pound can
  Green and black lithographed, flaking 22.00
  With 1886 patent date, poor condition 40.00
Austin Powder Company, ½-pound can, green with tan paper label,
  rare 75.00
Boston Powder Company, ¼-pound can, red stenciled, faded 60.00
Canadian Explosives Limited
  ½-pound can, black with upside-down falling duck labels 89.00
  1-pound can, black lithographed with falling duck
    Fine condition 34.00
    Good condition 32.00
  6-pound keg, green with red "Snap Shot" lettering 102.00
Curtis & Harvey
  1-pound flask, Curtis & Harvey's Gunpowder on paper labels 95.00
  2-pound can, yellow with blue paper Amberlite label. 48.00
Ditmar's Powder Company, 1-pound can, New Sporting powder paper
  labels. 89.00
E. I. duPont de Nemours Powder Company
  ½ pound can, red
    Golden Pheasant Gunpowder. 90.00
    Indian Rifle Gun Powder label
      Good condition 86.00
      Rust spots 50.00
  1-pound can
    Dark green, Ballistite Smokeless Powder
      Good condition 67.00
      Rust spots 46.00
    Red, Eagle Gun Powder paper label, scarce 213.00
    Schuetzen Smokeless
      Excellent condition. 50.00
      Good condition 40.00
  1 pound keg
    Green
      Black-and-white labeling depicting a dog 54.00
      "Shot Guns Only" label with dogs 51.00
    Red with deer on top label 30.00

Eureka Powder Works, 1-pound can with orange Imperial Gun Powder
label. 30.00
John Hall and Sons
    1-pound can, black with Tower Proof Gunpowder label,
        faded 113.00
    1-pound flask, red with blue paper "No. 6" label 118.00
Hamilton Powder Company, 1-pound lithographed black on gray
    Nobel's Empire Powder 112.00
Hazard Powder Company
    ½-pound can, red with Kentucky Rifle Powder label, torn. 38.00
    1-pound can
        Black with Kentucky Rifle Powder label, dirty label 45.00
        Red
            Hazard Electric Gunpowder, poor condition. 30.00
            Kentucky Rifle Powder
                Can flaked. 20.00
                Poor condition 22.00
    6-pound keg, red with Duck Shooting Gun Powder label, fair condi-
        tion 75.00
    25-pound can, red with "Cannon" label, varnished, good condi-
        tion 46.00
Hercules Powder Company
    1-pound can
        Black Sporting Powder on orange and black label 42.00
        Infallible Shotgun Smokeless, full label 12.00
    1-pound canister (round), Smokeless Rifle Powder. 86.00
    1-pound flask, orange lithographed Black Sporting Powder . . . 70.00
King Powder Company
    1-pound can
        Green with lithographed red and gold lettering 35.00
        Yellow with lithographed red banner. 31.00
    6-pound keg, red with Quick Shot paper label. 50.00
    Salesman's sample can, King's Smokeless, mint condition . . . 250.00
Laflin & Rand Powder Company
    ½-pound can, Orange Extra Powder
        Regular design. 22.00
        Round design. 25.00
    1-pound can
    Black
        Orange Ducking Powder label, good condition. 120.00
        Orange Rifle Powder paper label 42.00
    Lithographed Smokeless Powder in color 10.00
Mathewson's Gun Powder, 1-pound can with orange and black
    label 20.00–30.00
Oriental Powder Company, 1-pound
    Black with Texas Rifle Powder label, fair condition. 126.00

Maroon with black-and-white label with duck, fair condition   250.00
Robin Hood Powder Company, 1-pound can, green with white and red
   (Robin in red)
   Excellent condition 165.00
   Good condition but crazed paint 60.00
   Poor condition 60.00
The Schultze Gunpowder Company, 1-pound tin
   Black with Schultze Gunpowder paper labels 5.00
   Lightning bolt labels 5.00
Warren Powder Mills
   ¼-pound tin, Warren Sporting Powder Number 5 label 40.00
   1-pound tin, green with Snap Shot paper label, faded 96.00

CHAPTER 15

Knives

When I was a youngster back in the 1930s, a boy was undressed without his pocketknife. After all, we all wore knickers with lace-up "high-cuts" that had a knife pocket on the outside of the right boot, and it would be a poor lad that didn't have that pocket filled. A knife was just a knife to me in those long-ago days when mumblety-peg was played at recess, and many a fine blade was ruined in the rocky Connecticut soil. I have learned a bit since those well-remembered yesterdays, and it is safe to conclude that the old saying "too soon old, too late smart" is applicable to the value of fine knives. Today, as the prices of fine old knives continue to escalate, even the sharpest collectors and dealers get knicked now and then. One's knowledge must be well honed if he or she hopes to make the cut. I urge beginning collectors to learn all they can regarding collectible knives *before* buying any knife, for there is far more junk on the market than worthwhile blades. You should read the books listed in the appendix, go to knife shows, and do anything and everything to avoid being skinned.

Collectible knives come in all shapes and sizes and in all price ranges. The knives that are included here are, for the most part, sporting blades used in the pursuit of hunting and fishing, but no introduction to a chapter on knives would be complete without the Bowie knife, and that isn't going to be ignored here.

Historians disagree on the origin of the earliest Bowie knives that were handcrafted for Rezin Bowie, but it is fairly well accepted that the first of these blades was the work of blacksmith Jesse Smith and was finished by Rezin himself. Later makers included Henry Schively of Philadelphia, Rees Fitzpatrick, and James Black—and there are those who insist that each of these men, together with others whose names are lost to history, fabricated the knife that saved Colonel James Bowie's life in an 1827 fight with Major Norris Wright. Be that as it may, history tells us it was Schively who introduced the eight-inch blade, sharpened false edge, and slant clip, thereby becoming the "father" of the classic clip-point "Bowie knives" that followed. I could ramble on and on about classic and collectible Bowies but I have made my point—Rezin Bowie and his little brother started something that knows no end. Those of you who wish to pursue Bowie knives and their history will find Robert Abels's two books, *Bowie Knives* and *Classic Bowie Knives,* of great interest and well worth the time and expense of finding them on the used and rare book market. Any serious collector of Bowie knives should also consider David Hewett's enlightening and entertaining article about the "original" knife in the July 1990 issue of *Maine Antiques Digest.*

Considering the size and shape of things, it is a far step from a large sheath knife to a small folding pocketknife, but each arrived in our country with a long European lineage. Sheath knives are adaptations of the Spanish dagger, Scottish dirk, and other old-country designs. The common pocketknife has changed little since the 17th century. Folding knives can be traced to the first-century Romans and are documented in literature dating back to 1672. There is the little "Safety Hunting Knife," dating from 1902; many offerings by Union Cutlery Company, whose later blades carried the "Ka-Bar" markings; and, of course, the ever popular "Keen Kutter" knives made by the Walden Knife Company.

It would be impossible to conclude this all-too-short listing without naming two of America's most popular and widely collected knives—those manufactured by Remington and Winchester. Remington made and sold fine knives from 1920 until 1940 and the eve of World War II. Winchester entered the knife business when it merged with the E. C. Simmons Company in 1923 and moved the Simmons-owned Walden Knife Company to New Haven to manufacture—you guessed it—Winchester knives. The company made quality knives until 1933.

It was difficult to compile the list of collectible sporting-knife prices that follow—difficult not because there is a lack of material on the market but because there are so many non-sporting knives that are truly collectible from a knife-nut's point of view that it becomes necessary to draw a line between sporting and non-sporting blades. Sporting knives come in all shapes, sizes, and price ranges. There are skinning knives, fishing knives, bird-hunting knives, and stainless steel knives for saltwater sportsmen that come with and without marlin spikes in both sheath and folding models. Non-sporting knives include many models of both sheath and folding designs that serve no sporting purpose. I have not included daggers, boot knives, Rambo-style monstrosities, or any of the truly wonderful specimens inlaid with gold or sheathed in old ivory (sporting or not, only a fool would take a knife of that caliber out in the weather or expose it to the harsh treatment sportsmen give their tools). I trust my thin line is drawn where it will do you the most good in evaluating this or that knife.

Before perusing the following prices and buying or selling a particular knife, you should know that—unless stated to the contrary—the prices listed are for knives in mint or near-mint condition. Flaws of any kind greatly reduce the value, and heavily used or abused examples are next to worthless unless they are very, very rare. Sellers should realize that they can expect no more than half the listed price, and buyers should remember that the time-worn phrase caveat emptor is still sharp advice. I have kicked around the sporting collectibles scene for more years than I care to remember, and the sharpest dealers I encounter are those who prune the public with worthless cutlery. Know who you are dealing with and be sure they stand behind what they sell. You can put a Band-Aid on a cut, but your wallet and ego are not so easily repaired.

The following knives are listed alphabetically by maker. To avoid confusion, sheath knives and pocket or folding knives are listed separately. Sheaths are included unless stated otherwise.

Buck Knives

Sheath Knives
    Model 116, 3½″ blade, satin finish, as new 25.00
    Model 119ST, 6″ Bowie blade, satin finish 110.00
    Model 123 Lakemate, 6½″ filet blade, as new. 20.00
    Model 125 Streamate, 4½″ filet blade, as new 20.00
    3¼″ blade skinner, satin finish 40.00
Pocketknives
    Creek 4¼″ closed, 3-blade stockman, as new 45.00
    Model 110, Custom 5″ closed lockback, mint condition 135.00
    Model 317, 5¼″ closed, 2-blade jackknife, light use 110.00
    Model 513, 3⅜″ closed lockback, as new 40.00
    Model 515, 2⅞″ closed lockback, as new 35.00
    Model 531, 4¾″ closed 2-blade trapper, as new with sheath . . 125.00
    Model 560, XLT1 Titanium, 5 closed lockback, new with
      sheath 50.00

PASSING THE BUCK

Years ago a knowledgeable sportswriter stated that, in his opinion, Buck knives were the most overrated knives in America. Collector values mirror this opinion, so caveat emptor is good advice if one is looking for future values.

Camillus Knives, pocketknives

3¼″ closed lockback, wood scales, used 25.00
3⅝″ closed Cub Scout knife, used 25.00
4½″ closed
    Two-blade trapper, as new in box 35.00
    USA stainless sailor's knife, as new 30.00
    5″ closed A. G. Russell CM-2 granddaddy Barlow, as new 40.00

Case Knives

Sheath Knives
    Model 3-FINN 4¼″ blade, leather handle, as new 40.00
    Model 147 3¾″ blade, walnut handle, as new. 75.00
    Model 161 4½″ blade, stag grip, as new 125.00
    Model 208, 5″ blade with black rubber grips, as new. 100.00

Model 261-KNIFAX combination 5″ knife/4½″ ax, walnut
  grip 350.00
Model 317, 5″ blade with leather/fiber handle, as new 100.00
Model 392 4½″ blade with ivory handle, as new. 150.00
Model 561-deluxe 5″ knife/4½″ ax, stag handle, rare. 400.00
Model 661-KNIFAX, 5″ knife/4½″ ax, rare 500.00
Model 961-deluxe 5″ blade, imitation pearl handle, as new . . . 400.00
Model E-23 5″ blade with mottled pearl grips, as new 175.00
Model M3-FINN, 3″ blade, leather handle, as new 35.00
Model Machete made in 1942, as new 125.00
Model Midget 2¼″ blade, pearl handle, mint 175.00
Pocketknives
Display knife (pre-1940) 12″ blade, as new 1,200.00
Model 61213 5½″ swell center blade, green bone handle 500.00
Model M100 3¼″ press button slide blade, as new, various
  handles 100.00
Model 3165 5½″ folding hunter, yellow composition handle . . 400.00
Model 5165 5½″ folding hunter, stag handle 400.00
Model 5171L 5½″ folding hunter, switchblade, stag
  handles. 1,200.00
Model 6143 5″ Daddy Barlow, various liners/handles. . . . . . to 175.00
Model 6165 5½″ folding hunter, green bone handle 450.00
Model 11031SH 3¹⁄₁₆″ jack, walnut handles, as new 125.00
Model 61048 Sportsman's Jack
  Green bone handle 150.00
  Bone or red bone handle 50.00
Model Zipper 5½″ switchblade, mint condition
  Green bone handle. 4,000.00
  Stag handle. 3,000.00
Other folding hunter models . . . . 35.00 to 1,200.00

COLLECTING CASE KNIVES

Case not only made great knives before the company was bought out in the early 1970s, but there are probably more Case knife collectors than there are for any other type. Case products made prior to 1972 are valuable and highly collectible.

Cattaraugus Knives, pocketknives

Folding machete, 11¼″ blade, used and dull. 75.00
Model 11709 4″ blade Small Hunter, stag handle 75.00
Model 12099 4½″ Deer Slayer, stag handle, as new 150.00

Model 12819 5⅜″ King of the Woods, stag handle, mint
  condition 500.00
Model 21419 come-apart camp knife, 3¾″, stag handle, mint
  condition 125.00

Bob Dozier

Sheath Knives
  3½″ blade skinner, stag handle, as new 465.00
  3⅝″ blade Drop point, as new
    Micarta handle. 345.00
    Stag handle 485.00
    Surface ivory handle 745.00
Two New "Bare Bones" Knives
  DK-2CM 3¼″ drop point, Micarta scales, Kydex sheath 115.00
  DK-3CM 3¼″ drop point, Micarta scales, Kydex sheath, no finger
    groove. 115.00
Gerber Knives
Pocketknives
  3⅝″ closed midlock blade, wood scales 30.00
  4½″ lockback, brass frame with wood inlay, light wear. 35.00
Sheath Knives
  Blackie Collins model, 3⅜″ sawtooth blade, used 65.00
  R. W. Loveless design boot knife, as new. 150.00
  Model C-425 4¼″ blade hunter 75.00
  Model C-475 4⅝″ blade hunter 75.00
  6¾″ blade Guardian II, mint condition 85.00

Lloyd Hale, sheath knives (Lloyd Hale's folding knives are wonderful.
  They are also too expensive to go awandering and, therefore, are not
  included here.)

4⅛″ boot knife, Micarta handle, mirror finish. 475.00
5¾″ blade hunter, compass is stag handle, no sheath 395.00
12¼″ blade Bowie, nickel silver hilt, stag handle, no sheath 650.00
4″ drop-point blade hunter, stag handle, mirror finish 525.00

Ka-Bar Knives (Union Cutlery Company), pocketknives, Dog's Head
  Models

22 Bullet model 4½″ blade, stag handle. 500.00
66 Bullet model 4½″ blade, bone handle. 450.00
Model 6191LG 5¼″ blade, bone handle. 450.00
Other old Dog's Head models with various handle materials. . to 400.00
New Dog's Head knives. 50.00

Keen Kutter Knives, pocketknives

Model K170, 4¼″ (Barlow) single 3¾″ blade, as new 45.00
Model K0147 ¾″ Muskrat, two narrow 4″ blades 185.00

Model K0247, two 3⅞″ blades (spear and clip), as new 100.00
Model K01881 (Barlow) 3½″ spey and pen blades, stag handle   100.00
Model K01884 (Barlow) 3⅛″ spey and pen blades, stag handle   100.00
Model K02070 (Barlow) 3″ spey and pen blades, stag handle 50.00

THE K KNIVES

Keen Kutter and Ka-Bar knives are fine investments. Ka-Bar knives were made by the Union Cutlery Company and Keen Kutter by the Simmons-controlled Walden Knife Company, which merged with Winchester in 1923 after which the highly sought after Winchester name was used. It is worth the time it takes to learn all you can about these two "K" names.

Robert Loveless, sheath knives

3¾″
    (Lawndale) skinner, Micarta handle, used, fine condition . . 1,545.00
    (Riverside) drop-point blade, stag handle, mint condition . . 2,495.00
5½″ (Safariland) hunter
    Cocobolo handle, used 1,695.00
    Finger-grooved stag, used 1,695.00

BOB LOVELESS

The legendary Bob Loveless started making knives in 1953 when he went to the New York sporting conglomerate Abercrombie & Fitch to buy a Bo Randall knife. He was told there was a long waiting list for these blades and decided then and there to make his own. Within a few years his "Jersey Belle" knives were the A & F store's house knives and his fame was assured.

Marbles Knives

Pocketknives, folding hunter
    Hard rubber handle 700.00
    Stag handle 600.00
Sheath Knives
    Expert 5″ blade hunting knife
        Stag handle 195.00
        Without blood groove 125.00

Ideal

    5″ blade hunting knife, leather handle, fine condition 145.00

    6″ blade hunting knife, stag handle, very good condition   200.00

Woodcraft 3⅜″ blade,

    Leather handle and aluminum butt

        Good condition 115.00

        Mint condition. 175.00

    Stag handle

        Mint condition. 285.00

        Poor condition. 95.00

Morseth Knives

Michigan Sportsman 4″ clip-point blade, Micarta handle, used . . 150.00

Model 3 Alaskan Hunter 4¾″ blade, stag handle, mint condition 230.00

Model 4 Cascade Skinner 4⅛″ blade, stag handle, as new. 230.00

Model 5 Wilderness Knife 6″ blade, stag handle, mint condition 220.00

Model 8 boot knife 4¼″ blade, ivory Micarta handle, mint condi-
tion. 295.00

Pal Cutlery Company, sheath knives (Note: These designs and many others originated with Remington. In 1940 PAL bought the Remington stock and designs. They made knives until 1953.)

Model RH35 USN Mark I 5¼″ fighting knife

    Fine condition 100.00

    Used 60.00

WW II 4⅞″ blade fighting knife, fine condition. 125.00

Puma Knives, folding Fisherman's knife, scale and priest

Fine condition. 150.00

New in box 70.00

W. D. "Bo" Randall, sheath knives (Note: Older Randall knives in fine condition are much more valuable than the newer ones listed here.)

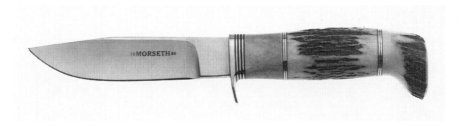

Morseth Model 3 Alaskan Hunter has a 4¾″ clip blade and is shown with an India stag handle. This fine knife is valued between $200.00 and $300.00.
Photograph courtesy of A. G. Russell, Springdale, Arkansas.

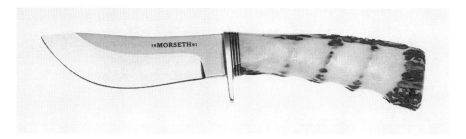

This Morseth Cascade Skinner with an India stag handle with finger grooves was made by A. G. Russell. The overall length of this fine knife is 8½" and it is valued at $275.00. *Photograph courtesy of A. G. Russell, Springdale, Arkansas.*

Model 1
    7" blade, mint condition
        Micarta handle. 295.00
        Stag handle 295.00
    6" blade, mint condition
        Micarta handle. 295.00
        Stag handle 295.00
    Model 5 Camp & Trail, stag handle, mint condition
        5" blade. 290.00
        6" blade. 290.00
    Model 7 Fisherman-Hunter, 5" blade, stag handle 285.00
    Model 8 Trout & Bird knife, 4" blade, used and pitted. 175.00
    Model 12 Sportsman's Bowie, 6" blade, mint condition 265.00

Remington Knives

Sheath Knives
    4¼" blade skinner, leather handle, used . . . . 55.00 to 60.00
    6" blade hunter, leather handle, very good condition   85.00 to 95.00

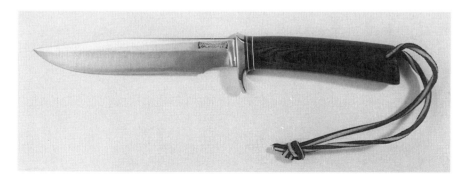

Randall Trout and Bird knife is available with a wide variety of handles. A 7½" knife with a 4" blade, this is one of Randall's most popular knives and there is usually a waiting list of up to one year for delivery. *Photograph courtesy Randall Made Knives, Orlando, Florida.*

OUT OF THIS WORLD

It's a long step from a Florida garage to the moon, but the journey was made when Bo Randall became what many consider to be "America's knife maker." This talented cutler was both out of this world and down to earth, and his knives command top collector dollars.

Model RH50 4½″ blade hunter/skinner, light pitting 60.00
Model RH251 4″ blade hunter, Girl Scout etching, worn. 75.00
Pocketknives
3¾″ closed knife with blade and screwdriver, wood handle,
    used 250.00
Boy Scout knife
    3⅝″ blade (broken, used and pitted 75.00
    3¾″ blade, used 100.00
    Model R213, bone handle, as new 200.00
    Model R293, brown bone handle, mint condition. 1,500.00
    Model R1253, brown bone handle, as new 1,200.00
    Model R6943 3″ closed pen knife, light pitting and use. 25.00

The following Remington pocketknives were made beginning in 1982 by Camillus and other manufacturers. The "bullet" models have appreciated in value, but the others. . . . Caveat emptor.

Model 1173L (1984) 3⅝″ closed lockback, new in
    box . . . . 200.00 to 275.00
Model 1303 (1984) 4½″ closed lockback, new in box. 190.00
Model R1173 (1983) 3⅜″ two-blade trapper, new in box 275.00
Model R1615 (1988) 5″ closed jackknife, new in box. 75.00

R. H. Ruana, sheath knives

4⅜″ skinner, green stag handle with grooves, made by Rudy . . . 300.00
4½″ blade skinner, stag inlays, scratched 135.00
5″ blade skinner, stag inlays, as new 275.00
5⅛″ hunter, stag inlays, owner's monogram, used 135.00
6″ blade hunter, stag inlay
    Made by Rudy 285.00
    Used 175.00

A. G. Russell

Pocketknives
    "Arkansas Toothpick" 3½″ blade
    Ebony handle, as new 60.00

Stag handle
    As new. 75.00
    Scratched 45.00
Sailor's knife, combination blade and marlin spike, as new. . . . 75.00
Sheath Knives
    Model AGMK 9½″ blade Bowie, Zytel handle, as new. 100.00
    Model AGMK-2S, 9½″ blade Bowie, stag handle 170.00
    Model AGST "Sting" 3¼″ double-edged blade*, rosewood
        handle. 55.00
    Model LV-DS (Loveless style) 3¾″ drop-point hunter, Micarta
        handle. 295.00
    Model LV-DBR (Loveless style) 3¾″ drop-point hunter, stag handle,
        new 375.00

THE CUTTING EDGE

In April 1974, *Knife Digest,* prior to publication of its first issue, named A. G. "Andy" Russell the first member of its Hall of Fame for his tireless work on behalf of others. Today, more than a quarter century later, Russell's good name continues. As a cutler, a seller, and a promoter of others' work, he has few peers. Any interested collector should subscribe to "The Cutting Edge" catalogs of pre-owned knives. Send $15 to 1705 Highway 71 North, Springdale, Arkansas 72764. Tell them I sent you.

Russell (Green River Works)

Sheath Knives
    Model 78 stag handle hunting knife, 6″ blade, pitted. 125.00
    Model 215 Cocobolo handle sheath knife, 4½″ blade, pitted. . . 85.00
    Model 1000 Bowie-style hunting knife, stag handle, no
        sheath. 175.00
Pocketknives
    Model 42 Barlow, two blades, white bone handle . . . . scarce
    Model 603 Barlow, single blade (3⅜″), bone handle, pitted   1,200.00

Schatt & Morgan Knives, pocketknives

Model 396 4″ clip blade, imitation stag handle, as new 150.00
Model 1166 3⅝″ blade, nickel silver bolsters, used 200.00
Model 37193 3⅛ ″ blade, nickel silver bolsters, new 50.00

*Note: Model 52 had buffalo-horn handles.

Schrade Cutlery, pocketknives

Model 114 ¾" fisherman's knife, 5" blade, stag handle. 300.00
Model 1083 sportsman's knife, 5" blade, stag handle, as new . . . 150.00
Model 1147 ¾" Barlow, 5" clip blade, pitted 125.00
Model 1514J dagger-style, clip-point, push-button, 4" blade*. . . . 150.00
Model 1543 ¾" hunting knife, folding clip-point, push-button, 4⅞"
    blade* 300.00
Model G1543 ¾" folding clip-point, push-button, 4⅞" blade*. . . . 400.00

Western Cutlery Company, sheath knives

Model L66 4½" hunter, leather handle, as new. 20.00
4" clip blade Boy Scout knife, BSA emblem, used, no sheath 55.00
5¾" blade fighting knife, leather handle, fine condition 50.00

Winchester Knives

Model 1060 Texas Jack 4⅛" blade, celluloid handle, mint
    condition 225.00
Model 1611 jackknife, 3¼" blade, scratched 50.00
Model 1920 folding hunter, 5¼" blade, bone handle, as new . . 1,000.00
Model 1950 clip-point lockback, 6¾" blade, stag handle, as
    new 1,200.00
Model 2701 Barlow, 3½" blade, bone handle
    As new 225.00
    Used 125.00
Model 3944 gunstock, 3¾" blade, fine condition. 250.00

The following W-15 knives were manufactured by Blue Grass Cutlery
    under license from the Olin Corporation beginning in 1987

One-blade Toothpick, new 100.00
1927 Lockback folding hunter, 5⅜" blade, new 100.00
3904 Whittler (3⅝"), new 100.00

The list goes on with lesser values. The most collectible, and therefore
    valuable, Winchester knives were made from 1923 until the early
    1930s.

+--+
| |
| **BANNED BLADES** |
| |
| Some states, several cities, and some towns have |
| outlawed double-edged knives as well as switchblades. |
| Check your local laws, not after you purchase such a |
| knife but before. The money you save will be your own. |
| |
+--+

*Push-button, or "switchblade" knives, are illegal in most states. In 1957 traffic in them was
banned by the federal government.

PART IV
DECOYS

CHAPTER 16

Duck Decoys and Decorative Bird Carvings

ecoys have been a part of my life since the early 1930s when, with my father's help, I made a crude example that only vaguely resembled any known waterfowl. Dad was never a decoy maker in the accepted sense; but, influenced by Joel Barber, Charles "Shang" Wheeler, Ted Mulliken, and others, he made his own fine gunning models and, as I grew, I contributed. In 1959 Dad and I started the North American Decoy Company and sold oversize decoys in sets of eight for $56 or $7 each. Plastics soon changed the decoy "business" forever, and small companies such as ours could not compete with "dollar-a-duck" look-alikes. Fine wooden duck and geese decoys left the water for the shelves of museums and collectors. A fine-condition example of the decoys my father and I made in the 1950s can bring as much as $200 at today's auctions—and that is a long way from the water—but it serves admirably as a personalized introduction to this chapter. Decoys, once merely tools of the trade, are big business, and today's collectors and potential collectors are cautioned to heed the timeless "Let the buyer beware."

SIGNED DECOYS

Collectors should be wary of "signed decoys." Few of the working models handcrafted by hundreds of able and skilled makers had any identification other than that of their owners. This is not true of all decoys. Many Crowells, Wards, and others did, indeed, carry markings; but, generally, old decoys can only be identified by experts. Buyers must know who they are dealing with and trust them and their judgment.

Many things, including the aforementioned plastics, have had a hand in making old and not-so-old decoys the popular collectibles they are, but for all intents and purposes it began when a New York City architect who knew nothing of guns and gunning "discovered" his first decoy in 1919. The architect was, of course, Joel Barber who wrote the first book on decoys in 1934 and coined the phrase "floating sculpture" to describe the birds that would wait until the 1960s to gain the attention of dealers and collectors. This is not to say that fine decoys were neither noticed nor collected during the first half of the century for, of course, they were, but many more were burned on cold winter nights or discarded.

Things changed quickly when Hal Sorenson began publishing his *Decoy Collector's Guide* in 1963, followed by Adele Earnest's and William Mackey's new decoy books in 1965. And in 1968 the first "all decoy" auction was held on Cape Cod. It had taken more than 30 years, but Joel Barber's "floating sculpture" had come of age, and he was correctly, albeit posthumously, termed "the father of the decoy." (Barber's, Earnest's, and Mackey's books on decoys are available in reprint editions and reading them should be a part of one's homework.)

The 1970s saw the two-year multi-part sale of Bill Mackey's extensive decoy collection where, for the first time, a decoy was sold for over $10,000. But this was only the beginning. In the 1980s a wood duck decoy by Joseph Lincoln sold in excess of $200,000 and was topped a few weeks later when a pintail by Elmer Crowell went for more than $300,000. The 1990s saw the famous Caines Brothers' mallards sell for more than $258,000, and private sales are said to put the aforementioned figures to shame. If these high prices scare you, they needn't. Good, inexpensive yet collectible decoys are still available, and an open mind is at least as important as an open account.

No one can tell someone else what to collect or what to expect to pay for this or that decoy, but if I were starting a decoy collection today, I would take a long, hard look at the various pre-plastic factory decoys. A fine collection of papier-mâché, decoys can still be put together for a reasonable cost, and ducks, geese, crows, and owls made of cardboard or cloth present today's collectors with interesting possibilities, as do the costlier wooden factory decoys that range in price from expensive Masons to Down East Decoys, Victors, and the three different Wildfowler Decoy makers that turn up occasionally. Cork decoys, other than those made by well-known mak-

Three stuffed-canvas Canada geese from southern Illinois with old repaint and several small tears sold for a total of $250.00. *Photograph courtesy of Guyette/Schmidt, West Farmington, Maine.*

ers such as Charles "Shang" Wheeler, have never been popular with collectors, and plastic has no place in a decoy collection. The choices are many; but, sad to say, the marketplace is not overrun with worthwhile material. Decoys in fine condition are hard to come by, and collectors seeking valuable or investment-quality decoys of any kind are pretty much forced to go to estate sales and decoy auctions where the prices are high. Quality decoys do occasionally turn up at barn sales, flea markets, and local auctions and antiques centers. In the past few years I have come across a variety of collectible decoys and miniature carvings by known decoy makers in these locations by being there first and knowing what I was buying; but beginning collectors will do well to buy from honest dealers and auctioneers, such as those listed in the appendix. Good decoys don't grow on trees nor are they often found along the side of the road—and when are, my earlier "caveat emptor" advice cannot be ignored. While we are on the subject of the buyer being wary, remember that ownership of auction items passes on the fall of the hammer and guarantees are only as good as the reputation of the guarantor. Know what you are buying and who you are buying it from.

I could ramble on here and tell you about the world of difference between retouching and repainting and between repairs and reheadings, but these, I think, are things you must learn for yourself. Go to decoy shows and exhibits; read the early books by the authors mentioned here and add Henry Fleckenstein's *American Factory Decoys* to your list of "must read" volumes. Invest in auction catalogs from the organizations specializing in decoy sales that are listed in the appendix. Decoys may or may not be your "thing," but no one can compete in this market unless he knows what it is all about.

The following list of decoy makers and manufacturers is only a beginning, but it will, like a pair of leaky duck boots, get your feet wet.

Andy Anderson, Chillicothe, Illinois

Canvasback pair, minor wear and an age crack in the hen 450.00

Anderson Decoy Factory, San Francisco, California

Pintail made of sheet metal, rare, old repainted condition 230.00

Ken Anger, Dunneville, Ontario

Black duck, original paint 950.00
Blue-wing teal pair, fine original paint and only minor wear . . . 1,750.00
Canvasback drake, signed on bottom, original paint 1,250.00
Mallard pair, working, original paint and showing average
   wear 1,800.00

Animal Trap Decoy Company, Lititz, Pennsylvania (Note: Wooden factory decoys by Animal Trap were made in both Pennsylvania and Louisiana and are priced from $35 to $75.)

Canada goose, papier-mâché
   Near mint, unused condition 65.00

Redhead pair by Ken Anger of Dunville, Ontario, in near mint original condition sold at auction for $2,000.00. *Photograph courtesy of Guyette/Schmidt, West Farmington, Maine.*

Showing light wear 40.00
Redhead, case of six, mint condition 225.00

Ferdinand Bach, Detroit, Michigan

Canvasback drake, maker's name carved in bottom, excellent condition
    with light wear 4,850.00
Redhead drake, outstanding paint detail, near mint condition 15,500.00

James E. Baines, Potomac, Maryland

Canvasback drake, old repaint. 50.00
Coot, made in the style of Bob McGaw, fine original paint 450.00

Willard Baldwin, Stratford, Connecticut

Black duck
    Minor repairs 550.00
    Retouched paint 550.00
Bluebill (scaup) drake, sleeper, original paint, fine condition   1,200.00

Sam Barnes, Havre de Grace, Maryland

Bluebill (scaup) drake, original paint, cracking 300.00
Canvasback drake, early 1900s, original paint, light wear 900.00
Charles Birch, Willis Wharf, Virginia
Black duck, hollow-carved, old "in use" repaint 450.00
Brant, hollow-carved, with checks and old repaint 350.00
Canada goose
    Completely repainted in Birch's distinctive style 800.00
    Solid body, removed old repaint 900.00

John Blair, Philadelphia, Pennsylvania

Mallard drake
    Repainted in Blair's style 450.00
    Restored paint 1,700.00
Swimming black duck, 1880s, fine condition with original
    paint 5,000.00

Canada goose by Charles Birch of Willis Wharf, Virginia, brought $5,750.00 plus 10% buyer's premium at a 1994 auction. *Photograph courtesy of Richard Oliver & The Ward Museum, Salisbury, Maryland.*

Roswell Bliss, Stratford, Connecticut

Black duck, signed at a later date 200.00
Bluebill (scaup) hen, "Bliss" brand burned into bottom, mint condi-
    tion. 500.00
Goldeneye drake, old repaint. 400.00

George Boyd, Seabrook, New Hampshire

Black-bellied plover, Mackey collection stamp, near mint condition with
    original paint 2,500.00
Black duck, oversized, fine original paint, some age marking 1,500.00
Canada goose, canvas covered, dark old varnish coating 1,450.00
Canada goose, miniature
    Pair. 1,400.00
    Single 900.00
Yellowlegs, fine original paint 900.00

Ned Burgess, Church's Island, Virginia

Baldpate drake, old repaint 250.00
Canada goose, replaced canvas cover, old repaint 100.00
Canvasback drake, oversized, old repaint 450.00
Ruddy duck drake, 1930s, fine original paint, light wear 4,700.00

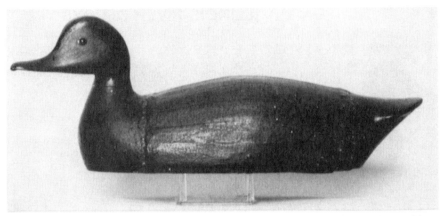

Canvas-covered black duck by George Boyd of Seabrook, New Hampshire, with some touch-up paint but in generally fine condition sold for $3,000.00. *Photograph courtesy of Guyette/Schmidt, West Farmington, Maine.*

Tom Chambers, Toronto, Ontario

Canvasback drake
    Original paint, moderate wear and darkening............2,750.00
    Repainted as a goose, restored to "original" coloration......600.00
    Redhead drake, near mint condition....................1,500.00

Nathan Cobb, et al. Cobb Island, Virginia

Brant
    by Elkanah Cobb (Nathan Jr.'s son), hollow, mostly original
        paint...19,500.00
    by Nathan Cobb, Jr., replaced bill, very worn paint.......2,250.00
    Hissing Canada goose, by Nathan Cobb, worn original paint, average
        wear...90,000.00

Ralf Coykendall, Jr., Manchester, Vermont

Black duck, miniature sleeper, signed, fine original paint......225.00
Canvasback, pair, miniature, signed, original condition........200.00
Labrador duck drake, miniature, signed on bottom, fine original
    paint...250.00

Ralf Coykendall, Sr., Weston, Connecticut

Black duck, hollow, carver's initials "RC" on bottom, fine original
    paint...250.00
Mallard drake, hollow, carved and branded initials on bottom
    board...600.00

A. E. CROWELL & SON

Collectors of Crowell decoys and decorative carvings should be aware that Anthony Elmer Crowell (1862–1952) was joined in the business, possibly as early as 1919, by his son Cleon. Many examples of the Crowells' work attributed to Elmer were the work of Cleon who continued to make and sell birds until his death in 1961.

A. E. Crowell & Son, East Harwich, Massachusetts

Black-bellied plover, lightly worn original paint 10,000.00
Canada goose, oval brand on bottom, restoration and fine original
    paint 2,500.00
Canvasback drake
    Crossed wing, rectangular stamp, original paint 8,000.00
    Miniature, feeding, near mint condition 1,200.00
Green-wing teal drake, miniature, near mint original condition. . 950.00
Hen scoter, miniature, scarce paper label, near mint condition 1,200.00
Large slat goose, old "in-use" repaint and repaired head 1,350.00
Merganser hen, oval brand, old coat of varnish, replaced bill . . . 450.00
Pintail drake, old repaint, considerable checking and cracking. . 700.00
Tern, life-size, decorative, raised wings, oval brand, original
    paint 6,500.00
Wood duck drake, miniature, rare, near mint original condi-
    tion 1,500.00
Yellow-legs
    Fine early and original paint 8,000.00
    Worn, cracking 1,800.00

Sam Denny, Clayton, New York

Bluebill (scaup)
    Drake, old retouched original paint 250.00

This pair of Crowell bluebills (scaup) were originally made as doorstops and both bear the Crowell rectangular stamp. They brought $2,900.00 at auction.
Photograph courtesy of Guyette/Schmidt, West Farmington, Maine.

Miniature waterfowl by the Crowells of East Harwich, Massachusetts, are (left to right): a running black duck ($500.00) and a very fine Canada goose ($1,800.00). *Photograph courtesy of Guyette/Schmidt, West Farmington, Maine.*

Hen, old worn paint, repaired bill 175.00
Redhead drake, original paint with some wear and chipping. . . . 350.00

John Dilley, Quogue, New York

Black-bellied plover, dry original paint, minor wear 10,250.00
Dowitcher, spring plumage, showing wear and repairs. 2,250.00

Unusual wooden wing ducks used to disguise the wooden wings of now-out-lawed sink boxes were made by Henry Davis of Perryville, Maryland, at the turn of the century. The drake (top) sold for $2,200.00 and the hen (formerly in the Mackey collection and so marked) sold for $2,900.00. *Illustration courtesy of Richard Oliver and The Ward Museum, Salisbury, Maryland.*

Dodge Decoy Factory, Detroit, Michigan

Black duck, original paint, light wear and old repair 525.00
Mallard drake, old original factory paint, age shrinkage cracks 600.00
Pintail drake, original paint, some dents and one old check in
   body. 850.00

Downeast Sportcraft Co., Freeport, Maine

Black duck, "sleeper" position, fine original paint with light wear and
   checking 275.00
Mallard pair, unusual swimming (feeding) positions, original
   paint. 400.00

Captain Ben Dye, Havre de Grace, Maryland

Bluebill (scaup) drake, made as a wing duck, painted over. 650.00
Redhead drake, Mackey collection stamp, old "in-use" repaint . . 450.00

Robert Elliston, Bureau, Illinois

Canvasback drake, partly removed old repaint. 300.00
Mallard drake, "round body style," fine worn original paint . . . 3,500.00
Pintail
   Drake
      Exceptional condition. 4,000.00
      Original paint, old bill repair 1,050.00
      Hen, good original paint 700.00

Evans Decoy Factory, Ladysmith, Wisconsin

Bluebill (scaup) drake, Evans stencil, original paint. 375.00
Coot, worn original paint 375.00
Mallard drake, "mammoth" size, Evans stencil, original paint and light
   wear. 450.00

Thomas Gelston, Quogue, New York

Dowitcher pair, relief carving, worn original paint and replaced
   bills. 1,050.00
Yellowlegs (2), cork, old original paint showing wear and tear . . 300.00

Bert Graves, Peoria, Illinois

Canvasback pair, fine original paint with "Graves distinctive
   weights" 3,500.00
Mallard drake, old black paint overcoat removed. 300.00
Pintail drake, fine original paint with "Graves' weight" 3,000.00

Miles Hancock, Chincoteague, Virginia

Black duck, near mint original paint 450.00
Bluebill (scaup) drake, original paint worn to wood in some
   areas 400.00

Mallard pair, miniature, signed and dated 1968 . . . . 250.00
Merganser pair, touched-up original paint and structurally
    sound 1,100.00

Hays Decoy Company, Jefferson City, Missouri

Black duck, fine original paint with Hays weight on underside
    Minor checking split 350.00
    Slight checking 450.00
Mallard pair, original paint with some wear and checking. 475.00

Herters Decoys, Waseca, Minnesota

Canada goose, 1940s, white check patch repainted 160.00
Canvasback pair, balsa bodies, worn original paint 110.00
Decorative decoys
    Red-breasted merganser 85.00
    Others. . . . . 75.00 to 125.00

James T. Holly, Havre de Grace, Maryland

Canada goose, c. 1890, fine original paint with only minor wear and
    roughness. 7,750.00
Canvasback drake, old repaint removed 550.00
Canvasback pair, cork bodies, excellent original condition with light
    wear 1,250.00

Two owl decoys: a large hand-carved example and a Herters factory decoy at the right sold for $500.00 and $300.00, respectively. Owls and crows are natural enemies and owl decoys attract crows. *Photograph courtesy of Guyette/Schmidt, West Farmington, Maine.*

Owl and crow set of decoys by Herters of Waseca, Minnesota, from the 1930s were in very fine condition and sold for $1,450.00. *Photograph courtesy of Guyette/Schmidt, West Farmington, Maine.*

REPAIRS AND REPAINTING

The phrase "old in-use" repair or repaint is an overworked cliché. Buyers should realize that both repairs and the application of a second coat of paint reduce a decoy's value. Many fine birds are "professionally restored" in one way or another without serious depreciation. Before you buy, be sure you know what was done and who did it.

This canvasback decoy (drake) was used by Milton Weiler as the model for his classic decoys series. It was made by William Heverin of Charlestown, Maryland, and sold with a fine watercolor of the decoy by Weiler for **$1,000.00.** *Photograph courtesy of Richard Oliver and The Ward Museum, Salisbury, Maryland.*

Ben Holmes, Stratford, Connecticut

Broadbill (scaup) drake, only traces of original paint 10,500.00
Red-breasted merganser, entirely professionally repainted. . . . 4,500.00
Whistler pair, old repaint 900.00

Rowley Horner, West Creek, New Jersey

Black duck
    Fine original paint 2,700.00
    Most of original paint on head but repainted body 750.00
Brant, fine original paint with minor wear, previously purchased from
    Mackey collection 4,500.00

Ira Hudson, Chincoteague, Virginia

Black duck, rounded body
    Fine original paint 1,200.00
    Old in-use repaint 250.00
Broadbill (scaup) drake, "football-style" body, original paint and light
    wear 2,250.00
Green-wing teal
    Drake, 1915–1920, exceptional original condition 50,000.00
    Hen, mate to drake above 32,500.00

Pintail drake, decorative, standing, wings, extended neck, fine original
  varnished paint. 32,500.00
Redhead drake, early rounded body, most of original paint
  intact. 1,200.00
Wood duck pair, miniature, old crazed and original paint. 3,150.00

Doug Jester, Chincoteague, Virginia

Black duck, "great" original paint with Jester's scratch
  detailing. 650.00
Bluebill (scaup) drake, worn original paint with minor checking and
  cracks 350.00
Goldeneye drake, old probably original worn paint 400.00
Hooded-merganser drake, old repaint. 350.00
Pintail pair, fine original paint and professional restorations. . . 2,000.00

Joseph Lincoln, Accord, Massachusetts

Brant, fine original paint with restoration to old check in back 9,000.00
Canada goose
  Fine original paint and only slight age check in bottom . . . 13,000.00
  Old repaint 800.00
Golden plover, tack eyes, shot marks, fine original paint 1,500.00
Hissing goose, miniature, original condition 1,250.00
Pintail drake, old repaint 550.00
Surf Scoter
  Canvas covered, old repaint and flaws in canvas 425.00
  Self-bailing, old repaint and minor wear 750.00
White-wing scoter hen, "outstanding" and original dry paint   25,000.00
Widgeon drake, old repaint. 1,000.00

Mason Decoy Factory, Detroit, Michigan

Bluebill (scaup) pair
  (Premier grade), fine original condition with slight rough-
    ness 2,100.00
  (Standard grade), tack eyes, worn original paint 350.00

Louisiana decoys have a character all their own as is evidenced by this pair of mallards that were made by Raymond Laine of New Orleans and were sold for $250.00. *Photograph courtesy of Guyette/Schmidt, West Farmington, Maine.*

This Canada goose by Joe Lincoln of Accord, Massachusetts, is a classic decoy in original paint with only minor wear and the expected body splitting on its underside. A fine example of Lincoln's work, it sold for $3,000.00. *Photograph courtesy of Guyette/Schmidt, West Farmington, Maine.*

Blue-wing teal drake (premier grade), near mint condition . . . 4,000.00
Canvasback drake (premier grade), Seneca Lake model, fine old original paint. 950.00
Golden plover, rare spring plumage paint, considerable wear and tear 1,500.00
Goldeneye drake (premier grade), fine old and original paint. . . 850.00
Mallard pair
    ("Snakey-head" premier grade), varnished original paint. . . 2,500.00
    (Standard grade), glass eyes, original paint and neck-filler repair. 350.00
Pintail drake (standard grade), near mint original condition . . 1,050.00

Mason Decoy Factory shorebirds in original paint are (left to right) yellowlegs with a hairline crack ($500.00), dowitcher hit by shot and with crack at bill joining ($500.00), and tack-eye robin snipe with minor cracking ($800.00). *Photograph courtesy of Guyette/Schmidt, West Farmington, Maine.*

Mason factory decoys. *Top row, left to right:* **Challenge grade mallard drake in original paint with chips ($550.00), challenge grade redhead drake in original paint ($950.00), challenge grade golden-eye hen in original paint with minor repairs ($900.00).** *Bottom row, left to right:* **Premier grade canvasback hen in fine original paint ($1,300.00), premier grade black duck with the rare "grade" stamping and in fine condition ($1,100.00), challenge grade canvasback drake in original paint with only minor fading ($1,200.00).** *Photograph courtesy of Guyette/Schmidt, West Farmington, Maine.*

Redhead drake (premier grade), worn original paint with tiny chips in
  tail 500.00
Redhead hen (premier grade), good original condition with one
  check. 900.00
Widgeon pair (standard grade), fine original paint with neck-filler
  repairs. 4,000.00
Willet (shorebird), fine original paint and only light wear 2,500.00
Yellowlegs, tack eyes, original paint 450.00

Early "slope-breasted" mallard pair (top) in the Mason Decoy Factory's top-of-the-line premier grade had very good original paint and sold for $1,700.00. The rare pair of challenge grade mergansers with repaint removed were bid to $1,950.00. *Photograph courtesy of Guyette/Schmidt, West Farmington, Maine.*

Premier grade Canada goose decoy by the Mason Decoy Factory of Detroit, Michigan, had original paint and bill repairs and sold at auction for $2,750.00. *Photograph courtesy of Guyette/Schmidt, West Farmington, Maine.*

MASON DECOYS GRADED

Collectors will enjoy these wholesale prices for Mason Factory decoys from a 1916 quotation:

Premier Model - hollow	9.00 per dozen
Mammoth Canvas Back - solid	9.00 per dozen
Challenge Model - hollow	6.00 per dozen
Challenge Model - solid	5.00 per dozen
#1 - Glass eyes	4.00 per dozen
#2 - Tack eyes	3.50 per dozen
#3 - Painted eyes	3.00 per dozen

Robert McGaw, Havre de Grace, Maryland

Black duck, fine original "scratch" paint and only light wear.... 750.00
Bluebill (scaup) pair, miniature, fine condition.............. 825.00
Canada goose, miniature, fine condition.................... 300.00
Canvasback, pair, worn and retouched old paint with repainting 450.00
Canvasback hen, miniature, fine condition.................. 275.00
Pintail pair, miniature, fine condition..................... 500.00

Madison Mitchell, Havre de Grace, Maryland

Baldpate drake, fine original paint, signed and dated
1975 .... 300.00
1982 .... 175.00

Oversized (20½") Delaware River black duck decoy by John McLoughlin of Bordentown, New Jersey, illustrates the so-called Delaware River style. Signed by the maker, this decoy sold for $1,900.00. *Photograph courtesy of Guyette/Schmidt, West Farmington, Maine.*

Black duck, miniature, walnut base, c. 1970, fine paint 325.00
Bluebill (scaup) pair, signed and dated 1972, fine original paint   625.00
Blue-wing teal pair, signed and dated 1975, original paint 400.00
Bufflehead pair, fine original paint. 550.00
Canada goose pair, one signed and dated 1979, fine original
    paint. 700.00
Canvasback pair, repainted by Mitchell 300.00
Coot, fine paint with minor wear 325.00
Redhead pair, signed and dated 1975 . . . . 350.00
Swan pair, original aged paint and the "barn door" keels 4,750.00
Widgeon pair, fine original paint 500.00

Davey Nichol, Smith's Falls, Ontario

Black duck, c. 1920, worn original paint with average wear. 900.00
Mallard pair, relief-carved wings, fine original paint and old
    varnish 1,200.00
Wood duck drake, relief-carved wings, fine original paint. 2,000.00

These decoys by Madison Mitchell of Havre de Grace, Maryland, were made for Phil Williamson of Cambridge, Maryland, in the 1960s. Pictured are (left) a pair bluebills (scaup) with minor discoloration ($275.00) and a fine pair of canvasback in near mint condition ($400.00). *Photograph courtesy of Guyette/Schmidt, West Farmington, Maine.*

These Canada geese by Madison Mitchell of Havre de Grace, Maryland,
were in fine original paint and sold for **$625.00 (top)** and **$500.00.**
Photograph courtesy of Richard Oliver and The Ward Museum, Salisbury, Maryland.

Charles Perdew, Henry, Illinois

Mallard drake, 1930s
    Fine paint by Edna Perdew and Perdew weight 6,500.00
    Worn paint by Charles Perdew 1,600.00
Mallard pair, decorative
    Full size, mint condition 5,500.00

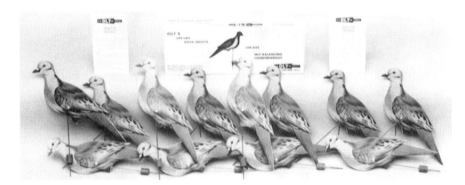

One dozen mint condition dove decoys by the Olt Company, which is better
known for their bird and game calls, sold for **$300.00** in their original box.
Photograph courtesy of Guyette/Schmidt, West Farmington, Maine.

Only eight merganser decoys made by Captain Charles Osgood (1820–1886) of Salem, Massachusetts, are known. The drake (top) was originally in the collection of Dr. George Ross Starr and the hen (bottom) was purchased from Adele Earnest. These outstanding decoys sold for $57,500.00 and $32,500.00, respectively. *Photographs courtesy of Guyette/Schmidt, West Farmington, Maine.*

Half size. 2,000.00
Miniature. 1,350.00
Pintail drake, old repaint 675.00

Peterson Decoy Factory, Detroit, Michigan

Bluebill (scaup)
Drake, early and fine original condition 425.00

Hen, worn original paint 425.00
Mallard pair, worn original paint 650.00

Pratt Decoy Company, Joliet, Illinois

Black duck, worn original paint and only moderate wear 85.00
Canvasback, worn condition 90.00
Coot pair, good original paint 170.00

Nate Quinlin, Rockwood, Michigan

Bluebill (scaup) drake, low-head style, old in-use repaint 1,650.00
Mallard drake, c. 1880, worn old paint and wear 1,250.00
Redhead drake, low-head style, paint restored in Quinlin's
    style 1,900.00

Benjamin Schmidt, Detroit, Michigan

Canvasback drake, fine and original paint and condition 600.00
Coot, preening position, fine original condition 450.00
Mallard drake, several cracks 250.00
Pintail
    Drake, near mint original condition with a few rough spots . . 800.00
    Hen, fine original paint with only minor wear and hairline
        crack 500.00
Redhead drake, original paint with minor wear and small
    checks 300.00
Wood duck drake, original mint condition with no wear 2,400.00

Frank Schmidt, Detroit, Michigan

Redhead drake, excellent and original paint with only minor
    wear 175.00
Ruddy duck, worn but strong original paint showing average
    wear 275.00

Canvasback pair by Benjamin Schmidt of Detroit, Michigan, was in near mint condition and sold for $1,050.00. *Photograph by Guyette/Schmidt, West Farmington, Maine.*

Harry V. Shourds, Tuckerton, New Jersey

Bluebill (scaup), old repaint
　　Drake 550.00
　　Hen. 350.00
Bufflehead drake, rare, fine worn original paint and fine wide
　　body 8,500.00
Canada goose, bill repair and repaint 300.00
Merganser drake, old in-use repaint with checks and cracks . . . 850.00
Redhead drake, c. 1910, vine original paint and only minor
　　wear 7,000.00
Yellowlegs (shorebird)
　　Very good original paint with only light wear 1,500.00
　　Wear and tear. 750.00

Stevens Decoy Factory, Weedsport, New York

Black duck, worn original "scratch" painting with minor check-
　　ing 600.00
Bluebill (scaup) drake
　　Moderate wear and minor paint touch-up. 950.00
　　Shot scars to head 700.00
Blue-wing teal drake, very good original paint and "Stevens" stencil on
　　bottom 7,500.00
Mallard drake, c. 1880, original paint and restored bill 650.00
Redhead drake, worn original paint with repairs and shot scars 750.00

CHECK IT OUT

　　You will often find the word "checks" or "checking" used when describing decoys. When wood dries and shrinks, cracks—often called "checks"—develop. Such lengthwise separations are particularly common in woods, such as white cedar, which were often used in making decoys.

Stratier and Sohier, Boston, Massachusetts

Folding tin, original worn paint with original stick (leg)
　　Ruddy Turnstone 250.00
　　Sanderling 200.00
　　Short-billed dowitcher 200.00
　　Yellowlegs 125.00
　　Others with original paint . . . . 75.00 to 300.00

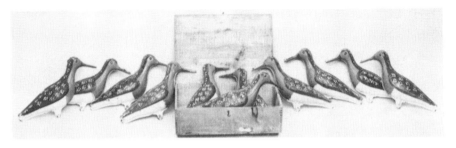

Eleven of the original folding-tin yellowlegs by Stratier and Sohier of Boston, Massachusetts, were auctioned together with ten original stakes (legs) in their original box for $700.00. *Photograph courtesy of Guyette/Schmidt, West Farmington, Maine.*

Rhodes Truex, Atlantic City, New Jersey

Black-bellied plover, original paint retouched in a few places . . . 375.00
Brant, worn original paint showing normal in-use wear 450.00
Yellowlegs, original paint with only minor wear and tear. 225.00

Obediah Verity, et al. Seaford, New York

Merganser hen, old working repaint and average moderate
wear. 500.00
"Peep," c. 1870, worn original paint with heavy shot marking . . 1,350.00
Yellowlegs, rare, outstanding original paint and original bill . . 4,600.00
Other shorebirds by and "attributed to" the Verity family of Long
Island fame . . . . 500.00 to 5,000.00

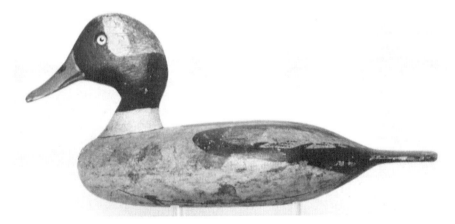

A rare 1880–1890s bufflehead from Stevens Decoy Factory of Weedsport, New York, in fine original paint with only minor wear and cracking sold for $7,000.00. *Photograph courtesy of Guyette/Schmidt, West Farmington, Maine.*

Very fine, c. 1940s pair of bluebills (scaup) by the **Ward Brothers of Crisfield, Maryland**. These working decoys are constructed with balsa bodies, show only minor wear, and sold for **$2,700.00**. *Photograph courtesy of Guyette/Schmidt, West Farmington, Maine.*

Ward Brothers, Crisfield, Maryland

Bluebill (scaup)
    Hen, turned head, near mint condition 1,800.00
    Pair, signed and dated 1972, fine original paint 2,750.00
Bufflehead drake, signed by Lem Ward, near mint original
    paint 2,000.00
Canvasback
    Drake
        Balsa model, fine original paint and some dents
            1936 . . . . 2,700.00
            1948 . . . . 1,400.00
        Signature and "L. T. Ward & Bro." stamp, near mint condi-
           tion. 1,100.00
    Hen, c. 1930, fine paint with average wear and checking . . . 8,500.00
Green-wing teal, standing, decorative, fine original paint with restored
    wing tip. 2,000.00

This fine, early (1930s) black duck decoy was made by the **Ward Brothers of Crisfield, Maryland**. It is signed in pencil on the bottom, has only minor wear and repaired bill, and sold for **$4,300.00**. *Photograph courtesy of Guyette/Schmidt, West Farmington, Maine.*

Pintail
Drake
Decorative, preening, signed and dated 1967, fine condition. 5,000.00
1920s, worn original paint with average in-use wear. . . . 16,500.00
Hen, mate to 1920s drake above 12,500.00
Widgeon pair, c. 1936, original paint with old darkening coating and touch-up 13,000.00

John Wells, Toronto, Ontario

Black duck
Fine retouched paint with some roughness to thin bottom board 1,800.00
Low head and very worn 850.00
Canvasback hen, original paint with one broken eye 900.00
Redhead drake, c. 1900, fine original aged paint 5,500.00

Charles "Shang" Wheeler, Stratford, Connecticut (Note: Wheeler shared his expertise and his patterns for decoys with all who asked, and many look-alike examples exist.)

Black duck, pine head and cork body, from Wheeler's shooting rig
Cracked neck 1,225.00
Good condition 2,250.00
Canvasback drake
Fine original paint, important provenance 10,000.00
From Jack Mitchell's fine collection, repaired bill. 9,000.00
Pintail drake, fine original paint with varnish overcoat 4,500.00
Whistler (goldeneye) drake, preening pose, mint varnished condition 18,000.00

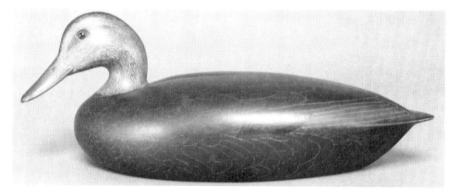

Pictured is an outstanding black duck decoy by Charles "Shang" Wheeler of Stratford, Connecticut, who many consider the finest decoy maker of all time. This decoy was given by Wheeler to the artist Lynn Bogue Hunt who in turn gave it to Milton Weiler who used it in his classic decoys series of paintings. The decoy sold for $29,000.00. *Photograph by David Allen for Richard Oliver and The Ward Museum, Salisbury, Maryland.*

Chauncey Wheeler, Alexandria Bay, New York

Bluebill (scaup) drake, retouched old paint and cracking 300.00
Canvasback, near mint original paint and only light use
    Drake (high head) 1,225.00
    Hen. 950.00
    Pair, oversized, near mint original condition. 5,000.00

Wildfowler Decoy Company

Old Saybrook, Connecticut
    Bluebill (scaup) pair, average in-use wear and tear 180.00
    Green-wing teal pair, near mint original paint and condition. . 700.00
    Mallard
        Decorative bookends, from Mitchell collection, mint condi-
           tion 375.00
        Pair, fine original paint 465.00
    Widgeon drake, fine original paint showing little-to-no wear. . 350.00
Point Pleasant, New Jersey
    Brant, "Harry Shourds model," mint paint 100.00
    Bufflehead pair, signed by Charlie Birdsall, mint condition . . 750.00
    Goldeneye hen, very slight wear. 175.00
    Mallard pair
        Mint condition. 350.00
        Oversized, branded oval 220.00
Quogue, New York
    Mallard
        Drake, fine original paint with "Quogue" stamping. 185.00
        Hen, fine original paint with "Quogue" stamping 150.00
    Pintail pair, fine original paint with light varnish overcoat . . . 245.00

Gus Wilson, South Portland, Maine

Goldeneye, made for "Lake Champlain"
    Drake 300.00
    Hen. 275.00
Merganser drake, old worn paint with head and bill restora-
    tions 1,250.00
White-wing scoter
    Oversize model, old in-use repaint and minor wear 1,100.00
    Preening, originally in Adele Earnest's collection, original
      paint. 5,750.00

NOT LISTED

There are thousands and thousands of fine decoys and hundreds and hundreds of worthy carvers that are missing from this book. They will be "discovered" in the books and auction catalogs listed in the appendix.

CHAPTER 17

Fish Decoys

ish decoys, those finned fantasies designed to lure real fish within range of the ice-fishermen's spears, splashed onto the sporting collectibles stage in the 1970s, starred briefly in the 1980s, and flopped off into the wings in the early 1990s. No other sporting collectibles have even remotely approached the "rags-to-riches-to-rags-again" fish-decoy scenario, and today's players need to know the score as the stage is crowded with bad actors, pushy promoters, and—yes—rotten fish. If, after reading this introduction, you are still determined to pursue painted perch and colorful carp, the following "origins of the species" may prove beneficial.

Fish decoys—honest fish decoys—have been around since early man used "fishy" lures made of bone and other natural materials to bring fish to the crude nets and rustic spears. It should be noted that these early decoys had no hooks nor do any honest-to-goodness examples from any era. Fish decoys were, and are, designed to bring fish within range of the ice-fisherman's spear. To this end, they must be weighted to sink and swim around beneath the hole the fisherman has cut in the ice. These weighted wonders run in size from a few inches to the large examples used to judge the size of the real thing. In Wisconsin, sturgeon decoys changed from 24-inch to 40-inch lengths when the laws were altered to protect the species, but decoys of this size are the exception. Average working decoys run from five to nine or ten inches in length and weigh a lot more than people expect. I once suggested that those sincerely interested in buying fish decoys should carry a pail of water with them and be certain the object of their eye sinks as it must to be the real thing. Try this sometime; you'll be amazed at how few "antique fish decoys" pass this simple test for honesty.

If you remember that a genuine fish decoy has no hooks and no indications where such hardware has once been and that it must sink below the water surface, you will be on the right track. Unfortunately, you still have the clouded question of the authenticity of any given fish decoy, and it is a question only you can truly answer.

When fish decoys first appeared on the collectibles scene in the early 1970s, they were hyped by a handful of individuals who had watched duck, goose, and shorebird decoys soar in price in a few short years from less than $100 to more than $1,000. By the early 1980s, fish decoys had found their way into many of the bird-decoy auctions run by Bourne, Oliver, and others; and, for the first time, fins and feathers shared the auction block. The 1980s were a time of plenty. Fine art soared and set record highs, and sporting collectibles followed suit. The now-famous Haskell minnow sold for $20,000; a Lincoln wood duck decoy was knocked down for $240,000; and four-figure fish decoys by heretofore unknowns, such as Harry Seymour, Kenneth Bruning, and Oscar Peterson, were gobbled up by a seemingly insatiable buying public. Sad to say, the last act was about to begin.

Every melodrama has at least one villain, and our rags-to-riches-to-rags scenario has more than its share. There is the auctioneer from New England who was discovered to have fresh fish on his hands, the midwestern collector who had not one but two shills hyping the price of his decoys at a New York auction house, and the writer from Texas who "aged" fish decoys in his birdbath. It would be difficult to pick a single villain from this lot, and the task becomes impossible when we examine the entire cast of this unusual production.

The meteoric rise in both price and popularity of the lowly fish decoy brought out the worst in people, and the market was inundated with all manner of minnows, frogs, and critters of all description. Buyers became confused; and, when the 1980s boom went bust, fish decoys sank and are only now beginning to show signs of recovery. Fish decoys will never again be the stars of a sporting collectibles stage, nor are they likely to ever again bring big bucks. But they are a part of our sporting heritage and, as such, deserve consideration in spite of their obviously spotted past performance.

Today's and tomorrow's fish-decoy collectors are faced with the option of amassing a collection of contemporary carvings or tempting the odds and trying to put together a collection of honest antique decoys. In the first instance, the buyer hopes that he or she has opted for a carver with a future, and in the second, he or she is after a past performer with a proven pedigree. Neither is a sure thing, but nothing else is either.

The following list of fish-decoy makers and manufacturers is in alphabetical order. The prices listed are up-to-date auction and/or catalog figures and do not include the 10% buyer's fee that is generally added to today's auction selling prices. Sources for additional information will be found in the appendix.

This fish decoy by the well-known Cadillac, Michigan, carver Oscar Peterson dates from the 1930s. *Photograph courtesy of John E. Shoffner, Fife Lake, Michigan.*

FACTORY FISH

Most companies that mass-produced fishing lures also made fish decoys. Several appear in this listing, and all should be considered both collectible and valuable if they are in good to excellent condition.

George Aho

6½″ sunfish with glass eyes, signed and dated 6/22/87 . . . . 115.00
11½″ walleye with button eyes, signed and dated 7/30/86 . . . . . 195.00

Ross Allen, Sr.

A carefully carved and well-scaled decoy with wooden top fin, excellent condition 775.00

Lawrence Bethel

7″ crappie with glass eyes, natural finish, mint condition. 35.00
8¾″ walleye, black/green/white, 1990s, mint condition. 45.00
11″ trout, double jointed, rainbow-trout finish, mint condition. . . . 70.00

Blackhawk Decoy Company

6½″ plastic decoy, black-and-white finish, 1950s, very good condition 45.00

Floyd Bruce

Rainbow trout, 1970, excellent condition. 70.00
9″ bluegill, 1983, excellent condition 135.00
12″ brown trout, signed and dated 1933 on the bottom, mint condition. 100.00
16″ grass pike, carefully painted natural finish, mint condition . . 125.00

Alton "Chubb" Buchman

11½″ herring, green/yellow, c. 1980, scarce, mint condition 395.00

John Fairfield

12″ sucker, brown and white with pinkish side stripes, mint condition. 175.00

"Tars" Geiselhart

5¾″
Silver-painted fish, 1930s–40s, rare, good condition 75.00
Sunfish, 1980s 50.00
7″ red-and-white fish, 1980s. 45.00
10½″ red-and-silver fish, 1980s 50.00

Heddon

4″ four-point ice decoy
    Complete but poorly repainted 150.00
    Shiner finish, very poor condition 150.00

UNKNOWN FISH

Few of today's plethora of phony fish are worth a second look, but there are exceptions. Look for honest wear, the lack of antiquing stains, and staining. Then, if you like it and the price is right, buy it.

Leroy Howell

Natural wood fish, white-painted fins, 1930s 375.00

Russ Hurlburt

7″ perch, green and white, 1930s, outstanding condition 750.00

Mike Maxson

11½″ rainbow trout, 1980s, near mint condition 85.00
12″ brook trout, near mint condition 95.00

John Motherway

Black-and-white fish with red spots, 1940s, excellent condition . . 85.00
5½″ black-and-silver fish, excellent condition 80.00
6½″ black-and-silver fish, excellent condition 85.00
7″ silver-and-red fish, 1940s 85.00

Jim Nelson

7″ brook trout, excellent condition 325.00
7½″ brook trout, white, signed and dated 12/93 . . . . 50.00
8″ rainbow trout, 1970s, near mint 145.00

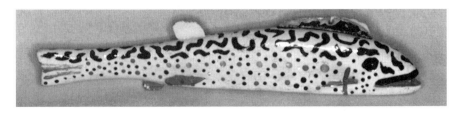

This is a 1940s fish decoy by Jim Nelson of Cadillac, Michigan. *Photograph courtesy of John E. Shoffner, Fife Lake, Michigan.*

Paw Paw

Red-and-white finished fish with checking, repainted red head. . . 40.00

Randall Decoys

Brown/gold scaled finish, paint chipping from fins, early 45.00
Red-and-white fish with brown spots, near excellent condition . . . 65.00

Slatten

5¼″ bass, metal, 1950s–60s, very good condition
    Green and black. 45.00
    White with multicolored accents. 55.00
6″ shiner, metal, black with multicolored accents, mint condition 60.00
7″ pike, metal, mint condition
    Green spots 65.00
    Red, white, and black. 60.00

Bud Stewart

8″ perch, poor condition. 60.00
10″ pike, multi-spotted, late 1980s, signed, near mint condition. . 125.00

Herman Stohr

6″ trout, glass eyes, brown, 1960s, mint condition 150.00
10¼″ pike, green spots, 1960s, mint condition 200.00

Walter Wester

8½″ sucker, red and white, signed "WWW," said to be the best
    example of Wester's work 100.00
14″ trout, green and yellow with lead fins, excellent condition . . . 75.00

An early (1930s) fish decoy by Michigan maker Bud Stewart. *Photograph courtesy of John E. Shoffner, Fife Lake, Michigan.*

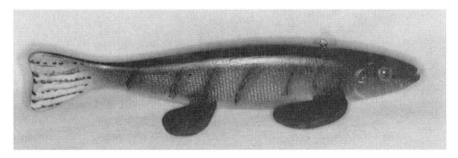

This fish decoy, which resembles a herring, was made in the 1940s by Andy Trombley. *Photograph courtesy of John E. Shoffner, Fife Lake, Michigan.*

SINKERS

Remember, fish decoys were designed to do their work below the surface and were weighted so that they would sink. Test any you are thinking of buying.

Appendix

The following list of sporting collectibles sources is intended for your edification and enlightenment. There are hundreds upon hundreds of people in this business who could, and probably should, be included. But the list is mine, and the names are included because these are the individuals and organizations I know and trust. And, with this final entry, I turn you loose to fend for yourselves. Good luck.

Decoy Auctions

Ted Harmon
2320 Main Street
West Barnstable, MA 02668

Gary Guyette-Frank Schmidt Inc.
Box 522
West Farmington, ME 04992

Richard Oliver
c/o The Ward Museum
Schumaker Drive
Salisbury, MD 21801

Decoy Dealers

Henry Fleckenstein
Box 577
Cambridge, MD 21613

RJG Antiques
PO Box 2033
Hampton, NH 03842

Duck Stamps and Duck-Stamp Prints

The Depot
Sullivan, IL 61951

Russell A. Fink Gallery
9843 Gunston Road
Lorton, VA 22079

Michael Jaffe
Box 61484
Vancouver, WA 98666

National Wildlife Philatelics
Box 061397
Fort Myers, FL 33905

Wild Wings
Lake City, MN 55041

Fishing Tackle Auctions

Bob Lang
Turtle Cove
Raymond, ME 04071

Fishing Tackle and Accessories
The American Sporting Collector
Arden Drive
Amawalk, NY 10501

Frederick Grafeld
297 Born Street
Secaucus, NJ 07094

Heritage Enterprises
22A 3rd Street
Turners Falls, MA 01376

Martin J. Keane
PO Box 288
Ashley Falls, MA 01222

John E. Schoffner
624 Merritt
Fife Lake, MI 49633

Woodruff's Old Corkers
Main Street
Jamaica, VT 05343

Fishing Tackle Museum

American Museum of Fly Fishing
Route 7A
Manchester, VT 05254

Shooting Accessories

Circus Promotions*
614 Cypruswood Drive
Spring, TX 77388

Robert Hanafee
29 Bedford Court
Amherst, MA 01002

James Tillinghast*
PO Box 19-C
Hancock, NH 03449

Calendars and Posters

Circus Promotions*
614 Cypruswood Drive
Spring, TX 77388

Robert Hanafee
29 Bedford Court
Amherst, MA 01002

Sporting Art and Prints

The Bedford Sportsman
Bedford Hills, NY 10507

Collector's Choice
10725 Equestrian Drive
Santa Ana, CA 92705

Russell A. Fink Gallery
9843 Gunston Road
Lorton, VA 22079

Hickok-Bockus
382 Springfield Avenue
Summit, NJ 07901

Petersen Galleries
9433 Wilshire Boulevard
Beverly Hills, CA 90212

Wild Wings
Lake City, MN 55041

Sporting Book Auctions

Oinonen Book Auctions
Box 470
Sunderland, MA 01375

Swann Auction Galleries
104 East 25th Street
New York, NY 10010

Sporting Book Dealers

Anglers & Shooters Bookshelf
Goshen, CT 06756

Anglers Art
PO Box 148
Plainfield, PA 17081

Judith Bowman Books
Pound Ridge Road
Bedford, NY 10506

Callahan & Co.
Box 505
Peterborough, NH 03458

*The untimely deaths of both Bob Strauss and Jim Tillinghast have left voids that, for now, are being filled by family.

Connecticut River Bookshop
Goodspeed Landing
East Haddam, CT 06423

Gary Estabrook
Box 61453
Vancouver, WA 98666

Fair Chase, Inc.
PO Box 880
Twin Lakes, WI 53181

Fin 'n Feather Gallery
Box 13
North Gramby, CT 06060

David Foley
76 Bonneville Road
West Hartford, CT 06107

Game Bag Books
2704 Ship Rock Road
Willow Street, PA 17584

Highwood Bookshop
Box 1246
Traverse City, MI 49685

Frank J. Mikesh
1356 Walden Road
Walnut Creek, CA 94596

Pisces and Capricorn Books
514 Linden
Albion, MI 49224

Ray Riling Arms Books
Box 18925
Philadelphia, PA 19119

Trophy Room Books
4858 Dempsey Avenue
Encino, CA 91436

Sporting Firearms

W. M. Bryan & Co.
PO Box 12492
Raleigh, NC 27605

Cape Outfitters
Route 3, Box 437
Cape Girardeau, MO 63701

Chadick's Ltd.
Box 100
Terrell, TX 75160

Michael de Chevrieux
PO Box 1182
Hailey, ID 83333

Griffin & Howe
33 Claremont Road
Bernardsville, NJ 07924

New England Arms Co.
Kittery Point, ME 03905

Sporting Magazines

Highwood Bookshop
Box 1246
Traverse City, MI 49685

Index